MW00815497

John T. McCarthy

M Aggie

Maggie's Angels

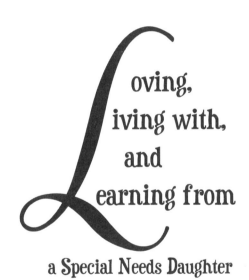

Loving,
living with,
and
Learning from

a Special Needs Daughter

JOHN T. MCCARTHY
Maggie's Dad

Maggie's Angels: Loving, Living with, and Learning from a Special Needs Daughter

© 2016 by John T. McCarthy

Note: Maggie's Angels is published with the understanding that the publisher and author are not engaged in rendering legal, accounting, or other professional service. If legal advice or other professional advice, including financial, is required, the services of a competent professional should be sought.

All rights reserved. No part of this book may be reproduced or used in any form or by any means without the written permission of the publisher.

Address inquiries to:

John T. McCarthy
DBA Maggie's Dad
8207 Brookside Pl.
Wauwatosa, WI 53213

E-mail: John@maggiesdad.com
Phone: 414-530-7963

Website: www.maggiesdad.com

Library of Congress Cataloging-in-Publication Data has been applied for.

Edited by Chris Roerden
Cover design by Delaney-Designs.com

Printed in USA

ISBN: 978-0--9979036-0-7

WORDS OF THANKS AND GRATITUDE

It takes a village to write a book. In the case of *Maggie's Angels*, a large, disparate, fascinating, genuinely nice collection of individuals contributed in important ways to bring this book to life.

Our Maggie recognizes and is happy this book is about her, even raising her arm when talking it up. Although she is a central character, there are many co-stars and even an assortment of angels making an appearance and adding to the storyline. I count over 60 individuals living strong despite intellectual disabilities who grace these pages.

In the writing process, I discovered that they, along with their parents, were excited to be in the spotlight, have their voices heard and inspiring stories told. I am sincerely grateful to all of them. The plan going forward is to use the book to trumpet their triumphs.

Special credit goes to my good friend Jan Lennon. This book would not have come into being without her constant support and strong belief in me and the story I attempt to tell. Her talent and ability to take my words in whole cloth and transform them into something I can be proud of continually amazes me.

Jan, you are indispensable, and I am in your debt. No way could I have pulled off this project without you being in my corner. Thank you.

Many thanks to my trusted professional editor, Chris Roerden, who persuaded me I had another book in me and important story to share. Chris encouraged me to venture forward with this book, sealing the deal stating she would enthusiastically be on board to do the editing. She came through, putting her immense talents and lifetime of accumulated wisdom to bear to bring Maggie and her angels to life.

Sister Edna Lonergan, despite having her hands full and big heart engaged with running and finding funding for St. Ann Center's two campuses, graciously read an early draft as well as a complete final proof of my book. From this effort she provided extensive valuable advice and guidance from the perspective of a caregiver. Sister gently reminded me to always remember to put the individual first over the disability. She also suggested I honestly express my feelings and frustrations as a special parent and caregiver.

Thank you, Sister Edna, and all the best on fulfilling the noble mission of St. Ann Center to serve the underserved.

I feel fortunate to have discovered Pamela Trush of Delaney-Designs to design the book cover and interior layout. Pamela put her talent and creativity to work to capture the spirit of Maggie for the cover. She succeeded in a wonderful way. Thank you, Pamela.

Over the course of the last decade, numerous friends, acquaintances and clients have taken an active interest in this fledgling book concept and were sincere in their encouragement. I owe a debt of gratitude to all of you.

My devoted wife Cathy knows me better than I know myself and knows and loves Maggie as only a mother can. Without her constant love and support over the long course of writing this book, this love story would not have come to light. Cathy being Cathy, went the extra mile, carefully reading the final proof and provided the attention to detail only a loving mother and spouse could.

Thank you dear. I love you.

Maggie's Angels is really a McCarthy family joint venture, with Maggie as honorary "Chair of the Board." All of our children are gifted. Martha and Jack are highly talented and intelligent young adults. They have in common a deep love for their special sister. Martha and Jack have been involved in the book project since the very beginning. They will continue post production in making the book a success, active in promotion, marketing and distribution.

Finally, I wish to dedicate *Maggie's Angels* to my family: Cathy, Maggie, Martha and Jack. You are true angels in my world.

CONTENTS

CHAPTER 1

MEET OUR MAGGIE

"It is not known precisely where angels dwell-whether in the air, the void, or the planets. It has not been God's pleasure that we should be informed of their abode."

Voltaire

The eldest of our three children goes through life carrying the burden of a cognitive disability. Yet anyone who meets Maggie realizes there is something truly special about her. I like the descriptive word *special*, believing it particularly apt for Maggie. So I invite you to join me in discovering, as I have, the wonders, joys, and challenges—along with the highs and the lows—of living with, loving, and indeed learning from a child with an intellectual disability. In our journey of exploration, I'll share with you the depths of unconditional love, the magic engendered by Special Olympics, and the healing power of art and music.

My Maggie is a central character on this virtual carpet ride, joined by a cast of several dozen remarkable, courageous, and inspiring individuals who are also living strong with special needs. You'll meet their equally special parents, as well. Come along to be enriched by a deeper insight, and perhaps come to believe, as I do, in the true angels among us. See how hugs are the closest distance between two friends. Be prepared for a few tears along with smiles and occasional laughter. Buckle up and settle in.

My wife, Cathy, and I are far from being alone in loving a special child. One in five Americans has a relative living with a disability, and one in ten has a relative with a severe disability such as Maggie's.

Our daughter possesses the best of childlike qualities. She is unconditional in her love, genuine in her feelings, lacking all prejudice, and totally unconcerned with status, material possessions, or appearances. Her American Girl doll Samantha holds a favored place with Maggie, sharing a pillow as a cherished friend.

After our second daughter, Martha, started driving, our third child, brother Jack, suggested his sister could now drive him to his soccer games. "Not this sister," Maggie reminded him in all seriousness.

Life for Maggie is simple, honest, straightforward. Her sense of humor is often at a heightened developmental level, and on occasion she displays incredible insight. Maggie likes music, musicals, sing-alongs, and drawing in her sketch book. She especially loves babies, speaking softly to them as she gently touches their tiny hands. One mother asked her, then a teenager, if she would like to babysit sometime. "Oh, no! That would not be a good idea," Maggie wisely replied.

Life with Maggie does have heartaches, but life is never dull. She possesses the enviable gift of never having outgrown childhood and all its wonder. She believes in Santa Claus and the whole magical experience he represents. It is a thrill to see her absolutely giddy at spotting and calling out to Santa at the mall.

Our now 30-something daughter is in many respects a woman child. Although she can easily pass for half her age, Maggie was recently diagnosed with osteoporosis. She is also sporting a few gray hairs.

Many times I wonder what goes on in Maggie's mind. When she reached puberty and began to use feminine hygiene products, I made the error of inquiring of her why this was necessary.

Exasperated at my questions, she gave me a strange look. "Because I am a lady. Don't you know that? Don't you know anything?" Chastised, I never dared bring up the subject again. If I do refer to her menstrual cycle, she quickly reminds me, "I am not a man."

Maggie continues to surprise, amuse, and occasionally frustrate those of us who love her. For one thing, you never know what will come out of her mouth. Once, I stopped to see her at the office while she was doing her part-time, make-work paper shredding job. I asked her, as I am wont to do, if I could have a kiss. "Can't you see I'm busy?" came her tart reply.

If I ask Maggie two or more questions in a row, she replies, "Are you giving me a test?" Maggie cuts to the chase when addressing people. Often, it can be a generic "Hello friend." Other times, it is more suggestive of words she's heard but might not have understood. Once while out taking a walk we paused to say hello to our neighbor at the end of the block. It was a warm day and he was cutting the grass shirtless and in shorts. So Maggie called out to him, "Hey, shorts-a-nagger."

In many ways Maggie's life is full. She looks forward every Wednesday morning to her weekly two-hour, special-needs art class at the Donna Lexa Community Art Center. For half her life, Maggie has been a part of what she refers to simply as "Donna." Over this span she has amassed quite a body of artwork, which has added significantly to her self-esteem. Recently, I remarked about her being an artist. She corrected me in her inimitable way, reminding me she is a "featured" artist. Owing primarily to her prodigious amount of work as demonstrated by her extensive portfolio, Maggie was indeed selected as featured artist for an open house at the Donna Lexa West Milwaukee Center. When I shared this fact with my sisters, anticipating a repeat of Maggie's response to me, Maggie described herself this time as a "starving" artist. Her aunts broke up laughing.

Maggie received a lot of speech therapy in her early years, and to this day likes to enunciate and fully sound out words. Her favorite baseball player was C.C. Sabathia, too briefly a Milwaukee Brewers pitcher. When we remind her that C.C. is now a rich man with the New York Yankees, she offers a pouty face, sticking out her lower lip. I have no doubt what she really likes is the rhythm of saying his name.

As a family, we were so blessed to have Tony and Shirley Leszczynski as friends and backyard neighbors for half of Maggie's life. She never missed an opportunity to emphasize every syllable in their last name. Their gentle golden retriever, Jake the wonder dog, had free run of our backyard and would romp over to visit whenever the kids were out. The family had an above-ground pool, and Maggie loved it when the powerful Tony would toss her up in the air so she landed with a big splash. A number of years have passed, but Maggie still recalls Jake, and talks about the happy times in their pool.

Maggie always made it a point to pair the names Tony *and* Shirley. So all of us found it hard and truly sad when Shirley succumbed to a particularly nasty cancer in the fall of 2014 after a heroic eight-year battle.

Shirley never hid the warm spot she held in her big heart for our Maggie. In the final months of her life, racked by pain and unable to sleep, Shirley often thumbed through a box of personal items and mementos. These included a photo of her with our Maggie sitting on a sofa in her home, her arms cradling Maggie. Their faces shine with the genuine affection and purity of their special relationship. Tony gave this picture to Maggie on her birthday as a way of remembering her late friend and neighbor. Cathy and I marvel at how Maggie was able to touch someone as good as Shirley in such a profound way.

A stark landmark in the life journey with a special needs child occurs when parents learn their loved one's pathway will not be normal.

Maggie was our first born, and by all accounts we were blessed with a very healthy, beautiful baby girl. Not until she was slow to develop as the months went by did we express mild concerns. The pediatrician felt there was no cause for alarm. Though our anxiety as new parents was understandable, in her professional medical opinion it was unwarranted. Maggie was thriving and would catch up. The good doctor reminded us that children develop at varying speeds.

At Maggie's first birthday, when other parents might celebrate their child's first steps, our girl was being evaluated at Children's Hospital of Wisconsin. A series of tests determined that our little one was "developmentally delayed." The blow was cushioned somewhat by the modifier "mildly."

This unwelcome news shocked and distressed us. A foreboding emptiness settled in my gut. Although Cathy was concerned about how I would handle being the father of a child who was "not normal," I knew that Cathy would be strong and devoted to Maggie no matter what, and this alone proved a great comfort.

Developmental disability, as we would come to know, is a condition that prevented Maggie from learning such basic skills as walking and talking as quickly or as easily as other children her age. So she qualified for some interventional therapy and ECD: early childhood development education and services. We hoped that with these services she would catch up. But with each passing six-month period, as she fell further and further behind, it became apparent we had a special needs child.

We continued to be proactive, and when Maggie was five we had her undergo a comprehensive diagnostic evaluation at the renowned Waisman Center at the University of Wisconsin-Madison. It is one of fourteen Eunice Kennedy Shriver Intellectual and Developmental Disabilities Research Centers associated with major universities.

The cause of Maggie's developmental delay remained a mystery.

At age eighteen, while attending high school in a special education curriculum, behavior, gait, and balance became bigger issues. Based on her symptoms, a neurologist at Children's Hospital of

Wisconsin suspected leukodystrophy. Cathy then took Maggie to the National Institutes of Health (NIH) in Bethesda, Maryland, for a week-long work-up with world-class specialists. I stayed home to care for Martha and our youngest child, Jack.

Truthfully, I chose not to learn too much about leukodystrophy, a rare genetic disorder I had never heard of. The whole idea of this change in our Maggie was too scary to contemplate. And little if anything was available to treat it. An added source of my apprehension came from the reaction of a neurologist acquaintance. When I told Dr. Fleming on the phone that our Maggie had been diagnosed with leukodystrophy, his quiet one-word response was "Wow!"

Eventually I learned that this five-syllable term describes a progressive degeneration (dystrophy) of the white (leuko) matter of the brain. The loss is gradual, difficult to diagnose, and can lead to a slowdown in physical and mental development, accounting for the onset of Maggie's cognitive, balance, and behavioral challenges.

According to the NIH website, treatment for leukodystrophy is symptomatic and supportive. I read this to mean there is no current cure. Treatment may include medications and physical, occupational, and speech therapies, along with nutritional, educational, and recreational programs. When I now read this list, I realize that Cathy and I have gone down every road available. We have provided our special girl with all of these multiple approaches.

Recently during an appointment with a new neurologist, I was shown an MRI or magnetic resonance imaging scan of Maggie's brain. I admit to not knowing what I was looking at. However, now I more fully appreciate that our girl, despite significant damage to the white matter of her brain, has learned to adapt and succeed quite remarkably. Sadly, this complex disease tends to be progressive-meaning it gets worse.

Thankfully, Maggie's condition seems to have stabilized. As one good example, she eagerly walks the entire 2.5-mile length of the local Fourth of July parade as a Wauwatosa Special Olympics team member, and she has been accomplishing this feat for the past fifteen years. Also, over the same period, her times in the 1,500-meter race walk competition have been consistent.

Rather than focus on what our daughter cannot do because of her disability, Cathy reminds me of how blessed we are for all she is able to do. Maggie not only can talk, but also is quite verbal and loves to sing. She can communicate how she feels, what she wants to eat or drink, and when she's tired and would like to take a nap. Maggie is fully mobile and can walk long distances. Our girl is toilet trained, feeds herself, has no difficulty swallowing, and sleeps well. Her hearing and vision are good. All of this—which should not be taken for granted—makes it much easier to care for her.

However, we must not leave Maggie home alone for any extended period of time. It's a safety issue. Should a fire break out, she would not know what to do. She also cannot be trusted to cross the street by herself or go outdoors without supervision.

What Cathy and I want most is for Maggie's behavior to improve. The fact is she is delightful 90 percent of the time, but the remaining 10 percent proves challenging. At those infrequent times she can be disruptive, throwing things, being loud, using profanity, and occasionally turning aggressive. Her psychiatrist gave her a diagnosis of intermittent explosive disorder to describe the meltdowns, as well as ADHD, Attention Deficit Hyperactivity Disorder, to explain her attention span and everyday actions. On top of this is oppositional defiance. Maggie will regularly let me know that "No means no!"

I must admit that Maggie's 10 percent negative behaviors often leaves me frustrated, disappointed, even angry. I am also frequently embarrassed by my daughter's antisocial actions in public settings. The fact is, her cognitive and physical challenges are ones we as parents can live with and accept. It is her disruptive behavior issues that are a real problem and that rock our world.

Owing to all these issues we have consulted and worked with

psychologists and follow a behavior management plan. The medicines Maggie takes are psych drugs. The newest psychiatrist has changed her drug routine. Once again, we hope to see improvement. Her behavior limits her participation in camps, classes, community programs and other public activities. To make a better life for Maggie, we need to make progress with her behavior.

On the bright side, Maggie is our bridge to memorable events and people. The highlight for the McCarthy family in 2010 was when we travelled to Ireland during spring break to join Martha while she spent the spring semester of her junior year in college studying at University College Dublin. We planned our trip to visit with Martha for her 21st birthday in the land of our Irish ancestors.

We are truly blessed that our three children, Maggie, Martha (sissy), and Jack (bro), clearly love each other. Anytime I ask Maggie who her favorite sibling is, she never fails to diplomatically answer "both." As parents, we have come to believe that Maggie has been a true gift to not only Cathy and me but also her younger brother and sister by teaching them greater appreciation of their own abilities. Maggie has also helped them to mature at an earlier age.

One of the highlights of this Irish vacation was a day spent on the remote island of Inis Mor located in the west of Ireland off the Galway coast among the Aran Islands. After a 45-minute ferry ride from the mainland, while the other tourists rented bikes, took horse-and-buggy rides, or hopped on minibuses to tour Inis Mor, our family resisted the multitude of vendors hawking tour services and instead opted for a leisurely lunch. Then the more adventuresome Jack, Martha, and Cathy rented bikes to explore this rugged island via pedal power, and I stayed behind minding our slowest eater, who was feeling tired. I seriously considered inquiring whether I could rent a room for the afternoon so Maggie could nap while I read a book.

However, Maggie rallied, as is often the case. We left the restaurant, mutually deciding to go on a buggy ride. But no buggies were available. As we continued walking along the road, with my not knowing what we would do for the next couple of hours, Maggie started a conversation on her own with a young woman minibus-driver awaiting the next ferry and its influx of tourists. Often, Maggie connects in her special way with strangers, so I have learned to expect this and go along with it. The next thing I knew, Maggie and I were climbing aboard the tour bus at the invitation of our driver and guide, Cliona Conneely.

Ordinarily, a driver waits until at least a couple of extra passengers show up, but we had this tour all to ourselves. Maggie and Cliona carried on a conversation the whole time, seeming instinctively to understand each other.

The high spot of the tour, literally as well as figuratively, was our stop at Dun Aengus, an ancient observation fort. Usually Cliona would stay behind while her passengers visited the gift shop and restaurant and the more able and physically fit tackled the steep climb to the thousand-year-old fort at the summit. Cliona asked if Maggie was capable of this rigorous climb. We have taken Maggie on several hikes in Arizona, and she competed in the 3,000-meter long-distance race-walk in Special Olympics, so I knew Maggie would be able to trudge to the top.

Halfway up, Cliona remarked how well Maggie was doing, adding that it would be much easier coming down. I had to correct her logical assumption, explaining that in Maggie's case the world is turned upside down. Up is relatively easy, down is more challenging. Things in life that the average individual finds hard, such as love, trust, acceptance, or lack of envy or prejudice, to Maggie come easily. On the other hand, what is second nature for most of us, such as navigating downhill, is for our girl difficult. Owing to problems with balance and depth perception, Maggie feels unsteady descending unless handrails are available that she can grasp with both hands.

We reached the top of Dun Aengus after half an hour. For the effort, our reward was a feast for the senses, starting with a spectacular panoramic view. We breathed in the fresh salt air and listened to the surf of the Atlantic ocean pounding the rocky cliffs below—all begun by Maggie and Cliona having smiled and exchanged pleasantries.

Over the course of our afternoon together, Cliona shared with us that her 75-year-old mother was named Maggie. That might explain the inexplicable bond between these two young women, but I don't think so. Our Maggie is an astute judge of people, and her parting goodbye hug with Cliona and telling Cliona she loved her, said it all. We left with a piece of Inis Mor forever etched in our hearts.

We have without a doubt been enriched as a family by having Maggie play a major role in our lives. Among the generous gifts she makes possible are the many wonderful people with whom we have crossed paths solely because of her. Maggie was only 12 when she first connected in her special way with a gentle man who has since become a dear friend to our entire family. A native of Nigeria, Emmanuel Udo is a Catholic priest who spent five years residing, ministering, and assisting in our parish church while completing his graduate and doctoral studies at Marquette University. At the conclusion of Sunday services, Father Emmanuel would stand in the back of the church shaking hands and greeting parishioners as they left. On her own, Maggie approached him and gave him a hug. From this simple act of affection developed a warm relation-ship that continues to this day with each member of the McCarthy family. As a spiritual man, Emmanuel has a place in his heart and in his prayers for our special child of God.

Father Emmanuel went back to his home in Nigeria, but more than three years later he returned for a visit to our Milwaukee community. It had been five years since Maggie's last personal contact with her African friend. Yet it did not surprise me that she instantly reconnected with him as if there had been no passage of time. For her, their connection was as simple and natural as turning on a light switch.

When we hosted two welcoming dinners at our home for Emmanuel, Maggie clearly wanted time alone with her friend. As the rest of our group milled around the kitchen and family room, Maggie and Emmanuel went into the quiet of the living room and shared an exclusive one-on-one conversation.

Maggie relishes personal attention, especially from someone who has the patience and basic goodness of Emmanuel to answer her oft-repeated questions as well as the willingness to work to carry on a dialogue. In many ways, talking with Maggie is like talking with a young child. Nevertheless, she has all the life experiences of a young adult. Emmanuel's English is good, but his native dialect renders his speech somewhat difficult for some to understand. Amazingly, these two appear to have no communication problem.

This caring priest is an attentive listener. Maggie senses this. In his opinion, Maggie is much more intelligent, observant, and insightful than is generally believed, characteristics revealed to only those few who give her the time and attention she craves. It is a beautiful thing to behold, Maggie and Emmanuel—two very different individuals—connecting on such a fundamental level.

At the conclusion of Emmanuel's month-long stay, Maggie enthusiastically accompanied me as I drove our mutual friend to the airport for his long journey back to Africa. At the departure area, my son, Jack, unloaded his bags while these very special friends offered each other heartfelt goodbyes.

"I love you, Emmanuel."

"I love you, too, Mah-gee."

A movie scene could not have been scripted any better or delivered in a more touching way.

Over the past year, I have given more thought than ever before to her sense of well-being. So on occasion I directly ask our girl if she is happy. To my relief, she consistently responds that, yes, she is happy. Pressing further, I ask what makes her happy, and she answers without hesitation "us." I take this to mean her family-mom, dad, sister Martha, and brother Jack. What a wonderful gift it is to know she is genuinely happy because of the love and the richness of her family interactions.

We are so blessed as a family that she is a happy part of "us." Each night as she heads upstairs to bed, Maggie sweetly says, "I love you, Dad," and I know for certain she means it. Frequently she adds, "Don't forget."

Always taken with emotion, I ask her if I can have a goodnight kiss. Her standard reply in the sweetest tone of voice is, "Of course you can!"

Maggie not only knows how to love but also that she is loved. Sadly, many people who have a whole lot more going for them than our daughter who is cognitively disabled do not know these truths. The Maggies of the world have much to teach us, if we are willing to listen.

Don't forget.

CHAPTER 2

A MAGICAL MYSTERY TOUR

It has been said, and I believe it is true, that caring for a vulnerable special needs person is the equivalent of adding a full-time job. It extracts a toll from the caregiver both physical and emotional. Taking care of our Maggie is a demanding and challenging 24/7 job. I readily admit this duty falls most heavily on Maggie's mom, my loving wife, Cathy. In fact, when I drive Maggie to a doctor's appointment, to a day program, or to get her hair cut, Maggie sometimes refers to me as "sub," as in substitute.

Childcare responsibility, especially for Maggie, was primarily shouldered by Cathy. I have not yet fully retired from McCarthy Grittinger Financial Group, the financial planning and investment advisory firm I founded when Maggie was ten, although I did transition to a less demanding role and work schedule these past two years, thereby allowing me to assume more care for our first-born adult child.

My plan includes taking Maggie on more excursions. Typical of our trips was a sojourn to Branson, Missouri. Maggie loves live music so the city's self-described Show Capital of the U.S.A made it seem a good destination. Thinking to spend some quality father/daughter time together and to create some memories for both of us, I looked on this short three-night away-from-home trip as both an adventure and a learning experience. I also wanted to provide Mom with a badly needed respite after a particularly rough patch with Maggie.

Probably the best thing about Branson is the people—warm-hearted, down-to-earth, genuine, and extremely nice to our special girl. We ate breakfast a couple of mornings at the local Branson Denny's. The hostess was welcoming and very friendly, but on our first visit neither of us could make out what Maggie was asking her to bring. Finally, I managed to interpret that what she wanted was that "coloring stuff." She knew Denny's offered crayons and a coloring book to keep children occupied. The next day when we returned, we not only were remembered but treated royally.

Although Maggie expects the children's coloring book at this family restaurant, as an adult woman she is also entitled to sit with her father in the hotel bar for the cocktail hour. In no time at all, she made fast friends with the bartender, John Michel. A Frenchman, he has two first names. For this special customer he made a fancy kiddy cocktail, and she quickly devoured the cherry. Noting this, a patron sitting in the corner of the bar told John Michel to give Maggie another on him, but this time to put two cherries in it.

Our kind benefactor then introduced himself as Jake. Maggie looked down the bar and inquired in all innocence if he was the Jake from State Farm, quoting a line from a clever television commercial shown frequently during the football games to which Maggie is exposed. The reference wasn't lost on the bar crowd, all of whom erupted in laughter. Maggie joined in, because like all of us, she enjoys being the center of attention.

Maggie for some reason likes to refer to certain fellows of John Michel's age and body type as Oz. As it turned out, we were having breakfast at the hotel the next morning when our new friend, John Michel, slid into the booth next to Maggie without saying a word, planted a big kiss on her cheek, then left. In response to this display of affection, my girl exclaimed happily, "Oz kissed me!"

Life with Maggie has its ups and downs. One Sunday when getting into the car after attending church with her mom, our girl experienced a bad fall on a treacherous patch of ice in the parking lot. Owing to her neurological condition, Maggie's impaired balance gives her very little body control in a free fall. Being a Sunday, Cathy hustled a surprisingly calm Maggie to Urgent Care for help.

As it was, Jack and I were away. We'd escaped Wisconsin's arctic blast to enjoy sunny Arizona when Maggie and Mom had this unwelcome excitement. By phone to us, Cathy downplayed the extent of Maggie's injuries, reasoning there was nothing we could do from a distance about a fractured collarbone and a deep gash on the forehead. So on returning home, I was shocked to see Maggie's bandaged forehead and a deep purple bruise covering her shoulder, neck, and face.

I consider a primary role as a father to be that of a protector, so I felt guilty that I had not been there for Cathy and Maggie when she got hurt.

Dr. Sobczak, Maggie's primary care physician, appeared in our lives when Maggie transitioned from pediatric care to adult medicine. A wonderful, caring doctor, he is a prime example of how to be in our girl's corner. For her follow-up appointment after the accident, I brought Maggie to his office so he could check her progress and remove the stitches from her head. We had to return a few days later because the stitches proved difficult to remove, having been crudely done to begin with. Maggie likes Dr. Sobczak and told him she would not "give him a hard time" on her next visit. Fortunately, her hair partially obscures the permanent scar she now has, a blemish that would cause much distress for most young women. For Maggie it is of no concern. However, the always thorough Dr. Sobczak prescribed physical therapy and a bone density test owing to Maggie's broken collar bone. All of this resulted in multiple trips to the Froedtert Hospital Specialty Clinics. There, she is remembered by the receptionists, nurses, therapists, and doctors because she interacts with everyone with a hearty chorus of "Thank you!" "See you!" and even "Love you!"

On one such visit we shared an elevator with a lone black man dressed in street clothes. He was massive and powerfully built, appearing as if he could have been a defensive lineman in the NFL. Our Maggie turned to him and said, "Hi, hon."

He smiled warmly and said, "Hi."

As we exited the elevator, Maggie added, "Have a nice day."

He responded kindly, "Thanks. You, too."

Although I don't know what this giant of a man was doing in the hospital that particular day, odds are it may not have been connected with a particularly pleasant experience. Maggie in her own special way had reached out to him and possibly made his day a little brighter.

Maggie possesses a beautiful soul. There is much we can learn from her and from other special needs individuals. For one, she has absolutely no prejudice. In fact, our girl feels a genuine warmth toward people of color.

Maggie has a fascination with media mogul Oprah Winfrey. Perhaps part of the attraction is the distinctive and singular name Oprah. Maggie has long been exposed to Oprah because Cathy regularly watched her TV shows. At Donna Lexa art class Maggie's favorite subject matter is Oprah. When we go to the bookstore, among the dozens of periodicals on the racks Maggie immediately locates *O* magazine. She has cut out every picture of the star she could find and created several collages as part of her art projects.

Maggie likes to keep to routines, and visiting her sister is one of her favorites. Over the last dozen years we made semi-annual trips to the Twin Cities to visit Martha, who went to college there and lives there now. We frequently stay at an Embassy Suites hotel in St. Paul, primarily because Maggie so enjoys the nightly complimentary cocktail reception offered to guests. A people person, Maggie over the years has developed a unique relationship with Lavera, the reception manager and bartender. It doesn't seem to hurt their friendship that Maggie likes to fill the tip jar.

Maggie and Lavera often call each other girlfriends. On some occasions Maggie refers to Lavera as Oprah. There is indeed a striking resemblance between the two women. When I shared this observation with Lavera, she said she took it as a compliment, especially coming from Maggie, adding she wished she could have even a tiny bit of Oprah's success. At the end of our stays it is beautiful to see Maggie and Lavera share heartfelt hugs.

Maggie's favorite singer by far is the country music star Darius Rucker, formerly known as Hootie from his days as front man in the popular group Hootie and the Blowfish. I admit to also being a fan. I like the fact that Maggie and I share this particular taste in music, but in addition to enjoying his music, our girl clearly digs the name Hootie. She has a handful of his CDs and can identify all his songs. Whenever he performs in Milwaukee we buy tickets to see him live. Maggie doesn't understand why he doesn't perform here all the time.

At first I had no idea he had any connection with the special needs community, but once again, Maggie was somehow ahead of the curve. I happened to catch Rucker on TV, and on a whim decided to do an internet search using his name and the words "special needs." It didn't take me long to choke up with emotion when I realized Hootie has a soft spot in his heart for the Maggies in our midst. To my delight, I discovered a powerful and moving four-minute video of Darius Rucker performing an original song, "Music from the Heart" at the 2011 Country Music Awards in Las Vegas.

What brought tears to my eyes, as it probably will to yours, was the on-stage, back-up choir for this rousing, heartwarming performance of 25 young adults, all dressed in black, all with developmental disabilities. They had originally come together at a special summer camp held at Vanderbilt University.

The opening lines of "Music from the Heart" is "Welcome to our lives, welcome to our hearts." Among all the celebrity country music stars sitting front and center that night, these talented young people shone the brightest and stole the show. They poured their hearts out in song while accompanying Darius at his finest. One particular young woman was shown on camera twice, tears of happiness streaming down her face. The charitable arm of the

Academy of Country Music has a program named "Lifting Lives." This highlight moment aptly demonstrates the power of music to do just that for these special young people, lifting their lives and ours.

The public posts to this inspirational video are equally touching. One mother shared: "This song is amazing. I have a four-year-old son that has cerebral palsy, seizures, past stroke, wears braces on his legs. What they say about music is true. He loves music. He can't talk much and we listen to music all the time. He dances and tries to sing what he can. He stood up smiling [watching the video] and got excited, which is wonderful to see. Thanks to everyone involved with this."

Lest you think Darius is a one-hit wonder with the special needs community, a 2013 story tells of him making a dream come true for a 16-year-old student with Down syndrome at a high school talent show in Charleston, SC. Judging from a grainy online video taken at Wondo High School, 16-year-old Frankie is a real showman. It seems he has been belting out the hits of South Carolina's native son Darius Rucker since the fifth grade. As his mom Debbie Antonelli says, "He is uninhibited and he loves to perform."

On this talent night, Frankie, wearing a Darius Rucker T-shirt, was doing his best rendition of his idol's song, "While I Still Got the Time." Halfway through his spirited performance, Frankie had the audience on their feet roaring with approval. He seemed unfazed when Rucker made a surprise onstage appearance. Arm in arm they finished the song in a duet that brought down the house.

Like many parents, the Antonellis had grown tired of hearing that their son couldn't succeed because of his condition. They resolutely pledged, "He can and he will." Anyone who sat in that high school auditorium or views its amateur video will attest to the truth of his parents' pledge and agree that yes, Frankie can! According to the boy's mom, "He is happy, he's healthy, he's funny, he's athletic…he is sweet and he is handsome. He just happens to have Down syndrome."

When I learned that Darius Rucker was coming to town to play at Milwaukee's 2014 Summerfest (dubbed the World's Largest Music Festival), I knew Maggie and I had to catch his show. As I have often said, life with Maggie is never dull and very often an adventure. This concert was no exception.

We arrived at the amphitheater early. To occupy Maggie for the half-hour or so until the show kicked off, she focused on enjoying a large box of popcorn. The first challenge of the night proved to be getting down to our reserved seats. As you now know, Maggie's neurological condition affects both her balance and depth perception, making it difficult—actually terrifying—to descend a steep flight of stairs, especially one without handrails. Unsympathetic ushers insisted we had to negotiate 40 rows of seats to reach our own. Although we tried, with me holding onto her, she was so frightened I knew I must find another way to accommodate her fear and her disability.

We carefully worked our way around by another route to the gated lower level, where I observed we would have an easy, one-row climb up to our seats. At this, I ran into another inflexible usher, who informed me the only way to reach these seats was to return again to the top and descend down the steps. Sensing this, Maggie got a little worked up and so did I. But then I thought what Mom would do. Calming down and taking a deep breath, I respectfully but firmly said there must be someone in authority who could help us.

After a few distressing minutes, the head security guard arrived. This tall, uniformed "brownish black" man quickly appraised the situation and told Maggie he would help her. He unlocked the gate and personally escorted Maggie and me to our nearby seats. He then instructed the usher to take care of us in any way we needed. Maggie was profuse in her thanks, and this kind man wished us an enjoyable time.

Seated next to Maggie in our row was an attractive young woman. Maggie offered her some popcorn, and from this simple gesture an unlikely friendship began. Introducing herself as Kim, she explained she was there with her husband and another couple enjoying a night away from their infant son. They were excited to see Darius Rucker perform.

Once Darius appeared on stage, Kim persuaded Maggie to stand up and bogey with her arm-in-arm, both singing raucously and having a good time. I was at best a third wheel. Darius put on a spirited show, followed by an intermission before headliner Brad Paisley was scheduled to top off the show. This seemed an opportune time to leave Maggie with her new friend while I used the men's restroom. When I am alone with Maggie in certain crowded situations, my leaving can pose a problem, but this situation seemed perfectly safe. Not more than 20 minutes could have passed before I returned to find Maggie and Kim carrying on as before and generally acting silly. It occurred to me then that Kim had been imbibing and was now showing the effects of a night of drinking. I decided this was a good time to leave. It was getting late—past Mag's bedtime—and we had seen the star we had come to see.

Maggie did not want to leave her new friend. Kim tried a couple of times to ask me why we were leaving early. The music was so loud I could not make out what she was saying. Soon, Maggie and Kim were hugging each other and saying heartfelt goodbyes. We managed to get out of the crowded aisle and, as expected, Maggie had no problem at all climbing up the 40 rows of steps. As we walked out of the amphitheater she sweetly thanked me for taking her to the Darius concert.

Not until the next morning did I learn the full story. According to Maggie, when I left her alone with Kim the previous night, Kim asked if she would like to share a beer. Maggie knows this is alcohol. Despite not even liking beer's "gross" taste, she quickly answered, "Sure!"

I admitted surprise to this telling of events and asked her how much she drank. "Too much," she answered with a mischievous smile. Maggie then went on to refer to Kim as "the Beermeister."

It dawned on me that what Kim had attempted to ask me was whether my decision to leave before the concert ended was due to her getting Maggie a little drunk. Although Maggie shouldn't have alcohol with all the medication she takes, I believe half a can of beer on a rare occasion is unlikely to be detrimental.

Kim is three years younger than Maggie, married, and a mother. Her life is far different from Maggie's, yet these two very different young women came together on an unforgettable night and connected as girlfriends. I believe there is magic to that memory, even in the retelling.

Maggie rarely fails to make us smile. For one thing, we never know what she will come up with next. A couple of years ago, Cathy and I took Maggie along with us to an industry conference in Las Vegas. With her heightened sense of humor, Maggie found it amusing to be eating a caesar salad while staying at the Caesars Palace Hotel.

While Cathy was attending some meetings, Mag and I took a stroll along the Strip and stopped for lunch at a modest outdoor café. There, we came across a fellow dressed up as a popular entertainer and was charging tourists for the privilege of having their picture taken with him. This scene caught Maggie's attention, of course. I don't quite remember, but she may have called him "boyfriend." That would be just like her. This familiar stranger came over and sat down with us at our table. Ignoring me completely, he turned his attention to Maggie, asking, "Do you know who I am?"

Without missing a beat, our girl said, "You're Elvis," and a moment later, for good measure, added, "Presley!" I sat amazed by the surreal conversation that took place between the Special Olympian and the make-believe King.

Back in Wisconsin the following week Maggie's classmates at Donna Lexa art class asked where she had been, adding they had missed her.

"I was in Vegas," she said.

"What did you do there?" they wanted to know.

"I saw Elvis."

At that, Phil, a 65-year-old in her class whom I refer to as the Weatherman because of his keen interest in the weather, piped up, "She couldn't possibly have seen Elvis."

"Yes I did," Maggie insisted.

"No you didn't! Elvis is dead."

"Maybe you saw an impersonator," Phil explained.

And that is why Maggie now refers to any reincarnation of Elvis as a "personator."

Our middle child, Martha, three-and-a-half years Maggie's junior, lives in the Twin Cities with her husband. From the very start of their relationship Maggie accepted Matt Krueger as a member of the family. I vividly recall Maggie lagging behind as all of us left a restaurant, very comfortably holding the arm of her six-foot-six future brother-in-law.

Whenever Martha is mentioned, Maggie is quick to pair their names as a couple: Martha *and* Matt. Maggie being Maggie now refers to her brother-in-law as the "Krugermeister." One night while heading up to bed, Maggie sweetly told him, "I love you, Matt."

Clearly taken, Matt answered, "I love you, too, Maggie."

For the wedding in the summer of 2015 Martha included her big sister in her big day. As sister of the bride, Maggie proudly wore a beautiful red dress for the occasion, just like the bridesmaids. It was a storybook event, and Maggie played her part. At the church, moments before I was to walk Martha down the aisle, Maggie would be the last to enter and be ushered to her seat in the front row. The music was playing, the bridesmaids, groom, and best man stood in their rehearsed places and all awaited the appearance of the beautiful bride. But Maggie cannot be rushed. Our girl took her sweet time getting to the front, casually stopping along the way to chat with friends and family, oblivious to the main event.

During the couple's solemn exchange of vows, a momentary silence occurred and Maggie blurted out, "Say it, Martha." Matt couldn't help but break up at this outburst.

Later, at the reception, Maggie enjoyed sitting at the head table. Apparently she was fond of the champagne. Whenever her name was mentioned in the toasts or table talk, she triumphantly raised her arm.

When Martha and Maggie were younger, I took them both to the annual father-daughter dinner dance held at a club in our area. It's been quite a number of years since we attended our last event, yet Maggie remembers those occasions fondly and regularly mentions them. The Wisconsin Club, where Martha and Matt recently held their wedding reception, staged a father-daughter dinner the previous spring. I asked Maggie if she wanted to attend. She quickly replied, "Sure."

Maggie was impatient for the night of the event to arrive. With Cathy's assistance she got all "dolled up," and a string of pearls from mom completed her ensemble. Maggie still remembers that in years past she also received a wrist corsage and that a picture would be taken of us. As expected, the photographer asked Maggie and me to look into the camera and give a big smile—not a good idea for Maggie. Experience has taught us: simply take the picture, please, because she naturally smiles at the right time instead of trying to manufacture one.

The band at the Wisconsin Club's father-daughter dance that night did a nice job of playing the 1960s hit *My Girl*, originally recorded by the Temptations. As we slow-danced to the music, I found myself singing along to the lyrics: "*I got sunshine on a cloudy day, and when it's cold outside I got the month of May.*" At this line I was truly overcome by a wave of fatherly love for my girl.

Another dad I've come to know, also of a special needs child, refers to it as a love like no other. And, indeed it is.

CHAPTER 3

THE REMARKABLE CINDY BENTLEY

No one forgets a first-time encounter with the remarkable Cindy Bentley. This charismatic, 50-something African-American woman with the dynamic personality stands out in any crowd.

Maggie and I met Cindy some 15 years ago when we boarded the bus from Milwaukee to our very first State Summer Games for Special Olympics. "State" has been the scene of much drama and many life-changing experiences for Maggie and me—as it has for all the athletes and coaches privileged to attend. For our girl, the bus itself and the three-hour ride to Stevens Point in central Wisconsin comprise one of the highlights of the whole joyful experience.

Sporting a team uniform, Cindy seemed to know everybody on the bus and managed to engage with us all. It quickly became apparent she was a leader. At first I thought she was either a coach or an official of some kind. Then I realized there was something "special" about her, too, and was drawn to learn more.

It turned out Cindy's presence that particular year was as a member of the Wauwatosa Special Olympics soccer team. Like all teams it is co-ed and its athletes represent a wide range of ages. Because it is not uncommon for athletes to occasionally switch teams, Cindy Bentley later went on to compete and play for another area's Special Olympics team, but through the years we regularly ran across each other. Maggie and I didn't know it that first year, but we had begun to cross paths with a Special Olympics legend.

Shortly after our first brief encounter on the bus to Stevens Point, I happened to hear someone call in to a local talk radio program. I realized the caller was the same woman athlete we'd met on the bus. I listened intently as Cindy, in her recognizably slow and occasionally slurred speech, told the tragic story of the first stormy years of her life.

She started life in 1957 in Milwaukee with brain damage and a resulting intellectual disability. Her birth mother had abused both drugs and alcohol during pregnancy, and this infant—diagnosed with fetal alcohol syndrome—barely survived. Her father subsequently abandoned her, and her mother was sent to prison for drug offenses.

Alone and unloved, this precious child floated like driftwood among a number of foster homes. According to Cindy, when she was three a disturbed foster mother attempted to kill her by setting her shirt on fire. The child survived but suffered extensive burns, endured nine surgeries, and was hospitalized for six months. To this day those scars are a visible reminder of that cruelty.

At the age of eight Cindy was placed by social workers in the Southern Wisconsin Center for the Developmentally Disabled, some 30 miles south of Milwaukee. She spent the next 18 years there. Life was not happy for Cindy at what she referred to as "the institution," or even more derisively as "San Quentin," the prison. She rebelled, cried a lot, and had behavior problems. Cindy, who likes colorful outfits, with purple and red as favorites, was given no choice of what to wear. And relishing soul food, especially catfish, she had to eat whatever she was given. To this day she disdains oatmeal, a mainstay in her bland institutional diet.

No one at that time, including Cindy, could ever in their wildest dreams have thought she would be able to live alone one day and thrive independently. Now on her own, she adores her two cats, a Siamese named Blossom with a serious attitude, and a black and white named Oreo, that she refers to as her problem child.

Fast forward to the fall of 2013. Cindy Bentley was honored by Life Navigators, a non-profit agency dedicated to improving the quality of life for individuals with developmental disabilities. She was also a featured speaker at Life Navigators' annual fundraising dinner.

At that same event the year before, Cindy had approached two former board members of Life Navigators, Brian Lanser and me, to tell us how truly special she found our daughters Jessie and Maggie and how much she loved them both. She had gotten to know our girls through her work in programming for Easter Seals. For Brian and me, the fathers of special needs daughters, Cindy could not have told us anything of greater value.

Cindy makes it a point to never speak ill of anybody. We can all learn from this wonderful, faith-based woman, who told me, "I always see the best in people. We are all different. It is not what is on the outside but the inside. People need to be more patient and meet people where they are."

In 2013 Life Navigators broke tradition from honoring former governors and business leaders by turning the spotlight on Cindy Bentley, someone who benefited from the services of the organization and knows how to pay those benefits forward. I thought she was an excellent choice and was excited for her to gain this well-deserved recognition. Unfortunately, Cathy and I had a scheduling conflict and had not planned to attend the event that year.

A month before Cindy's big night, Maggie and I were doing one of our father/daughter rituals and attended the Wisconsin State Fair, held annually on the fairgrounds a little over a mile from our home. Maggie likes to snack on a giant pickle, corn on the cob, and a chocolate-covered pretzel, and to ride on the sky glider. Walking through the crowded exhibit hall, who did we run into but a smiling Cindy Bentley. This amazing woman was on her way to meet friends at Bingo. She seemed genuinely excited to see us and greeted us warmly.

I congratulated her for the much-deserved honor she was

receiving. She looked me in the eyes and asked if we would be attending. No way could I say no to Cindy. Cathy and I changed our plans and sent in our reservations for three, adding Maggie. I am so glad we did because Cindy's acceptance speech knocked the proverbial ball out of the park. Everyone in the audience was greatly enriched by experiencing this outstanding event and her inspiring words.

It occurred to me someone could and should write a book about Cindy Bentley. Fortunately, I wasn't the only one with this thought. *Cindy Bentley: Spirit of a Champion* was published by the Wisconsin Historical Society Press, funded in part by the Wisconsin Board for People with Developmental Disabilities. I purchased an early copy directly from Cindy and eagerly read it cover to cover. I became even more inspired by the many life lessons of the book's heroine.

The turning point in Cindy's life occurred at age 22, when an angel appeared in the form of Chris Ziegler, a recreational therapist who came to Southern Center. A recreational therapist is trained to help people who have disabilities, like Cindy, Maggie, and Jessie Lanser, by using sports, art, music, dance, games, and other activities to improve their lives. Chris saw potential in Cindy and offered encouragement, stayed positive, and slowly helped her build self-confidence. For the first time in her life Cindy had, in Chris, a consistently caring person and a friend. She blossomed and her life changed.

Had Chris not entered her life, Cindy earnestly believes she would have ended up in the criminal justice system. Talk about one person making a difference—this is a perfect example.

Then there is Special Olympics. Cindy is not shy about claiming this, too, saved her life. "Special Olympics is my hero," she proclaims. She poured herself into training and competing year-round in sports such as soccer, track, tennis, bowling, basketball, tennis, bocce, softball—even snowshoeing.

At age 34, Cindy Bentley was chosen 1991 Special Olympics

International Female Athlete of the Year. In 1995 she carried the U.S. flag and competed in tennis at the Special Olympics World Summer Games held that year in Connecticut. The following year she was named Global Messenger and traveled to Greece and Holland. She went on to be the first athlete on the board of directors of Special Olympics Wisconsin.

Maggie and I ran into Cindy again at the 2014 State Summer Games. I asked her if she was competing in soccer. "No," she said, "race walking." She floored me by saying she changed sports because for the past year she had to deal with breast cancer. Cindy Bentley is a fighter and a resilient survivor. As Cindy says in the book written about her, she loved sports and Special Olympics so much that she made a promise to herself: "I am going to compete until I die."

Would you believe Cindy has been to the White House not once, but twice and that she met both President Bill Clinton and President George W. Bush? In her meeting with the Clintons she sat next to First Lady Hillary Clinton, and animal-loving Cindy turned the conversation to the White House pets, Buddy the dog and Socks the cat.

Cindy blushes as she also tells how President Bush gave her a kiss on the cheek after she presented one of her gold medals to him for helping keep the country safe after the terror of 9/11. Understandably, the President was deeply moved by this heartfelt gesture. First Lady Laura Bush, visibly teary, sent Cindy a beautiful thank you note. Cindy, an avid reader, expresses deep admiration for this former First Lady for her extensive work promoting literacy.

On the subject of visits to the White House, I read that President Kennedy was the first head of state to have met publicly with someone with an intellectual disability. A 1962 photo shows JFK shaking hands in the oval office with nine-year-old David Jordalen of Shrewsbury, Massachusetts. This picture made David a national symbol as the poster child of the National Association of Retarded Children. He passed away in 2006 at age 52.

Invitations to the White House aside, the standing ovation Cindy received after her acceptance of the Life Navigators Award was well deserved. However, her success at the podium came as no surprise, as she had spoken before 15,000 people in Chicago at a Lion's Club International Convention, a major supporter of Special Olympics. Despite having had speech therapy to correct a speech impediment and being understandably nervous at the size of the audience focused on her, Cindy Bentley had somehow summoned the strength to make that hallmark speech. In Cindy's own telling words, "I'm a fighter. I am a determined person. If I can't do something right the first time, I try until I get it. I never quit, and I never say I can't." Those words capture the spirit of a true champion.

In my opinion, Cindy's most amazing accomplishment is that she lives a full life independent—albeit with her two cats—in an apartment of her own. Moreover, she has lived in the same apartment for at least 28 years and thoroughly enjoys her neighbors and neighborhood. Significantly, she also feels safe and secure. At first, never having experienced adulthood outside the sheltering confines of an institution, living on her own in the real world was indeed daunting. She admits to having been overwhelmed at the prospect and a little afraid. At the age of 26 she had to learn many basic life skills, from simple safety measures such as locking the door to setting an alarm clock, from shopping and cooking to using public bus transportation.

A woman of strong faith, Cynthia Bentley has made it her mission in life to be an inspiration to others and serve those in need. When I last caught up with Cindy she was on her way to a Feeding America volunteer service project. She told me, "My life started rocky but I am a good person and proud of who I am."

Cindy never dreamed that one day she would be director of an organization such as People First Wisconsin, a grassroots nonprofit run by and for people with disabilities, especially intellectual disabilities. But she is. For her wish to leave a rich legacy, she is definitely on track.

Sister Edna, a compassionate caregiver and president of St. Ann Center for Intergenerational Care in Milwaukee, counseled me to be conscious always of putting the person first, and to remember that people are primary and the disability secondary. Whereas a disability is natural, no one is their disability. Maggie has helped teach me that an individual with a disability is much more like a person without disabilities.

I was privileged to run into Cindy Bentley at a 2015 Life Navigators golf event. She was volunteering as a host and goodwill ambassador at this fundraiser. She told me she had just returned from Washington D.C. where she had received yet another award and an opportunity to hear President Obama speak at a function. She said the trip was good, but observed good-naturedly that on her return home the cats were mad at her over her extended absence.

Cindy recently shared with Brian Lanser and me that she is now serving on the board of Life Navigators. She is a wonderful addition. Any group, but especially a non profit organization serving special needs individuals, is only as good and effective as its leadership. Life Navigators is fortunate for the past dozen years to have had Vicki Wachniak as its Executive Director. Vicki has also been a close personal friend and mentor to Cindy over the last 20 years. According to Vicki, Cindy is "one of her favorite people on the planet."

Cindy Bentley has overcome the almost insurmountable odds against surviving, let alone thriving. She is a symbol of hope in ways few people ever achieve. She touches lives one person at a time-as a friend, a colleague, and when needed a protector.

Cindy greeted me warmly at that golf event and inquired about Maggie, telling me again how much she loves our girl. She declared as well that if anyone crosses Maggie, they will have to answer to Cindy Bentley. This remarkable woman is one more angel in Maggie's life and in the lives of so many others.

CHAPTER 4

THE WHEELCHAIR GIRLS

*"We are each of us angels with only one wing, and we can
only fly by embracing one another."*
Luciano De Crescenzo

When Maggie was about to turn eight, Cathy, the devoted mother of a special needs child constantly alert for opportunities to enrich our daughter's life, discovered Lions Camp. Once, at a swim class for special needs children, Cathy struck up a conversation with another mother while both waited for the lesson to end. This is how she came to learn about the camp for special needs kids ages 8 to 18 at the lake and woodland property of Wisconsin Lions International.

Cathy also discovered the Wisconsin Lions runs a spring and fall weekend Family Camp. She investigated and registered Maggie and me to attend and check it out. I admit to concern about not knowing what to expect and am typically wary of something new. But over the years I wisened up and learned to appreciate my wife's good judgment on these matters. The fact is, Lions Camp and the family weekends turned out to be a real find in the lives of Maggie and all our family.

For one thing, it was at Family Camp in May 1993 that Maggie and I crossed paths with the mighty Berendes family and their twin eight-year-old daughters, Nicole (Nikki) and Jennifer (Jenni). Maggie, in her special way, immediately took to these girls. For the more than 20 years since then, she has affectionately referred to them as "the wheelchair girls."

Lions Family Camp is open to Wisconsin residents who have one or more members with a cognitive disability. It is a great place to get to know some incredible families, learn of their own trials, and celebrate their triumphs. Such was the case with the wheelchair girls' mom and dad, Diane and Bob.

You are likely familiar with the proverb, "I felt sorry for myself because I had no shoes, until I met a man who had no feet." Cathy has often remarked how fortunate we are that Maggie is mobile—she walks. Because she walks and does not need a wheelchair, Maggie does not believe she is handicapped.

In Nikki and Jenni we found not one but two children Maggie's age born with cerebral palsy, both requiring a high level of care. As parents, we are reminded often that many parents such as Diane and Bob cope with far more severe situations than we do with Maggie.

A number of years had passed since we'd last seen Nikki and Jenni, but I was reminded of them while staying in St. Paul, Minnesota, at an Embassy Suites, a hotel configured around an open courtyard with corridors visible from all interior sides. While waiting for an elevator I encountered a young mother with her special needs son, about age 12, who was strapped into an electric wheelchair for support. I held the elevator door open, we exchanged pleasantries, and I learned from the boy's mother they were in town for some doctors' appointments at the nearby regional medical center. She then pointed out her husband and this boy's twin brother, also in a wheelchair, who at that very moment were taking the elevator on the opposite side of the courtyard. Later, I saw them all together at the hotel's complimentary breakfast.

I have since come to learn that cerebral palsy tends to be associated with premature and multiple births and may result in disabilities ranging from mild challenges to more serious mobility, intellect, communication, and vision issues. I became aware of everything mom and dad had to do that day to ready, toilet, dress, feed, and transport their twin sons who are disabled. Going to each medical appointment had to be a major production, and I felt a small degree of fatigue just watching them maneuver their sons into the two elevators. This chance encounter reminded me again of the wheelchair girls.

Because the May dates of Family Camp frequently fell on Mother's Day, the best gift we could give Cathy was some quiet time to be alone and to celebrate with her own dear mother, Kay Korevec. So these camp weekends with our three youngsters became a daddy thing.

Maggie stories always amuse her grandmother, Kay. While Maggie cannot read past the most elementary level, she can correctly spell a couple of hundred words. If I spell out a three or four-letter word, she can tell me what it is. Recently, I asked Maggie to spell Kay for me. She answered by saying the letter "K" and added her usual "duh" to indicate I should know better. Properly chastened, I decided to not pursue the discussion any further.

Our Maggie has been fascinated by wheelchairs from an early age. She even owns a toy wheelchair for her doll. Her closest friend in elementary school was Andy, who used a chair. To this day, Maggie says Andy is her boyfriend, despite not having seen him for some 10 years.

Maggie's neurological condition may at some point cause her to lose her mobility. When Cathy and Maggie flew to the National Institutes of Health (NIH) in Bethesda, Maryland, the goal was to have top specialists do a workup on Maggie and assess her very rare genetic disease. In advance of seeing her, the team of experts reviewed her records and test results. They asked whether she could walk. Not only does she walk, we responded, but she also competes in the two-mile race walk for Special Olympics. We added, she even won a gold medal in that long-distance event. Such mobility, given her diagnosis, surprised the experts.

Reminded by the two boys in wheelchairs of Nikki and Jenni,

the wheelchair girls nicknamed as such by Maggie, I realized
we had not seen them for about a dozen years. In the late 1990's
we'd gotten reacquainted with the Berendes a handful of times at
Family Camp. We even visited them at their home in 2002 when
we took a family bicycling vacation in Sparta, the self-proclaimed
"America's Bicycling Capital." Despite the passage of time during
which our family had no contact with them, Maggie occasionally,
out of the blue, inquires about the Wheelchair Girls as if she'd
seen them only yesterday.

In writing this book, I found myself thinking more and more
about them and wondering how their life journey had played out
over these past dozen years. Part of me harbored a fear of discovering them not doing well.

So, I made contact with Diane Berendes and quickly learned to
my delight that all was well with the girls and the family. We made
arrangements to reconnect for dinner at their home. On a cold and
dark November evening, Maggie and I drove to Sparta and enjoyed
a warm welcome by the family. Encountering the bright smiling
faces of the Wheelchair Girls, now adults, was exciting, especially
seeing that Nikki and Jenni were doing so well. For Maggie and
her old friends, their connection was instantly renewed.

It is hard for parents to realize that our daughters, especially as
firstborns, are 30 years old. Diane pulled out a scrapbook from the
first Lions Camp we attended back in 1993. As we reminisced, I
too felt as though we had last been there only a month ago.

Taking in all the progress made, I marvelled at how Bob and
Diane had created such a happy home, although I do recall Diane
having admitted to being overwhelmed at times. Very understandable. A wooden sign prominently mounted above their living room
window read: "Life isn't about waiting for the storm to pass, it is
about learning to dance in the rain."

A beaming Diane explained that this sign was a Christmas gift
of a few years past from their son, Paul. "I loved it the moment I
saw it," she said, having been especially taken by the usually stoic

Paul telling her that its message so reminded him of her and her motherly resolve.

These very special parents discovered their own coping mechanism. They no longer feel it necessary to go someplace if doing so is not conducive to the needs of the family—if it is a hassle, too crowded, or not enjoyable. They learned from experience to be more selective in choosing their destinations, politely turning down certain invitations.

As the Berendes family demonstrates, we learn through experience to dance in the rain. I came across a similar inspirational quotation from 19th century novelist Louisa May Alcott: "I am not afraid of storms, for I am learning how to sail my ship."

Though Nikki and Jenni are twins, their mom shared with me some of their differences. Jenni is bigger, and much more verbal, outgoing, and capable than Nikki. A vocal fan of the Green Bay Packers, she sported green and gold Packer garb the night we visited to show her allegiance. In her room is a football autographed by Brett Favre. The football-loving Berendes family had attended training camp in Green Bay the summer after the Packers, led by MVP quarterback Favre, won the 1997 Super Bowl. After practice, the superstar quarterback noticed the girls in their wheelchairs behind the fence on the opposite side of the field. To the amazement of the hundreds of fans gathered around, he came all the way across the field to present the twins with this cherished prize.

Jenni has held various jobs and likes working and making friends with coworkers. Her mom recounted how Jenni had suffered a bad fall at a summer camp when she fell out out of her chair and crashed head first onto the pavement. After high school Jenni was moved into a group home 25 miles down the Interstate to LaCrosse. After about 18 months of living separately from her sister and parents, Jenni opted to return home. It occurred after a short visit home, when Diane, driving Jenni back to the group home, made the final turn in the road. Jenni became so overcome by emotion she started sobbing. Through her tears she told her parents she missed home and did not want to return to the group home.

Nikki enjoys a beautiful relationship with her special friend Michael. She is also a champion hugger and likes having her shoulders rubbed. It was warming to see Maggie and Nikki affectionately hugging each other. Despite being nonverbal and visually handicapped, Nikki doesn't miss much. You can tell she takes everything in because she turns her head up, opens her mouth, and flashes a trademark smile. As a family, the Berendes enjoy regular outings, such as going to the movies. Although Nikki is legally blind, Diane believes the movies are a feast for her senses. She takes in the sounds, smells, and atmosphere, and eats popcorn.

Whereas Nikki doesn't speak much, her twin sister Jenni makes up for it. She couldn't wait to spill the beans to me that her brother, Paul, was about to become a father. Jenni is excited to have a baby in the family and be an aunt.

Nikki, who was quite thin when we'd known her as a young girl, now looked healthy. Although her verbal responses are one-syllable utterances, she clearly was part of our dinner table conversation. Her father Bob shared with me how truly happy Nikki is. During our visit she displayed a constant smile. This quotation is so true of her: "I have never seen a smiling face that was not beautiful." According to her dad, Nikki wakes up smiling and is in love with life. What a special gift.

After a satisfying dinner of lasagna, garlic bread, and salad (Maggie loves salads), the Berendes family took us on a tour of their home. As we entered the rear living quarters of this cozy one-level ranch we passed through wide privacy doors to find a track system installed on the ceiling. A hoist moves the girls between an exercise therapy room, their bedrooms—each decorated in their personal styles—and a bathroom adapted for their disability.

But before we left the Berendes family we couldn't say goodbye without making plans to stay in touch and see each other again. Maggie invited her long-lost friends to come to our house and see her bedroom. I suggested they could come to Milwaukee and catch a Brewers baseball game at Miller Park. Home plate is only three miles from our door. I was quite sure I could work with the Brewers to secure good seats to accommodate the Wheelchair Girls, especially since they have a fear of heights. A visit to the Milwaukee County Zoo was ruled out because Jenni and Nikki also have some fear of animals. Our Maggie has a fear of escalators, and her friend Jessie Lanser fears the sounds of a saxophone.

Mom and Dad reminded me that they do not travel much these days, as overnights at hotels prove challenging. Diane wrote in a follow-up, "We really need some accessibility options in an overnight stay. More than just a room with bathroom handrails." As I have come to learn, where there is a will there is a way. I have also pleasantly found that in the special needs and disability community it is a small world after all.

It so happens that my old friend Diane Miller runs a nonprofit bed and breakfast in Newburg, 35 miles northwest of Milwaukee. She is executive director in residence of Welcome H.O.M.E.— House of Modifications. I suggested the Berendes family could stay there while visiting us and catching a major league baseball game. Maggie and I enjoyed spending nights there and knew it would be perfect for the special needs of our Sparta friends. In discussing this suggestion, Bob and Diane recalled that they had stayed at a B&B similar to this, but many years before. I wondered whether it might have been the same place.

On my return home, I called Diane Miller, who was excited to confirm the earlier visit of the Berendes and forwarded me a picture that captured their original stay. She added "I have a door covered with guest photos...so this was easy to find. It's a family that has always remained clear in my mind. It was taken in September, 1999—the first year we operated the B&B!"

I shared this 15-year-old picture with Diane Berendes. "Jenni asked me immediately after you left if we really could come to Milwaukee for the game and stay possibly two nights at the

Welcome Home bed and breakfast. I really would like to make this happen. When the schedule comes out in spring, let's connect to see what might work for our families."

Game on!

CHAPTER 5

DIANE MILLER—STILL KICKING

L et me tell you more about Diane Miller. It was in the years right after college when we met and developed our friendship. You couldn't help but notice her resolute demeanor in using hand crutches to get around. Being the same age, we are growing older in tandem. We've managed to stay in touch because of Maggie and our regular stays at the B&B.

In August 1955 a polio epidemic broke out in Milwaukee. Diane, then three-and-a-half years old, contracted this dreaded, disabling disease. Every mother of young children in the early 1950s was acutely aware of such a fearful epidemic. Years later when my mother met Diane, she realized that my friend—like me—was among the very last generation of children at risk for this life-changing condition. In 1954, only a year before the epidemic hit, Jonas Salk developed the vaccine that essentially eradicated polio. The problem was one of manufacturing sufficient quantities of this miracle vaccine. Consequently, the limited supply was rationed, with school-age children the first to receive it. Because Diane was of preschool age, she probably just missed being vaccinated. Knowing this, I asked Diane if she ever felt cheated because of her disability. She replied honestly that she harbors no bitterness, as this is the only life she has ever known.

As a student of history, I am aware that Franklin D. Roosevelt, our country's only four-term president, had contracted polio later in life, at age 39, leaving him paralyzed from the waist down and needing a wheelchair for mobility. Although his illness was common knowledge, he purposely downplayed the extent of his disability. The Secret Service did not allow photos showing him in a wheelchair, and the media and press corps helped guard the "state secret." FDR thought if the public was aware of the severity of his paralysis it would suggest a lack of vigor and leadership capability and hurt his political ambitions.

Interestingly, Eleanor Roosevelt said her husband's polio was a "turning point" that "proved a blessing in disguise, for it gave him strength and courage he had not had before." So it is possible FDR might never have reached the highest office in the land, from which he became recognized as one of our country's greatest presidents, had he not been disabled.

Although FDR is widely regarded as the public face of polio, researchers now believe he may have been paralyzed by Guillain-Barre syndrome. No one is absolutely sure of the actual cause of his paralysis. However, even if the correct diagnosis had been different, his treatment would not have differed much because neither disease had a cure.

Keith Veronese, a PhD chemist and freelance writer, says, "While we will never truly know if Roosevelt suffered from polio, the attention Roosevelt brought to the illness ended the most rampant cause of death and paralysis in human history, a disease dating to Ancient Egypt. Not a bad outcome for a possible misdiagnosis."

These days Diane Miller must use a wheelchair. Rather than feel sorry for herself, she has purposely elected to make lemonade out of the lemons in her life with the Welcome Home bed and breakfast.

As could be expected, the home is a wheelchair-friendly living laboratory. Its modifications include wide doorways, sloped floors, louvered doors, height-adapted countertops, and reachable faucets and controls that allow those with disabilities to live independently. Similar adaptations to their own home have helped the Berendes family, and others like them, to live strong.

During our regular stays at Welcome Home, Diane gets a real kick out of our Maggie. She enjoys Maggie's brand of humor, and we share a lot of laughs while Maggie devours a salad with all the fixings. Maggie is very comfortable with Diane and obviously fond of her.

But in the game of life, as we discover again and again, one never knows where a connection will help to open a door. Cathy and I worry about what the future holds for Maggie, considering her baffling neurological condition. Seeing how Diane has learned to adapt and function so well despite not being able to walk gives us, Maggie's parents, inspiration as well as a roadmap to follow.

Diane has been very supportive of my book project. In a note to me she writes, "Thanks for sharing Maggie with us. Reading about her I can't help but smile." Diane has also offered valuable input, especially about a few terms that particularly rattle her. "Wheelchair-bound" is at the top of her list as a no-no. "It is used often, I know, particularly by the media. To me (and others) it portrays a very negative mental image—someone who needs to be tied into their wheelchair, or worse yet, bondage."

I asked this intelligent, master's-degreed social worker her thoughts on the use of the term "confined." She does not especially care for it but was more ambivalent toward it. "Unfortunately, I don't have a great alternative to offer, but here are a few: mobile by wheelchair, wheelchair-user, wheelchair-mobile."

During my most recent phone conversation with my friend I asked how she was holding up. "John," she replied, "I'm still kicking."

Recently I readily accepted an invitation to serve on an investment committee for Independence First in Milwaukee. This community-based, non-residential Independent Living Center (ILC) is one of the largest in the country. A nonprofit, it is a resource for people with disabilities of all kinds, at all ages, offering 20 programs and services. It also operates a mobility store that sells a wide variety of quality refurbished equipment at reasonable prices. More than 50 percent of its staff, managers, and board members live with disabilities themselves. When I was introduced to the President and CEO Lee Schulz, he shared with me that he was well aware of the contributions of my friend Diane Miller and Welcome Home.

I am happy to report that the Berendes family did make it to Milwaukee for what the twins' mom referred to as the girls' Brewer adventure weekend. It felt good to have made this happen. In our busy lives too many of us too often run out of well-intentioned next years. Not only was a great time had by all, but we witnessed a historic 17-inning victory by the home team. We stayed only two extra innings to the 11th at the ballpark, which is when diehard sports fan Jenni relented to leave. We did catch the game in its entirety at home.

My eyes were opened by observing the amount of work it takes to care for Jenni and Nikki—two adult women. Both require assistance to eat. Watching Bob and Diane operate as a well-oiled, two-person tag-team proved instructive. It is quite a production, but these self-taught parents have it down pat. Visiting our house before the game meant getting each twin up two steps to our front entry. Jenni's electric chair with its battery is too heavy to lift. Diane Miller once again came to the rescue, providing a portable ramp for us to use. We appreciated having the twins able to come into our home. Maggie would have liked her friends to also see her bedroom, but it is on the second floor. However, all were able to partake of the pregame luncheon prepared by Cathy.

The Berendes conversion van is outfitted with a ramp and lift to accommodate the chairs. Maggie got a thrill out of riding up on the lift gate and down again. We were able to park close by the entrance to the ballpark with the handicapped plates—a good thing since the late May weather was unseasonably blustery. Also welcome was Miller Park's retractable roof.

Because Cathy chose to stay home, we purchased six tickets specifically designated ADA—which refers to a provision of the

Americans with Disabilities Act. Never before had I sat in this designated area. We were treated quite well, including being directed to the nearby First Aid station where we could use the handicapped-accessible bathroom, large and clean. I didn't know about this option before and was pleasantly surprised by its availability.

For those readers not familiar with the American with Disabilities Act, it was signed into law in 1990, and its protections cover an estimated 55 million Americans. The intent of this monumental legislation was to protect people with disabilities from discrimination in employment and enable them to participate fully in their communities.

When we took our seats, Maggie sat next to Nikki and happily ate a large box of popcorn Bob purchased for her. She had taken to calling her friend the "Nikster." Nikki rarely speaks, so Maggie inquired of her friend if she could talk. Diane was amused when her daughter clearly answered Maggie in the negative with the word, "No."

Reflecting on our time spent with the indomitable Berendes family, I related to the phrase "To walk a mile in my shoes." Experiencing, even for those few intense hours, what it means to be immobile, deaf, blind, and completely dependent does cultivate a keen sense of empathy. And to witness the Berendes family—and my friend Diane Miller—manage as well as they do is life affirming and humbling.

In 1945, during the frantic days of WWII, FDR, as commander-in-chief, was quoted as saying, "Once you've spent two years trying to wiggle one toe, everything is in proportion."

Dealing with the challenges of our children with special needs helps us keep everything else in proportion.

CHAPTER 6

FATHER PROTECTOR

I was blessed to have had a great paternal role model in my life. My father showed me through his actions how to be a courageous, unselfish father, faithful husband, and solid man. Numerous studies have demonstrated that fathers are crucial to the growth, development, health, and happiness of their children. Those raised without a father may be at a disadvantage. Without an active, loving father figure in the picture, a child is more likely to drop out of school, experience poverty, receive welfare, commit delinquent acts, use drugs and alcohol, have children out of wedlock, and be incarcerated. One could argue that much of society's ills are due to a breakdown in the responsibility of fathers.

Ken R. Canfield, PhD, is president of the National Center for Fathering and a father of five. He authored *The 7 Secrets of Effective Fathers*. I found much good advice in this book, but I don't believe it is as secret as the title suggests.

The author describes an effective father as one who maintains a long-term commitment and gives quality time to his children. He advises "don't ever underestimate your power as a father."

In Canfield's words, "Effective dads view the word father as a verb, not just a noun. It is possible 'to father.' We have always talked about 'mothering' but 'fathering' is a new term on the block."

The author lists secret #5 of an effective father as loving the mother. At my father's funeral service I quoted the late Reverend

Theodore Hesburgh, iconic president of the University of Notre Dame. According to the perceptive Hesburgh, "The greatest gift that a man can give his children is to love their mother." My father gave that gift to his children, as did my father-in-law. I believe that a loving marriage might be even more important for the parents of a child with special needs.

The book *Married with Special-Needs Children* opens with the commonly held perception that having a child with a disability puts such strain and stress on a marriage that the risk of divorce is magnified. The co-authors, Laura Marshak, PhD, and Fran Pollock Prezant, M.Ed., walk the talk, as each is the parent of a child with disabilities and is in a longstanding marriage.

The divorce rate in the population as a whole is 50 percent, meaning one out of two marriages fails. Margaret Atwood, a Canadian poet and celebrated novelist, had this to say: "A divorce is like an amputation: You survive, but there's less of you."

No doubt, parenting special needs children causes a marriage to be more complicated, but divorce is no more prevalent among such parents than the average for other couples. Indeed, many marriages have grown stronger as a result of the challenges. This aligns closely with my personal observation and experience.

Marshak and Prezant point out that parenting a child with special needs does have a large impact, amplifying emotions. Caring for an autistic child, for example, wears on both parents physically and even more so emotionally. This is also true for the behavioral issues with our Maggie.

The co-authors emphasize the heightened importance of open communication in forging a healthy marriage.

Author and essayist Anne Lamott tells us, "A good marriage is where both people feel like they're getting the better end of the deal." Marshak and Prezant suggest practicing non-threatening communication every day.

As a husband of 34 years and counting, I am not at all surprised by the contention of these authors, who are also wives and mothers, that in the vast majority of marriages—80 percent—it is the female spouse who raises the sticky communication issues. Males, on the other hand, try to avoid communicating whenever possible. There is even a term for a husband's deer-in-the-headlights look: stonewalling. I plead guilty.

I do not pretend to be an expert on marital matters. The combination of being married with parenting of Maggie are challenging. Cathy and I often disagree, and I stonewall. But we have instituted a Wednesday date night for which we have a companion care for Maggie while we get out of the house and spend some quality time together. The better we are together, the better it is for Maggie. Cathy is undoubtedly correct in her belief that Maggie can pick up on any tension between us.

A good marriage necessitates effective communication, compromise, and mutual respect. Whatever can make it easier for one's partner/spouse to talk is beneficial. Accept differences of opinion and adjust together. To adequately protect a child with special needs, a solid, long-term marital partnership is not only ideal but required.

When Cathy and I were new parents, each of us working to financially support our young family, we struggled to find quality child care for Maggie. She was more demanding than most children her age.

We went through a series of child care providers, primarily young mothers who worked out of their homes. All ended up telling us they no longer wanted to care for our child. Obviously, this situation was very stressful for us. Martha was born when Maggie was almost four. We had more success by hiring a couple of retired grandmothers to help us in our own home with our two young daughters.

When Maggie was age 30 months, we discovered a daycare center associated with a hospital in Milwaukee, and enrolled her. All seemed to be going reasonably well, and Maggie had developed a special connection with Connie, a young caregiver.

Things changed dramatically six months later. I was called to come pick up our three-year-old in the hospital's emergency room located directly across the street from the day care center. I was told that Maggie had been playing outside, where a large truck tire lay in the middle of the playground sandbox. The caregiver on duty heard Maggie softly crying, went to check on her, and saw that a four-year-old boy had Maggie wedged against the tire and was biting her face.

I raced to the ER, my anxiety relieved to find Maggie calmly sitting in a chair. But as I cradled her in my arms, thankful she was okay, I was shocked to see the severity of the attack on her. This was not a cut or a single bite. Instead, her pretty little doll face showed multiple bites. It is still hard for me at look at the photo taken of her that day. Bite marks and broken skin covered both cheeks. One eye was badly bruised, the skin around it bloody. Maggie's condition was far worse than I had been led to believe.

In order to collect my thoughts and control my emotions, that evening I put together a letter to the director of the day care center. I wrote that we could not comprehend how this attack—for that is what it was—could have gone on to the extent it did and for such a duration without supervisory intervention. I also told the director that Maggie would not be returning unless the offending child was removed. I believed this four-year-old boy would attack again, and I would not and could not subject our girl to this real possibility.

My subsequent meetings with the day care and hospital administration did not go well. They continued to understate the incident and flatly refused to even consider removing the aggressive boy. Connie, the young woman caregiver who had grown fond of Maggie, felt terrible and soon left for other employment.

Maggie's bite wounds healed, but the fear I harbored of her being abused in the future has never left me. I readily admit this real fear is top-of-mind whenever I consider the possibility of having to place Maggie in a group home. As for my being the suspicious father and protector of a special needs daughter, I am far from alone in this worry. Bob Berendes, father of twin daughters Nikki and Jenni, experienced Jenni's relocation to a group home after high school. One time when Jenni was at a restaurant with others, two of the caregivers got into an argument with each other that turned physical, and one of them left. Jenni was shaken by the fight between adults whose responsibility it was to take care of her.

Bob observed—and I concur—that a group home is only as good as its staff. Rapid turnover is a big problem. In a period of only 18 months he counted 24 caregivers coming and going. As a father/protector, Bob raised the fear we parents harbor that it takes only one "bad apple" to put a loving daughter at risk.

As parents, when we put our loved ones in the care of strangers, we have to trust they will be safe. Before Cathy and I discovered the two grandmothers as caregivers for our young girls, Cathy hired a recently divorced young woman. Something in her demeanor struck me as having problems in her own life. One day Cathy learned this woman had allowed an unemployed boyfriend to come to the house. I did not trust this situation and promptly fired her.

The fall following Maggie's third birthday, she started a half-day early childhood development (ECD) program in the local school district. It was very hard for us to put our little one on a school bus and have her transported all the way across town. To this day, I deliberately make solid eye contact with bus drivers, introduce myself, take their names, and generally let them know this special child has a father protector in her corner.

My friend, my client, and a special parent Larry Maloney has two adult children, daughter Shawn and son Tim, both living with Down syndrome. I inquired whether as a father protector he felt differently about his daughter, than his son. His wife, Nancy, piped up that Larry had told her more than once over the years that if somebody abused Shawn, he was prepared to kill him. Larry nodded and did not dispute Nancy's account. My friend is a genuinely nice, mild-mannered, 70-year-old gentleman, but I can relate to how he feels on a visceral level.

Discussing this father protector stance with several other fathers of special needs daughters, I found that they uniformly backed Larry. I had thought my own protective instincts for Maggie were outside the norm. They are not.

I am writing this book from a father's perspective, as you know. Our now 30-something daughter is a child in a woman's body. Her favorite dolls share her bed, but she is also a full-figured woman who fills out a swimming suit. I've heard that Maggie looks somewhat "showy" when she wears a fashionably low-cut dress. Believe me, I harbor a nightmare fear of someone sexually abusing my daughter.

Cathy and I travelled to Ireland in 1997 to celebrate our wedding anniversary. We were part of a tour group of mostly retired seniors. After dinner one night in Donegal, with a couple of hours of daylight still left, a group of us went outside to the town center to enjoy the pleasant May evening. Joining us was a widow of about eighty. A local teenaged boy, eyes glazed, either drunk or stoned, made a beeline toward this frail stranger and rested his head on her shoulder.

Witnessing this, I could tell by the look of shock on her face she was terrified by this unwelcome intrusion, and my first instinct as a man was to grab this delinquent by the neck and yank him away. Just as quickly I found myself instead channeling what my deceased maternal grandfather might have done.

John Fleming was born and raised in the west of Ireland, arriving in the United States aboard the *Lusitania* in 1912. When this ship was later sunk by the Germans off the coast of Ireland, it precipitated America's entry into WWI. Grandpa enlisted in the U.S.army, served in France, and became a decorated war hero. Physically strong, he went on to serve and protect as a Chicago cop.

Echoing what Grandpa might well have said at that moment, I bellowed, "Be gone with you now."

It worked surprising well. The young man immediately straightened up and snuck off, bothering us no more. Our elderly fellow traveller was greatly relieved, maybe more so that the incident did not escalate into a physical confrontation.

My own late father was also a solid man, a tough guy with a soft heart. From him, I learned the duty of being protective of the most vulnerable—the elderly, women, children, and the disabled. Thank you, Dad.

An organization taking prudent and responsible steps to protect the athletes under their care is Special Olympics. All coaches and volunteers undergo periodic Protective Behaviors Training. The program's stated goal is to train essential methods to prevent physical, emotional, or sexual abuse.

Each volunteer is subject to a background check. In addition, several basic common-sense principles are to be followed. Under no circumstances is a coach or volunteer permitted to date any athlete. All profanity is prohibited. Appropriate hugs are actually encouraged but it is important to avoid touching any athlete on any areas covered by a traditional swim suit. As noted by Special Olympic trainers, sexual predators come in all shapes, colors, sizes, ages, and genders. This respected organization wants a safe environment.

It advises dealing with athletes in public view. If that is not possible, such as in the shower, two volunteers should be present. If abuse is suspected, it should immediately be brought to the attention of leadership. If abuse is observed, it is the observer's duty to immediately report it to law enforcement authorities.

The notorious Jerry Sandusky, a long-time and respected assistant football coach at Penn State, was convicted and sent to prison for life on multiple counts of sexual abuse of minors. This well-publicized national scandal should provide a warning as well as a stark lesson that vigilance is paramount in all situations involving those in one's care.

We suffered a health nightmare with Maggie when she was

10 years old. Maggie and her sister, Martha, were roughhousing in the family room. Maggie was the instigator and the one hurt by falling off the couch. Because it happened on a Sunday, Cathy and I took Maggie to Urgent Care. As we suspected, she had broken her collarbone. The doctor also addressed an ear infection Maggie had developed. Since it was part of a series of such common child-hood infections she had endured, the physician prescribed a more potent antibiotic.

All seemed to go well until a few days later. Maggie started experiencing diarrhea and stomach cramps. We took her to her pe-diatrician, who alertly took stool samples to test if the symptoms were related to the antibiotic. The results came back negative. Maggie was told to drink plenty of fluids, and we all expected her to improve.

After two weeks, Maggie's condition did not improve. In fact, it worsened. Cathy, a registered nurse, wisely suggested I take our ailing daughter to the emergency room while she stayed home to care for six-year-old Martha and six-month-old baby Jack. Our thought was she would receive fluids for dehydration and all would be well.

It was a cold Sunday evening in February when I carried our weak and miserable pajama-clad child to Children's Hospital of Wisconsin, only a mile from our home. To our great surprise, this emergency room visit developed into a six-day hospitalization.

In the book by Ken Canfield, I read that a father is likely to face a crisis or series of crises in the course of raising a loved one. I contend this crisis scenario is even more likely and pronounced for the father of a special needs individual. Very often it centers on a health emergency. Canfield, in the role of father protector, sug-gests the following: "When a crisis occurs, fathers take a leader-ship role in dealing with it calmly, effectively, and constructively, and in restoring stability in the family." Easier said than done. This unexpected hospitalization was my siren-in-the-night moment.

I will never forget that first harried night Maggie was admitted and hospitalized. Not until two in the morning did she fall into a deep slumber, totally exhausted. This being a teaching hospital, a young-looking medical student entered our room, matter of factly informing me he was going to wake Maggie to examine and evaluate her. He was taken aback when I adamantly refused. Maggie had been in the room for hours at this point and been fully evaluated by a number of doctors. I reminded him he could have seen her an hour earlier, but didn't. The best for Maggie at that moment was to sleep undisturbed. You bet I prevailed.

The next morning I noticed a handful of young doctors huddled together outside the room. I sensed from their expressions they were at a loss to explain what was happening to my little girl. As a father protector, this was a defining moment to come to the aid of my child. It was no time to be passive or meek. So I approached this group of white-coated health professionals and passionately but in a controlled way pleaded that they do whatever it takes, consult with whomever they needed to, and arrive at a coordinated and effective plan of action to save my first-born.

The nurse caring for Maggie witnessed me take this initiative with the doctors. Greatly concerned for her seriously ill patient, she actually thanked me for intervening and attempting to light a fire under the medical team.

I spent Maggie's first three nights in the hospital by her bed. In a sleepy fog, I witnessed angel nurses care for her. The days were a flurry of activity, with a squad of medical specialists probing and testing, seeking to solve the mystery of what was happening to this very sick little patient. To my alarm and dismay I recall being told Maggie might have Crohn's, a chronic gastrointestinal disease. They were preparing to do exploratory surgery to confirm this. I was all too familiar with Crohn's disease, having watched my developmentally disabled cousin Brian suffer with it during his too-short 33-year lifespan. I vividly recall having cried as I shared this news with my dad. He knew, as I did, that Maggie might be facing the same terrible fate as his nephew Brian.

As is often the case for families during hospital stays, Cathy and I rode a roller coaster of emotions upon hearing each result of a medical test and each update. A positive lift came from a pediatric G.I. specialist who confirmed to our relief that Maggie definitely did not have Crohn's disease. Rather, he had discovered "clostridium difficile," a bacterial infection in the gut, more commonly known as C-Diff. The potent antibiotic our child had been prescribed for an ear infection by the Urgent Care physician had wiped out her own defensive good bacteria and caused her severe abdominal pain. Thank heaven we had taken her to a top-rated pediatric hospital with first-class Medical College of Wisconsin physicians. Had we not been there, we very well could have lost our Maggie.

Although Cathy and I were greatly relieved to learn this positive news, our roller-coaster ride was not yet over. That evening was the first I did not stay overnight at Maggie's bedside. Early the next morning we received a chilling call from our pediatrician, who solemnly informed us Maggie had endured a difficult night and was in guarded condition, with her kidneys close to failing. Cathy and I looked at each other, terrified once more by the realization we could actually lose our first-born. I believe I aged a couple of years at that very moment.

We learned that a young female medical student—surely another angel in our daughter's life—had maintained a vigil at Maggie's bedside and closely monitored her condition throughout the night.

The next day brought more hopeful news. Maggie had responded well to drugs to combat the C-Diff, and thanks to God and her medical team, she survived her struggle and her six-day hospital ordeal and came home.

As I said before and look forward to saying again, Maggie is blessed to have angels come into her life on a regular, as-needed basis. One such angel is Heidi Krahn, Maggie's middle school teacher. Heidi was a recent graduate of the University of Wisconsin's School of Education, and Maggie was to be her very first student in a brand new program instituted in our school district. The arrangement was not without its challenges—such as the time Maggie pulled the fire alarm and the entire school had to be evacuated.

Heidi and Maggie developed a unique bond. To this day Maggie refers to Ms. Krahn as her favorite teacher. While Maggie was in eighth grade, Heidi married. In our daughter's bedroom hangs a photograph taken at the wedding showing the beautiful bride hugging her beaming, prized student, Maggie.

When Maggie moved on from the relative security of elementary to middle school, I admit to having felt some trepidation. Students at this stage are teenagers, with all that entails. Heidi, as a new teacher in a new program, was given little initial support by the principal or the administration at the district level.

A couple of weeks into the fall semester that first year the facilities for Heidi and her two special students were not yet set up. Distressed, Cathy told me our Maggie was spending her school days in what amounted to a windowless, basement-level, tight-quartered broom closet. A meeting was subsequently held at school to address these concerns. Present were Heidi, the principal, district administrators, and Maggie's mom and dad.

Seated at the conference table in the principal's office, I soon got the impression the man was doing a splendid job of talking without saying anything. After too much of this, I calmly and respectfully asked him a simple question: "Is the room where you are educating these students with special needs up to fire code?" I then shut up and let him quiver.

After an uncomfortable moment, he stammered and answered, "I don't think so."

I did not reply but simply stared at him. He then proceeded to assure us that these students would be immediately transferred to a suitable classroom. We had gotten his attention.

Maggie went on to spend three happy years at Longfellow

Middle School, with her angel, Heidi, as her teacher. Heidi worked hard to make Maggie and the other special needs students on her watch a part of this school and the student body. Although these days Heidi and Maggie see one another only occasionally, they continue to hold a special place in each other's heart.

Heidi's success in having made her students a part of the school was evident at the middle school graduation ceremony. I was touched to see Maggie and her special needs classmate Joy given a resounding ovation by their more able classmates as they crossed the stage to receive their diplomas. Heidi has confided to me that she learned so much from our Maggie, and I suspect our girl taught some of the other regular students important lessons, too.

Maggie moved on to high school, once again with some bumps in the road. We had been spoiled by Heidi. Her new teacher was a no-nonsense veteran teacher. She and Cathy crossed swords on occasion during those high school years. It seems to me that younger, more energetic, and idealistic special education teachers are most likely to become disillusioned when there is a lack of support from their administration and its bureaucracy. They quickly burn out and choose to go in a different direction.

At age 16, and in grade 10, our Maggie was disciplined and suspended from school indefinitely—for a minimum of three days—pending the outcome of a parent conference. Granted, Maggie's inappropriate behavior can be disruptive. It is the number one challenge holding her back. We can't predict when these mysterious eruptions may occur. Perhaps the cause is hormonal, or triggered by prescription drugs, or maybe even the result of chemical reactions in her brain. Maggie is on medication to help control her behavior, and we have worked extensively with psychiatrists and psychologists. These measures have helped, but we are still frustrated when facing the occasional meltdown.

The incident that brought Maggie's suspension was triggered by an encounter with a new aide in a high school program held off campus. When I heard the aide was threatening to file assault charges against Maggie, my fatherly protectionist instincts kicked in. She complained of back pain after allegedly being pushed by our girl. I smelled a rat. I fired back, coming to our daughter's defense by hiring an attorney. Attorney Patricia Engel represents students and their parents in school law matters and special education issues in the State of Wisconsin. A former special education teacher, Ms. Engel is uniquely qualified to understand and address the difficult issues that families encounter, including matters of disability and discipline. Clearly we had the right advocate in Maggie's corner.

During an initial phone consult with Attorney Engel, she informed me of an alarming trend toward increased suspensions and expulsions of cognitively disabled students. Of our large extended family, I was never aware of a member expelled from school. Maggie would be the first.

Once I informed the high school administration we had an attorney, we received greater respect. Simultaneously, the aide, someone we never met, dropped plans to press charges against our then 85-pound, disabled, medicated, nonviolent child. It was then revealed that this aide had not followed protocol. She subsequently transferred to another school.

Fortunately, the story ended well. Maggie's suspension was lifted, and we thankfully had no other major incidents over the course of her high school years. I shudder to think what might have happened had we not had the will, resources, and ability to have the backing of a qualified attorney to protect our Maggie.

CHAPTER 7

GOLDEN MOMENTS

O ver the years, I have been inspired by merely being around Special Olympians, observing, coaching, and getting to know them as they participated in events. I appreciate that the late Eunice Kennedy Shriver, its heart, soul and founder, artfully managed to name this wonderful organization Special Olympics and not Disabled Olympics.

For the past 20 years I have attended the State Summer Games held each June in central Wisconsin on the University of Wisconsin-Stevens Point campus. Maggie attends as a member of the Wauwatosa (Tosa) Special Olympics Track Team, and I am there as a volunteer coach. This three-day event is the highlight of the year for me, never failing to yield a new collection of memorable and inspiring stories of these amazing special athletes.

At "State" for the Summer Games, they do things "big" for the 1,000 qualifying team competitors in track, swimming, and soccer. One year for the opening ceremony we thrilled to the sight of a Army helicopter landing in an adjacent field to deliver the Olympic flame. This was followed by Special Olympians reciting their oath: "Let me win. But if I cannot win, let me be brave in the attempt." A young man with Down syndrome, representing all the athletes, then took the microphone, and with the verve of Rocky Balboa, told them all to "Go for it!"

Skill, Courage, Sharing, Joy is the Special Olympics motto, and it appears on all participatory ribbons and medals awarded with much fanfare at athletic events. I would like to share some of the amazing stories behind a number of golden moments I have happily witnessed during my 20-year affiliation.

Our Maggie, at age 20, trained hard so she could move up and compete in a long-distance 3,000-meter race walk. She was fortunate just to qualify for State at the area meet held earlier in May. Two of her fellow athletes and teammates had been forced to pull out of the event because of a death in one family and a health problem in the other. Usually, the top three finishers qualify to compete in this particular event. So when only three athletes lined up for the start of this qualifying race, coach Eileen and I hugged. Eileen and I both realized Maggie would be headed to State.

Eileen Sherburne is typical of the many volunteers who make Special Olympics such a resounding success. A veteran nurse and rehab specialist at Children's Hospital of Wisconsin, Eileen is an accomplished athlete in her own right. Her major athletic claim to fame was qualifying for, competing in, and amazingly finishing the Ironman Triathlon in Hawaii. This grueling super bowl of tri-athlons combines a 2.25-mile ocean swim followed by a 115-mile bike ride with the topper: an exhausting full marathon run of 26.2 miles. A highlight of Coach Eileen's 25-year Special Olympics career was representing Wisconsin as a coach at the 2003 World Games held in Dublin.

As a training technique, Coach Eileen occasionally holds Maggie by the arm for balance, and runs with her to raise her heartbeat. For this exercise, Maggie refers to Eileen as "The Dragmeister." Maggie likes her track coach, and Eileen is equally fond of our daughter.

The night before Maggie's big event at State, while we walked back from the dance to our dorm on the Stevens Point campus, her soft voice said to me, "I really hope I win a gold medal." Because I honestly thought there was absolutely no chance of that happening, listening to her voice her dream sent a profound sadness through me. Although Maggie works hard and goes the full distance, her disability and balance are such that she doesn't have much speed. Maggie is motivated and could complete 5,000 meters if she had to, but only at her own plodding pace. I told Maggie to simply try her best, adding that even a ribbon would be great. Then I repeated and reminded her of the oath: "Let me win. But if I cannot win, let me be brave in the attempt."

The next morning Maggie put on her track uniform and her identifying bib number. At the staging tent we learned Maggie was slotted in the third division, which was for men and women from across Wisconsin who had posted the slowest qualifying times. Divisioning allows every competitor, regardless of ability level, to be placed in a competitive race that offers a legitimate chance to earn a medal, even gold.

The beauty of Special Olympics is there are no semi-finals—each race is a final. In this way a greater number of Special Olympians experience the pride of being winners. A lot of medals are awarded. Maggie's event had five competitors, meaning she had to finish ahead of only two of them to place third and earn her first-ever medal.

The gunshot sounded and the race started. All three divisions were grouped together, because this two-mile race walk takes up to a half-hour to complete. The mass start made it difficult to determine who was in what place. Halfway through this long race, it became apparent that Maggie needed to pick up the pace to have any chance of earning a medal. So Eileen encouraged Maggie to speed up and pass the competitor in front of her. Maggie gave a resolute one-word response—"Fine"—meaning if that is what you want. She then stepped into a higher gear to better position herself.

It looked to Coach Eileen and all of us Tosa rooters that Maggie would still need to pass yet another racer—a woman who had about a 20-yard lead on her—to move into third place and earn a bronze medal. Quite a thrilling spectacle was to see Maggie's teammates gather on the sidelines to shout encouragement to her to pass the race walker ahead of her. Sidney and Lee, two younger and talented sprinters, had come over from the track stadium to support Maggie. She was their teammate, after all, and wore the same uniform. These young guys walked alongside her, actually screaming encouragement to her.

Amazingly, spurred on and determined, Maggie passed the woman ahead of her in the final lap and crossed the finish line.

Thrilled that Maggie had persevered to earn a bronze medal, Coach Eileen and I headed over to the awards ceremony.

The officials helped our girl to the top step, hung a *gold medal* around her neck and announced Maggie McCarthy as the first-place winner. Together we asked the race officials if they were sure, believing that perhaps a mix-up had occurred. The June day was hot and humid, and a couple of the older men competing in her division had apparently started out fast but were unable to go the distance and dropped out. Maggie was indeed the sure, if improbable, winner.

As her name was announced, Maggie triumphantly raised her fist in the air. Once the medal was placed around her neck, Maggie took a long moment to admire it. Eileen and I stood by with team-mates and parents and witnessed our girl's expression of pure hap-piness. Still holding her precious award, Maggie beamed a smile of unadulterated joy. No athlete at any level, on any Olympic podium, was happier at that moment than our Maggie. And as a proud parent, I was overcome with happiness for her. I did not cry, but recall Coach Eileen being moved to tears. She had indeed won the gold medal she hoped for. Her dream was fulfilled.

Exhilarated, we couldn't wait to phone home to give Mom the unbelievably exciting news. Holding the receiver, Maggie said, "Guess what, Mom? I won a gold medal!"

On the other end I could hear Cathy understandably reply, "No way."

Without missing a beat, Maggie countered, "Yes, way."

Although Maggie's siblings, Jack and Martha, were accom-plished students and athletes who competed at the elite State level for their high schools, we all felt that by overcoming her disabilities to be the best she could be, Maggie was, and is, truly a champion.

One of the best life experiences I have each year is marching alongside Special Olympians in the Fourth of July parade in our Wauwatosa community. This grand parade is a slice of Americana. Our 40-member uniformed team steps off some 2.5 miles down the main street of North Avenue, along with rousing high school marching bands, vintage cars carrying local celebrities, horses (watch your step), and dozens of floats. Thousands of parade watchers line the route and pour out their loudest approval for the disabled citizen athletes as we pass by, surrounded by a sea of adulation, clapping, cheering, saluting, even standing up in waves for the Special Olympians.

As I continue to admit, I am always inspired and enriched by getting to know some very special people. One such individual is Tim Maloney, the son of Larry and Nancy. Tim is an exceptional athlete and a natural leader. To me, this redhead with Down syndrome is the face I put on Special Olympics.

Tim often leads our team in the parade, carrying the American flag and revving up the crowd. A few years ago on a very warm day, Tim was feeling under the weather. Yet he was determined to do his duty as flag bearer. Slumped in the shade of a tree prior to our group's being signaled to set off, Tim looked even paler than his normal bone white complexion. Conferring with his dad, I thought it prudent to summon one of the nearby emergency vehicles to attend to Tim. As he was taken away in an ambulance, we had to assure his worried teammates that their hero would be okay. After Tim was checked out and treated for dehydration, he was sent home in fine shape. The next year I made sure to fully hydrate Tim before and along the parade route. We obviously succeeded, because at the end of the route Tim anxiously told me, "John, I really need to use a bathroom."

My rookie year at State, I was not prepared for all the goings on. The whole bus empties, the athletes locate their gear as best as they can, and all of us are assigned sleeping rooms in the dorms and given keys. Then, this unwieldy group of up to 40 people shuffles up four flights of stairs. It is like herding cats. Thankfully, the dorms now have elevators and air conditioning.

Individual roommates are assigned rooms by sex, but the dorm floor is coed. Later that first day I was standing in the middle of one wing on our floor when I was surprised to see one of our male athletes sauntering down the hall without wearing any bottoms. Not knowing what to do, I turned to Tim, standing beside me. To my relief, he took charge, commanding this autistic athlete by name to "put some pants on."

The next day I was eating lunch with Maggie in the cafeteria when Tim approached me and asked whether I was in charge. Sheepishly I looked around and spotted no other coaches or volunteers, so I said, "Maybe. What am I supposed to do?"

"Well," he said, "we should probably be at a staging area at two pm."

"Thanks, Tim," I replied.

Over the past 38 years, Tim has participated in scores of Special Olympics events. He has a boatload of ribbons and medals attesting to his skill. At my very first State Summer Games, I stood next to his mother, Nancy, as he competed in a hotly contested 400-meter race walk sprint. Perennial winner Tim was trailing his athletic competitor, and it looked as if he would have to settle for second place. I asked Nancy if her son would be able to live with this disappointment, and she said she hoped so.

In the final turn, Tim took the inside lane, put his head down, tilted to the left in his own unorthodox style, and accelerated to the finish line. He won by a step. It was as exciting as anything I have seen in sport. Breathlessly, I ran over to congratulate my hero, telling Tim I thought it was an amazing race effort. Sweating, he told me in his halting voice, "John, I was not to be denied."

Tim's competitive nature is so strong, he pushes himself to the absolute limit. Superstars Lebron James, Aaron Rodgers, and Tiger Woods don't have bigger competitive hearts than does Tim Maloney. This stalwart went on earn the honor of being selected to represent Wisconsin and the USA in the 2007 World Special Olympic Games held in Shanghai, China. He trained hard under Coach Eileen, got super fit, and in the finest Olympic tradition gave it his all. His best turned out to be good enough for sure. Upon returning from China, Tim and his dad came to my office to show me the gold and silver medals he had won. Holding these world medals in my hands was extremely humbling.

The 2010 State Summer Games heralded yet another amazing year, in which our Maggie trained, competed well, and brought home a bronze medal. Having previously won gold and silver medals in the same 3,000-meter race walk, Maggie's stated goal that year was to bring home a bronze. The race went down just as she called it. Maggie was happy, and her coaches and teammates were proud of her. Cathy and I think she secretly likes the sound of the word "bronze."

But the really remarkable story of that particular year's State track meet belongs to Maggie's friend and teammate Diane Schuller. We had met this young woman, age 22 at the time, a couple of years earlier when she joined the track team. It broke my heart to learn at our Special Olympics holiday party that Diane was undergoing cancer treatments. Although she showed up at the party with her head bald from the effects of chemotherapy, she was all smiles. I was greatly relieved to hear from her mother, Mary, that things were going pretty well in her fight against a particularly ugly cancer. My first instinct was to plant a kiss on her bald head, but I held back until her younger sister, Corey, gave me the green light, saying, "They do it all the time."

Siblings Corey and Diane are very close. A National Honor Society scholar, Corey headed off to college that fall to pursue a career in nursing. She said it was Diane's health issues that motivated her to become a nurse. Maggie took a liking to Corey. The three girls went out for pizza a couple of times and attended a Rascal Flatts concert with special guest Darius Rucker. To see Corey, Diane, and Maggie stand up and boogie while singing along and enjoying a great time at the indoor concert was a heart-warming sight. It was also good to observe how fantastic the country music fans were to the girls.

Like Maggie, Diane participated in track and competed in the area's qualifying meet the same May as Maggie qualified for the long-distance race walk. Diane's event was the 400-meter race walk. Unlike Maggie, she did not initially qualify to move on to State. However, owing to a variety of fortuitous factors, several spots opened up. Like almost all the athletes, Diane very much wanted to go to State and experience all it offers. Her mother, on the other hand, was understandably worried about sending her daughter to Stevens Point alone. Knowing Diane's eagerness to attend State, I offered to intercede with her mom. As a chaperone and assistant coach, I told Mary I would be riding the bus and staying in the dorm with the team and would keep a close eye on her girl. With this assurance, she gave her permission. When I passed the word at track practice that her mother had given her okay, Diane thanked me profusely.

At the bus departure point in the school parking lot, the Tosa Special Olympics team got a rousing send off. Diane took a seat across from Maggie and beamed ear-to-ear. Her mother, as I could see through the bus window, was teary-eyed. Certain she was happy for Diane, I also knew this was the first time her special daughter would be somewhere overnight without her.

As it turned out, Diane proved to be independent as well as a terrific teammate and leader. She reveled in all that encompasses State—the dance, the pizza party, and the camaraderie of just hanging out in a college dorm. At the Friday night dance, she had the time of her life dancing with Theo, her friend since elementary school. When I overheard another athlete remind Diane that Theo had a girlfriend back home, she smiled coyly and said, "I know that."

All this activity was only a build-up to the big moment on Saturday morning when Diane would line up for the 400-meter race walk. Although Diane's speech is somewhat difficult to understand, I fully understood her professed dream to capture the gold. Coach Eileen and I had lower expectations, based on past performance. Moreover, seven others would compete in the same race who had the same goal. At best, Diane would be a long shot for a medal.

Her heart surely pounded as she lined up and moved from the staging tent to the race course. I noticed that her position was on the far right of the starting line. If she was going to be successful in this walk-sprint, she would need to get out quickly. The gun went off. Diane, a determined look in her eyes, demonstrated sheer effort. With her lumbering gait, she bolted to the lead and got the inside track. Coach Eileen and I watched open-mouthed at her strong start. The race was still early and very much an open contest, with all seven of the equally determined special women athletes breathing down her neck. She managed to keep a slim lead rounding into the final stretch. Watching this drama unfold, I thought how great it would be if she somehow could hold on and fulfill her quest. Yet, I held back my hope, not wanting to be disappointed or to superstitiously jinx her chances.

On this day and in this race, like Tim, Diane was not to be denied. As she triumphantly crossed the finish line, I raised my arms instinctively in a victory salute. Coach Eileen and I looked at each other and marveled at the performance we had just witnessed. Top athletes speak of wanting to be champions so much they can taste it. That must have been true for Diane Schuller, as her skill, courage, and especially joy were on full display that Saturday morning as she achieved her goal. She was indeed a champion.

Proudly wearing her gold medal after the race, a still-beaming Diane phoned her mom and sister in Wauwatosa to deliver the good news. Corey later shared how their conversation went. A jubilant Mary yelled upstairs to Corey, "She won the gold!" Her younger sister either couldn't hear this or didn't believe her ears. So Mary, breathless, yelled louder: "She won the gold!" Corey finally got the message and echoed excitedly, "She won the gold!"

On the bus ride home, Diane told me, "I can't believe I won the gold." But indeed she had, just as Maggie had won the bronze the same day to complete her own matching set of medals. Two tired young Special Olympians had lived their dream.

During the State games, I encountered many groups of athletes from throughout Wisconsin all decked out in their team uniforms. As the games go on, it is common to see many of these athletes adding new medals to round out their attire. When Maggie and I strolled back to our dorm one afternoon, we came across Bill, according to the name shown on the I.D. that every athlete displays, wearing the uniform of—if memory serves me—Manitowoc. Bill was about 35 years of age, personable, bearded, and parked in his wheelchair soaking up the festive atmosphere and the abundant sunshine. He smiled warmly at us, said hello, and showed off his medal.

Noting this, Maggie said, "Congratulations, Bill."

He replied, "Thanks, Maggie."

Bill then asked Maggie if maybe he could have a hug. She leaned into his chair and gave Bill a gentle hug.

Emboldened, Bill upped the ante. "Maggie, how about a kiss?"

Without missing a beat, our girl proceeded to give Bill a peck on the cheek.

"Thanks, Maggie."

"Bye, Hon."

Observing this sweet interaction, I thought this could well be the best day of Bill's life. I suspected Bill, having found a good spot and a productive act, was going to enjoy both for as long as it lasted.

Each year the adventures at State deliver magic. The golden story of 2012 revolved around one Danny Zalewski. One of the younger athletes, Danny joined team Tosa at age 15, still in high school. Because his intellectual capacity is quite low, he doesn't speak but communicates in grunts. Always friendly, he seems to enjoy being part of the team and is quick to give a high-five slap.

Despite cognitive shortcomings, Danny is a pretty good endurance athlete and started to do well in the 3,000-meter race walk. His father, George Zalewski, is a good man who worked hard and patiently with Danny to help him understand how to conduct this race. Many Special Olympians find it challenging to do the turns, stay in their lane, refrain from running in the race walk, and continue across the finish line. Not as easy as it sounds. Any of these would disqualify the athlete.

While Maggie was still in high school, she initially competed in the 100- and 200-meter dash. What held her back was her tendency to freeze at the sound of the starting gun. Running the 200-meter race one year at State, she stopped at the 150-meter mark, pointed up into the stands for some quirky reason, then continued the race to the finish line.

Once Danny came to a better understanding of what he needed to do in this particular long-distance event, his greater speed effectively knocked Maggie out of qualifying for State in that event. Coach Eileen, to her credit, is always seeking events in which each athlete can find success.

One of many good things about Special Olympics is that the events are always free and open to the public. So that momentous year at State, Danny had a large contingent of extended family members present to cheer him on. As the race started, dad anxiously paced the side of the road where the race is held, attempting to keep his son on task. Danny needed to keep going, stay on the road, and make sharp turns around each cone. Each time he did, Danny raised his hands above his head and clapped. This show of emotion got a warm response from the spectators. Despite some anxious moments during the half-hour event, Danny managed to complete the race and succeed in capturing the gold.

Paraded over to the podium, a sweating Danny had a gold medal draped around his neck. True to form, he clapped for himself and with a grunt showed his happiness. His family members, teammates, coaches, and indeed all the spectators and officials were thrilled for this Olympic hero.

When Maggie and I originally became involved with Special Olympics, one of the first athletes we came to know and like was Ryan, the only child of great parents Mary and Gary Gannon. If Maggie hears the name Ryan, she is sure to pair it with the name Gannon. Ryan was a runner who possessed good speed, despite an unorthodox running style. He also had a competitive streak and wasn't above a little trash-talking. Ryan adores sports, and has amassed a prodigious collection of sports memorabilia. A long-term Goodwill employee, Ryan is also blessed to have an extended family of aunts, uncles, and cousins, with whom he is very close.

Ryan's speech can be difficult to understand and poses an obstacle to engaging with him. I got to know him by conversing with him while he walked around the track warming up. By giving Ryan my attention, listening closely, and patiently interacting, I developed a friendship. Over the years, I attended a handful of Milwaukee Brewers and Marquette College basketball games with Ryan. He was very observant of the whole experience and missed none of the action, both on and off the field and the court.

Some years back at a State event, Ryan, along with the track team and the coaches, gathered in the community room of the college dorm to enjoy a ritual Friday night pizza party. It was also a send off of sorts for our long-time coach Jim Balzer and his athlete son Mike. Jim had recently retired, and his family, including Mike, were about to relocate about 150 miles away after some 15 years as a part of the Tosa Special Olympic track team. The athletes took turns giving Jim hugs and sincerely thanking him for being their coach. Several said they loved him. They all said they would miss him.

Ryan was the last to approach his coach. Scheduled to run the mile race the next morning, for Ryan, a sprinter, this step up in distance was a new and challenging event. He boldly announced to the coach, whom he'd regularly called "Old Man," that he was going to win the mile and give his gold medal to his departing coach to remember him by.

It is not uncommon for Special Olympic athletes to give away their gold medals. Ryan fulfilled his boast and handed an emotional Jim Balzer his gold medal, a moment I will never forget. Similar to Cindy Bentley with President Bush, Ryan Gannon's selfless act was like giving away a piece of an athlete's heart, and it was priceless.

Countless memorable moments occurred at the 2015 State Summer Games. In race walking, a couple of our women athletes achieved standout performances. One was Jenny Van Valkenburgh, a fascinating young woman of 26. But in 2014 at her first State games, Jenny so relished her independence that she went off on her own without telling anyone—much to the chagrin of us coaches. We pride ourselves on not losing any of the special athletes under our supervision. The following, most recent year, Jenny's mom took me aside as we were boarding the bus to leave for State. Nancy told me she had gently threatened her daughter that she would be taken home if she got out of line. I am happy to report that Jenny became an exemplary roommate, teammate, and competitor.

Moreover, at the first practice session for the track season I was struck by Jenny's significant fifty-pound weight loss. Coach Eileen, a nurse and a strong health advocate, gave Jenny a deserved shout out in front of the assembled group of parents and athletes. Jenny had been on a supervised weight-loss program over the past year and looked great, and she also enjoyed the dividends of improving her general health, self-esteem, and athletic performance.

Jenny competed well and brought home two gold medals. Perhaps her greatest thrill was the attention showed her by teammate Theo, highly popular with all the ladies. I heard from Nancy that her daughter has taken to referring to Theo as "Her man, Theo."

Caroline Loose, age 22, is one of the newest and younger members of our Tosa team. She is a good athlete, but when she first started competing as a runner, she experienced the dreaded side aches, so she prefers race walking. Success in this endeavor is what really motivates her. Caroline's times have shown such marked improvement that only Tim Maloney now outclasses her. Because this tiny blond athlete is small in stature, she was dwarfed when lining up in a division with the likes of her teammate Mike Spenner, almost three times her size.

Caroline's devoted mom, Kathleen, has patiently guided her socially reticent daughter during practice sessions and at meets, which were particularly challenging for the young woman the first year or two. Seeing the progress she has made is exciting. At the final practice prior to State, as Caroline completed her lap, she pleasantly surprised me with an unsolicited high five. Seeing this breakthrough, her mom looked at me and flashed a happy smile.

At State, this blossoming athlete is now quick to give her teammates congratulatory hugs. As her coach, I merited a fist pump—which is real progress, but I'd been holding out for a hug. I am thrilled to report Caroline gave me a hug at the post-season track party. It made my day!

As the saying goes, "A hug delights and warms and charms. That must be why God gave us arms."

According to Caroline's mom, her daughter not only has Down syndrome but is very likely on the autism spectrum. She travels to State by car with her mom instead of by bus, and they stay at a hotel. We have seen progress this year as Caroline felt comfortable enough to visit briefly with her teammates on the dorm floor. I learned that although autism is not typical for those with Down syndrome, this dual diagnosis is becoming more prevalent.

I have since come across a description of *"Down syndrome with a slice of autism."* The mother of Nick, a 21-year-old who was also given this dual diagnosis, writes a personal blog, and in one post, this provocative question is asked: *"What is normal?"*

An answer posted there is this quotation from no less an authority than Whoopi Goldberg:

"Normal is just a setting on a washing machine."

Pure gold.

CHAPTER 8

DONNA DREAMED BIG LEAGUE

As parents of a special needs child, we are constantly on the lookout for programming to enrich our daughter's life. Maggie's mom deserves all the credit for discovering Donna Lexa Art Centers (DLACs). Our aspiring artist has been attending special needs art classes there for more than 15 years—a creative outlet that has been a godsend for her and for us.

A determined woman named Donna Lexa founded a community art center in our neighboring City of Waukesha, Wisconsin, in 1985. A newly minted art therapist and struggling single mother, Donna dreamt big by striving to provide art instruction for people with special needs. Her center was modeled after one she was familiar with in California. She started small, one day a week in a church basement, and word soon spread about her offering innovative adaptations that allowed students with disabilities to participate. She felt passionately about the initiative that says: "Artwork is an extension of the person. If the artwork is accepted, the artist is accepted. This stimulates independence, self-confidence, and motivation."

Donna's son, Joe Randa, has proudly recounted how determined his mother was to fulfill her dream. Joe tells of growing up in what he referred to as a dysfunctional family. He and his two older sisters lived without the influence of their father, who was divorced from their mother. "For a good while, my mom had to do it all for us, and I am going to use her lessons. Stay focused. Keep driving. She always pushed everything to the next level."

Standing just under six feet tall and weighing 165 pounds, Joe Randa was a very good four-sport high school athlete. Lacking an edge, however, young Joe was limited in achieving his dream of playing professional sports, so he gravitated just to baseball. While his dream of reaching the major leagues seemed slim, Joe went on to hone his baseball skills in college, drawing inspiration from his mother's passion for the art center and the special needs art students he encountered. "My mom's best lessons were about never giving up," Randa said in an interview.

As in baseball, life throws curves that sometimes come at one out of left field. Sadly, this wonderful woman was minutes from home when her car was hit from behind and pushed into an oncoming third vehicle. Donna Lexa was killed May 16, 1996, age 52, soon after celebrating the 10th anniversary of her successful Community Art Center. She'd also recently seen her son improbably become the starting third baseman for the Kansas City Royals—on track to be named an All-Star rookie. At least her tragic death did not stop her legacy from continuing to inspire, imbuing her spirit in the art center she had birthed. Three area art centers, Waukesha, West Milwaukee, and West Bend were re-named for her (DLACs) and now serve some 1,000 special needs students, including our Maggie.

Joe Randa went on to hit .300 that difficult year, and ended up playing a total of 12 solid seasons in the majors. He gained a reputation for always smiling and playing the game as it was supposed to be played. For this he credits his dear late mother and her special needs art students.

I highly recommend that parents search for art outlets for their children at an early age in their development. Art and special needs art classes could well be an enriching, positive life experience for any disabled loved one of any age. Whatever the talent of the artist, engaging in art allows for individual expression.

Pablo Picasso, perhaps the most influential artist of the 20th century, is a case in point. Born in Spain in 1881, Picasso was deemed stillborn by the midwife in attendance. She left him on a table, blue and unmoving, to tend to his mother. His uncle Don Salvador, a doctor, went upstairs to look at the lifeless baby. As Picasso himself recounted many years later: "Doctors at that time used to smoke big cigars, and my uncle was no exception. When he saw me lying there he blew smoke in my face. To this I immediately reacted with a grimace and a bellow of fury."

Having had his life so improbably saved, Picasso lived to age 92 and is widely considered the greatest artist of his time.

Picasso was diagnosed later in life with dyslexia, possibly the result of a lack of oxygen at birth. This common neurological disorder causes the brain to process and interpret information differently. Not surprisingly, young Pablo was a terrible student. He was punished by being sent to detention or solitary confinement, but eagerly took his sketchbook with him, drawing incessantly. "I could have stayed there forever without stopping," he recalled years later. His own father ridiculed him for his "silly" art and for "mistakes" such as placing eyes in the wrong place. Yet, from this inauspicious beginning Pablo Picasso become recognized as a genius who transformed the world of art.

Like Picasso, our fledgling artist Maggie has her own unique style, frequently drawing "outside the lines." She owns a collection of several hundred pencils. Whenever I go on a trip, Maggie is tickled by having me return with some new pencils for her. She spends part of each day sharpening her pencils, and has been known to burn out more than a few electric pencil sharpeners. We make sure a supply of sketchbooks is always handy for our girl. She quietly and happily spends hours intently creating pencil sketches, her left hand working with a purpose. A sketch book is packed into her school bag for use at her day programs or camps and brought with us as a useful diversion on car or plane trips. Sketching calms Maggie, and she thoroughly enjoys this exercise in art.

Maggie rightly considers herself an artist, and her body of work consists of dozens of art pieces now adorning our home, in her bedroom and on a gallery wall in our basement. There are even a couple of pieces of office art displayed at McCarthy Grittinger Financial Group as well as at sister Martha's office in the Twin Cities.

Maggie's lead art teacher, Kurt Meinke, had this to say of our girl. "Maggie is an amazing artist. Her drawings are full of energy, excitement, and passion. Maggie has an innate sense of color and composition. She works fairly quickly and has developed a very recognizable personal style."

For the past 10 years, she has attended a two-hour art class held every Wednesday morning at the Donna Lexa West Milwaukee Center. Her fellow students may be challenged by cognitive, physical, or developmental disabilities as a result of age, illness, disease, or accident. To say this class is the highlight of her week is an understatement. Our girl eagerly looks forward to what she refers to simply as "Donna."

I have the privilege of driving Maggie to this class, and admit this task has evolved into a favorite part of my week. It is a joy to be exposed weekly to this diverse group of up to a dozen students for whom art is truly therapeutic, lifting spirits and opening exciting doors in life. The phrase "opening doors" is a wonderful metaphor for enriching and making fuller the lives of the disabled.

Each member of Maggie's special art group has a compelling life story worthy of an Oprah profile. I believe a gifted writer or playwright could produce a beautiful story around such a remarkable cast of characters. Cathy has taken to referring to this weekly gathering as a "love fest." Our Maggie is a central figure in it despite being one of the youngest and least capable.

The students form a special bond, and I have been uniquely privileged to get to know her classmates Janet and Jane. Maggie affectionately refers to this pair of fifty-something women as "the art wheelchair girls." I'd like to tell you a little about each.

Jane is a sweet, soft-spoken, attractive woman with a classy sense of style. She was 27, a graduate of Milwaukee's Mount Mary College and a professional social worker, when her life was drastically altered by an accidental prescription drug overdose from which she suffered a grand mal seizure that almost took her life. She barely survived and was left with a traumatic brain injury. Paralyzed, and now in a wheelchair, Jane creates as her specialty decorative fine arts, which she lovingly crafts as gifts for her nieces and extended family.

According to her art instructor, Kurt, Jane possesses an eye for detail and design. This kind woman also volunteers many hours at a nursing home. For the holidays, she crafted two dozen original coffee cups as gifts for all the volunteers and staff at the home. Jane has expanded her repertoire to painting.

On more than one occasion, Jane has told me how much she loves Maggie. It is so nice to be told your child is genuinely liked, and I welcome her comments about our girl. Not until a couple of years ago did I learn that Jane's older sister, Judy, with whom she lives, was an executive at M&I Bank when I worked there 25 years ago. Judy and I have now reconnected, brought together again by these two unlikely friends, Jane and Maggie.

It is refreshing to see a more able classmate, "smiling Bill," pushing Jane in her wheelchair to the elevator at the end of class. Being a gentleman, he also opens the outside door so she can get to the transport pickup area. Inevitably, once the nice weather arrives, one finds Jane soaking up the sunshine as she awaits her van. As Maggie and I head to our car and pass Jane, Maggie tells her friend she loves her, and Jane responds in kind. These friends then simultaneously say, "See you next week."

During each class, Maggie sits right next to Janet Kleser, the other art wheelchair girl. For the first couple of years, the only thing I knew about Janet was how artistically talented she is. Dedicated to her art, the instructors need to gently pry the paintbrush out of her hands at the end of class, so immersed is she in her work. I assumed Janet's severe disability was from birth, like Maggie's, or perhaps like Jane's, caused by accident. I came to learn her life story was much more dramatic than theirs and her disability even more senseless and tragic.

Until August 1978, Janet was a typical, fun-loving teenager, vibrant and healthy, the whole world wide open ahead of her. One summer night she excitedly headed to an Aerosmith concert in downtown Milwaukee. After midnight, when she would ordinarily have been home, a driver stopped his car along a rural county road, having spotted what he thought, in the dark of night, to be an animal lying off to the side. There he found an unconscious young woman, her body gruesomely shattered. In what is still an unsolved mystery, she had apparently been beaten with a blunt instrument, maliciously dumped from a vehicle, and left for dead. This unidentified crime victim, dubbed the "mystery girl" by local TV media, was taken by ambulance to the hospital. Miraculously, she survived her extensive and traumatic injuries.

I learned of Janet's incredible story from Kurt Meinke, who possesses a heart of gold. Kurt himself is yet another inspirational story and one of the reasons the DLACs are such a treasure. A veteran art professional, Kurt saw his own life dramatically change course when the art college he was employed by for more than 20 years changed administrations and dismantled his department. Days later he experienced a brain aneurism.

At the time he was fortunately with his partner, Ben, an Intensive Care nurse. Ben attended to him with life-saving emergency medical attention. Later enduring rehabilitation, and able to work at only a reduced level, Kurt found salvation in being part of these Donna Lexa special needs art classes. One of his prized students is Janet.

As is true for Janet, Jane, and Kurt, you never know what life is going to throw at you. Another example of such randomness is their classmate Kayla, who was just 18 and enjoying her first day of college when her car collided with a bus. She suffered a severe brain injury. It has been three years since Kayla joined these art classes, alternately accompanied by either her mom or her grandmother. Kayla possesses a beautiful smile, and her incredible progress is a testament to the power of art to heal.

The web site tagline for Donna Lexa Art Centers sums up that power succinctly: Inspiring abilities, transforming lives.

Yet another of my favorite art students is Penny. As a mature woman of 48, Penny welcomes a kiss from me as a warm greeting among friends. Like Kayla, Penny was also 18 when she sustained a traumatic brain injury in an accident. Now using a walker, she lives with her devoted mother. I once asked Penny whether she was alone in the car at the time of the accident. "Just me and God, who saved me," answered Penny.

Janet requires round-the-clock care, so she resides in a group home. For some reason, perhaps it was too large, the group home wouldn't allow her to display her signature masterpiece, an exquisite floral arrangement in a vase. Because of the situation surrounding this piece of art, Kurt had occasion to meet and visit with Janet's mother, Geraldine Kleser, at her modest Milwaukee home. The frail, widowed, 80-plus Geri pulled out the family scrapbooks and over the course of several hours told Kurt of Janet's heartwrenching yet inspiring tale.

Janet's connection with Maggie is warm and tender, akin to that of a big sister. On those occasions when Maggie gets out of line by being loud or profane, Janet, in her halting voice, gently and effectively admonishes her with an "Oh, Maggie!" Owing to this connection, I felt motivated to purchase the priceless work of art-without-a-home, which now hangs at our firm. Janet, like any struggling artist, was thrilled that her work had found a buyer.

Kurt and I sensed that Janet's mother, in declining health and nearing death, desperately wanted Janet's triumph over tragedy told before she passed on. I enlisted Maggie's sister Martha, who runs a social media marketing business in the Twin Cities, to help tell the story of Janet's rebirth through art.

Geri recounted how her youngest, still only a teenager, endured four months in the hospital, followed by additional time in rehab. The doctors were certain at the time that Janet, who could not move or speak, was destined to be no more than a vegetable for the rest of whatever life she had left. Close to 40 years later, mother and daughter, both fighters, would very much like to tell those doctors how wrong they were. For Janet is a skilled and accomplished artist, having found a latent talent, a passion, and a new meaning in her life through art.

Geri remained an inspiration in her own right until her death in 2013 at age 83. She never stopped being a ferocious advocate for her disabled adult daughter. During the toughest stretches of Janet's life, Geri encouraged her, repeating she was strong, and together they would make it through and survive.

Maggie's sister Martha, using her own media connections, managed to get a TV feature on Milwaukee's Channel 6 News profiling Janet's remarkable triumph through art over an unimaginable tragedy. In this three-minute piece, filmed at the art center, Geri is shown touchingly stating how glad she was that Janet is alive. Janet admits that initially dealing with her situation, "I used to get really, really angry, but no more." In a testament to the healing power of art and the love of a mother, she offers: "How much I have improved, really happy now."

If Janet can be happy, anybody can. Sitting rigid in her electric wheelchair, in her halting voice and using hand gestures for effect, Janet proclaimed: "You just gotta …otherwise go downhill." Geri rightly said on camera how proud she was of Janet for overcoming great odds and producing such beautiful works. Her daughter's courageous triumph through art embodies why Donna Lexa's art center fills a vital need and remains a success.

Erin, a young master's trained art therapist, is a paid assistant at DLAC. A true treasure, she is yet another angel appearing in Maggie's life. Recently married, this angel is now Erin Hein, as Maggie is quick to correct me, no longer O'Leary. Whenever Kurt

Meinke needs to be away, Maggie humorously refers to Erin as the "head honcho." Maggie idolizes Erin, a sweet woman who also works as a companion for Maggie. Her presence has been a priceless gift to Cathy and me, allowing us to regularly get away on Wednesday nights while she spends quality time with her devoted art student.

Margaret is another beautiful person and dedicated volunteer who helps make DLAC such a wonderful place for Maggie, Janet, Jane, and all the other special art students. Like everyone associated with the art center, Margaret also has a compelling personal life story. Dealing with a difficult cancer herself, she views helping out as her own effective therapy. I asked this diminutive fifty-something woman, who observes she is shorter than Maggie, if there is something I could do for her.

"Just keep bringing Maggie to class," she said.

Wow! I will.

Last fall, Janet was absent from class for about six long weeks, having something to do with a mix-up between her group home and the transit provider. This would not have happened had her mother Geri still been on the scene. A day without art for Janet is like a month without sunshine for anyone else. So we were all happy when Janet returned to class, no one more so than our Maggie.

Margaret, who is Jewish, told me it was endearing to witness Maggie and Janet carrying on and kibitzing like two old ladies. "Kibitz" is a well-known Yiddish term for chatting. To monitor her cancer, Margaret receives scans every three months. This beautiful woman has taken to giving me a thumbs up to signify her positive news, also smiling and proclaiming she earned another "get out of jail card for the next quarter." Here is hoping all the cards turn up winners.

For a lunch treat in the spring and fall, I have made it a ritual to bring sandwiches from Schlotzsky's for the art group. We have now taken to celebrating Jane's and Phil's birthdays. Maggie wants me to repeat this lunch party every week. I suspect she really likes hearing the name Schlotzsky's. After the most recent lunch, Janet handmade a thank you card for Maggie and me worthy of Hallmark. In it she wrote, across the top, "Love grows and we all need love." She went on to say, "I want to thank you so much for sitting next to me in art class, Maggie." She ends with "All my love to you and of course your family, Janet Kleser 11-11-2015."

CHAPTER 9

NEW FRIEND JACOB

Maggie enjoys musicals, with *Annie* her absolute favorite. She never tires of the movie version of this classic Broadway show. It is based on an adorable 11-year-old character from the comic strip *Little Orphan Annie*. Our Maggie can always be counted on to belt out a spirited version of the song "Tomorrow."

Maggie has viewed this movie, which stars Carol Burnett as Miss Hannigan and Albert Finney as Daddy Warbucks, well over a hundred times. In addition, she often watches the 2011 modern-day remake of this classic on her own small DVD player.

Cathy and I take Maggie to live musical productions whenever we can. We're thrilled to watch Maggie's excitement with the music, costuming, lighting, and staging. We attended the Disney stage productions of their animated films *Beauty and the Beast* and *The Lion King*. Maggie sat in awe, intently listening to the songs, including "Can You Feel the Love Tonight" and "Hakuna Matata." To our girl, these fantasies are real.

A couple of years ago I took Maggie to a local matinee production of *Joseph and the Amazing Technicolor Dreamcoat*. Maggie loves to sing along. Grandmas and moms have been known to remark how well Maggie sings, admitting she adds to their enjoyment. Such was the case at a performance of *Jesus Christ Superstar*, held as a benefit at a local church. A woman sitting in front of us made it a point of telling Maggie after the show how well she sang. While Maggie's brother, Jack, and her sister, Martha, have excelled in life—academically, athletically, and socially—Maggie is the better singer, as she can actually carry a tune. This is one area where gifts were spread around.

When Cathy and I attend plays together with Maggie, we have her sit between us. However, when I alone took Maggie to *Joseph,* I felt some trepidation as we were ushered into our back row seats in the sold-out theater, the last two tickets available. Right away I could see a special needs young man, along with his mother and what I assumed was his grandmother, occupying the seats next to ours.

I felt relief, but also curiosity, because this young man displayed a big smile, clearly excited to see Maggie. Perhaps they knew each other from some program, school, or camp. People frequently recognize our Maggie and remember her. But I discovered from talking to his charming mother, Kristen, that this smiling, happy young man, Jacob, was from neighboring Racine County. To the best of our knowledge they had never before met.

Jacob and Maggie immediately decided to sit next to each other, so Kristen and I talked over the heads of our adult children, then facilitated a get-to-know-you conversation for us all.

We learned firsthand that Jacob's favorite costume and character is Elvis. This came as no surprise. I've often delighted in observing how intellectually challenged individuals, free of inhibitions, enjoy putting on costumes and stepping into another's character. Our Maggie also has a fascination with Elvis. At dances held at the Special Olympics State Games there are always several athletes dressed up as the King, who—despite having died in 1977—lives on in spirit, especially in the world of certain special needs individuals.

The curtain rose and the musical, *Joseph*, began. Whenever the character of Pharoah imitated Elvis, Jacob got all charged up. He twice awarded these performances with a standing ovation. According to his mom, Jacob mimics his icon with near perfection, complete with Elvis wig, sideburns, jumpsuit, and sunglasses. Kristen remarked with some pride: "He is still working on the hip thrusts, but has the majority of the swag down pat."

She further informed me Jacob does not even require a costume to get into character. "He really believes some days that he is Ryan Seacrest hosting *American Idol* in our living room. He 'eliminates' contestants weekly, and sometimes gets very emotional having to 'send them home'."

Jacob's imagination, she said, knows no limits. "He has bins of costumes, including Santa Claus, a variety of scary masks, 1970s attire, rock stars, cowboys, and even wrestlers."

I have since learned, somewhat to my surprise, that WWE pro wrestling is extremely popular among many Special Olympians, especially young men. WWE was the theme of a Special Olympics dance I attended at which the athletes enthusiastically got into character, donning their wrestling gear and t-shirts. As an aside, I later met Justin, a 25-year-old with Down syndrome, whose mother told me her son is absorbed in all forms of this wrestling entertainment and spends hours engrossed in looking at glossy wrestling magazines.

During intermission, the five of us, now friends, stayed in our seats and got to know more about each other. We looked at a photo gallery of Jacob in costume. In turn, these nice people remarked on Maggie's being a good singer. Even when our girl doesn't know the words, she does an admirable job of singing along. We exchanged contact information and made plans to stay in touch.

At the rousing *Joseph* finale, with the music building to a crescendo and the entire cast triumphantly marching onto the stage, Maggie became extremely excited and loudly roared her approval. She repeats this same behavior every time at performances. For example, we happened to be seated front row center at a quality high school production of *Legally Blonde*, put on by the always talented drama students at Milwaukee's Pius XI Catholic High School. Cathy and I had to literally hold Maggie back. She was so charged up at the lively finale, we were certain she would jump right onto the stage.

We thoroughly enjoyed *Joseph,* and the company was an unexpected treat. A follow-up email from Jacob's mom, Kristen, said: "It was magical meeting both of you. I often have a great deal of anxiety trying to find outings that are 'Jacob friendly,' and I knew the moment you sat down I was in good company. I, too, had the thought Maggie and Jacob knew one another. He is still talking about his new friend. I would love to get together."

Kristen went on to share how special this play was for Jacob and how our Maggie warmed her heart. "It has been quite a journey with Jacob thus far."

Kristen admitted to shedding tears at the start of the play, because there was a history behind this play for her family. "In April of 2011 we had tickets to see *Joseph* at a high school production. Jacob became ill and was hospitalized the morning of the play. I'm not sure how much Maggie has trouble letting things go, but missing that play he had so anticipated was very difficult."

That hospitalization turned into a month-long nightmare of fighting a diagnosis of double bacterial pneumonia. "Jacob was on a ventilator for a few weeks. We nearly lost him. When he 'came to,' one of the first things he asked for was to see *Joseph*. I promised we would. Saturday, I kept my promise."

I'm glad Maggie and I were able to share his recovery celebration because it is a sad fact of life that at some point a high percentage of the special needs population will—often relatively early in life—require hospitalization. As was Jacob's challenge and that of our own Maggie, the experience can be life-threatening. Special needs parents remain on high alert to guard against the dangers these health crises represent.

Elvis lives.

CHAPTER 10

PEACE OF MIND

My own life story took an abrupt turn in May 2000 when a surgeon pronounced three chilling words: "You have cancer."

That his message was not just a bad dream, reality hit home when I was wheeled from post-operative recovery to the hospital's oncology floor. My diagnosis was squamous cell carcinoma, an aggressive head and neck cancer my medical oncologist referred to ominously as "Major League." The survival rate was only fifty percent.

At the time I was a healthy, just turned 49-year-old lifetime non-smoker. Blessed with a wonderful wife and three beautiful young children, I had a whole lot to live for. Maggie was barely 14, Martha 11, and Jack not yet six. Cathy recalls harboring a real fear I would leave her a widow to raise our children alone.

Melvin Konner, a physician and author whose own wife lost out to cancer, leaving him to raise their three children solo, wrote, "Cancer is our most feared bodily assault."

Weeks earlier I had discovered a mysterious lump on the left side of my neck. Fortunately, heeding the sage advice of my wife and a trusted doctor friend, I promptly brought this concern to the attention of my primary physician, who knew that a lump in the neck was a warning sign. He referred me to a surgeon to "cut this sucker out and find out what we were dealing with."

The source of the malignancy was a tonsil. Cancer had spread to my lymph nodes, causing the ominous lump in my neck. The best way to combat my cancer was determined to be radiation. In June 2000 I began seven weeks of intensive radiation to destroy the rogue microscopic cells invading my body.

The book *No Such Thing as a Bad Day* relates Hamilton Jordan's journey surviving three different bouts of cancer—all before the age of 50. His book gives voice to me and others who face the terror of this disease. His words, "All I ever wanted was a fighting chance" ring true.

During my darkest days that summer, I found comfort in reading the account of this survivor, best known as former President Jimmy Carter's Chief of Staff. I prayed that I, too, would join the ranks of the cured. I was determined to fight this deadly disease.

Maggie never really understood the seriousness of what I was experiencing, which was probably for the best. Martha, on the other hand, was keenly aware of what her father faced, although she did not express her emotions outwardly. Cathy became aware of how scared our middle child was that I would not survive. In her short life experience, she associated cancer with the three funerals she had attended for grandparents.

Hamilton Jordan, himself the father of young children, writes that a child under seven does not remember much about a parent who dies. I read this observation during the bleak days of my own cancer odyssey. I especially remember the Fourth of July, when I lay on the family room couch too weak and fatigued from treatment to go to the park to watch our five-year-old son compete in foot races. Cathy and Jack returned home with smiling faces and a trophy to show me for his having won the race. While this definitely picked up my spirits, I worried whether I'd survive to see our children run other races and reach adulthood.

Today I make it a point to refer to myself as a *fortunate* cancer survivor. Although Martha and Jack are now grown, independent, and well on their own paths in life, I believe our Maggie still needs both her father and mother to be in her life to love and care for her.

The following year, when I was mostly out of the woods, my internist, Dr. Christopher Drayna, reminded me during a routine physical that I was indeed lucky to have "dodged a bullet." My oncologist believes that had my doctors and I not been proactive about the suspicious lump on my neck, the cancer would likely have spread and with it the loss of all hope. He said, "John, if you were a physician, it is likely you would have procrastinated and waited six months, and it would have been too late."

I confess that while lying awake during the darkest hours of my brush with life-threatening cancer, I felt some comfort knowing I had a substantial life insurance policy in place—something no one can purchase once it's really needed. That is why it is high on the "must have" checklist when others depend on you, especially when one of those dependents has special needs.

Life insurance in its most basic form is protection in the event of the insured's premature death and the financial hardship imposed by that death on survivors. And here I will don my professional hat to speak from my experience as a financial planner.

A major goal in financial and retirement planning is to acquire a sizeable living estate, aka net worth. If financial independence has not already been reached, a plan needs to be in place to provide for those survivors who depend on the insured.

When I was diagnosed with cancer at 49, Cathy was 43, we carried a hefty mortgage, faced future college expenses at two private schools, and had not yet managed to build a self-sustaining investment portfolio. Life insurance is unique in that it provides an instant liquid estate at precisely the time of need. It makes one's family financially whole in the event of death.

As a case in point, my friend Mike Cary, our family's dentist, loving husband, and father of five, died suddenly and way too young of a brain aneurism at 49. His wife, Char, was devastated, in shock. His children, family members, dental patients, and many friends were left grieving and heartsick.

In what became his final act of love, Mike had exhibited the foresight of acquiring substantial insurance on his life. At the time, however, the generous life insurance payment was of little solace to Char. She felt strongly—and justifiably—that this trade-off was not a fair trade.

Nevertheless, the insurance proceeds did help the surviving Cary family financially, filling a gap caused by the loss of their sole provider. Life insurance put the family in a position close to where they would have been financially had Mike lived, worked, and continued accumulating wealth over the next 15 or so years until normal retirement and financial independence.

Today, some 14 years after their tragic loss, the Cary children have all completed college, and a couple of weddings have taken place. Char is financially secure and relishes being a grandmother. Still, Mike Cary was one of the most caring individuals I have crossed paths with on my life's journey, and I miss him greatly. Cathy and I had sought his help at critical junctures in our own lives, and he had been there to mitigate our challenges and allay our fears.

One of those junctures was when Maggie took a bad fall. She was in high school at the time, age 16, when her neurological condition worsened and increasingly affected her balance. She lost her ability to ride a bike and moved from being a sprinter in Special Olympics to a race walker. The day she fell she'd been getting off the school bus in our driveway. The fall caused the loss of a front tooth— which also made her mouth a bloody mess. I was at work, but Cathy was home and quickly on the scene, calming and attending to Maggie.

Cathy wisely called Doctor Mike. He instructed Cathy to clean Maggie's mouth and immediately bring her and the tooth to his office. Incredibly, Mike was able to save the tooth, care for Maggie, and comfort Mom. That evening, in his typical caring way, he called the house to inquire after our Maggie. Although the next day was a Saturday, Mike opened his office just to examine the tooth and thoroughly cleanse Maggie's mouth to protect against infection.

To this day Maggie has this tooth, which we can identify in her smile because it is slightly discolored. For almost every young woman such imperfection would be an issue, but for Maggie it is insignificant.

Mike, being Mike, went out of his way to take care of me, as well, when—prior to the start of extensive radiation treatment to combat my oral cancer—the oncology team wanted me to have some immediate dental care and a teeth cleaning. Mike kept his office open after hours and scheduled a hygienist to work overtime.

Cathy, for the most part, was able to keep her emotions in check during my cancer ordeal. But she broke down crying to our friend Mike Cary. After Mike passed away, I could no longer enter his office building, finding it too painful not having Mike greet me with his genuine smile and inquire of my family, especially Maggie.

As parents of special needs children, the 64,000-dollar question is: What does the future hold?

Realistically, our Maggie at age 30 has a permanent disability. We are long past the stage of believing that some miracle would cure her, although we still hope her quality of life can be maintained and we see marked improvement in her behavior. Maggie will always require a high level of care. The truth is we do not know her life expectancy.

The good news is that individuals with cognitive disabilities are living much longer these days. Indeed, the average lifespan of people with an intellectual disability is now 67, triple what it was in the 1930s.

So the reality for us is to openly face and even embrace our own mortality and the unknown future financial requirements of an extraordinarily vulnerable and needy dependent adult child. We must have a solid peace-of-mind plan in place to assure that our cherished loved one is well cared for after we are gone.

Many special needs parents face the same predicament as the 56-year-old single mother whose 20-year-old son has cerebral palsy and epilepsy. She laments being overwhelmed by the sheer cost and complexity of planning for her son's future. "I'm afraid for Michael," she says, "which is why I have to live forever." Such a fervent wish is not uncommon, but it is hardly a plan.

Families of special needs children require specially designed financial and estate plans. The truth is, this kind of planning is tricky and complex. A poorly drafted or clumsy estate plan, such as a will or beneficiary election, could actually make a disabled person ineligible for bedrock government benefits.

A foundational tool families might strongly consider is establishing a **special needs trust**, sometimes known as a **supplemental needs trust**, specially designed to preserve the child's eligibility for crucial government benefits. Assets placed in a properly drafted trust are not counted against the current maximum $2,000 to remain qualified for SSI and Medicaid.

Supplemental needs trusts are used to supplement, or pay for the extra costs over and above the basics that Uncle Sam provides. This extra allows funds for life-enhancing extras, such as travel, entertainment, additional medical therapy, motorized wheelchairs, modified vehicles, internet service, music and art lessons, media devices, personal grooming, and the cost of a private room versus a shared room at a health facility.

A special needs trust can serve as the basis of a long-term financial and care plan for a disabled loved one. I am proud to report that Cathy and I, as part of our overall comprehensive financial and estate plan, wisely put in place a special needs trust to benefit Maggie. This trust will be adequately funded from our accumulated estate assets and life insurance payouts.

A caveat: use an attorney who has the skill, experience, and expertise in crafting a special needs trust so you neither jeopardize your loved one's government benefits nor conflict with your plan's overall vision.

Life insurance can be a very effective means of supplying the necessary financial support after you are gone. It is an excellent funding source, because it provides certainty that coincides with the death of the provider/caregiver. Be sure to coordinate insurance with your overall estate plan, including the naming of beneficiaries on life policies and retirement accounts.

Primary questions to consider are how much life insurance protection to have and on whose life. Should this be an individual policy, or joint first-to-die coverages, or a survivor second-to-die policy? Further, what type or combination of insurance makes the most sense in your situation: term (pure) or whole (permanent) life?

An effective risk protection plan is to combine a Supplemental Special Needs Trust with permanent life insurance. This is a powerful combination that can ensure there will be financial resources available to pay for a special needs loved one's care over the long term.

Gabe Prospero is a fine young man from our parish and neighborhood who I have watched grow up. Having now graduated from college, Gabe has taken a position as a financial representative with Northwestern Mutual. This Milwaukee-based firm is a national force in financial services.

Gabe's older brother had been stillborn and would have otherwise been a Down syndrome child. His anguished new parents, Tony and Holly, worried about the survival of their next child, Gabe. He arrived healthy, but the Prospero's history of his lost special needs brother has stayed with him throughout his life and influenced his choice of a career. Gabe wants to help individuals plan for the future and uncertainty, thereby he chose a career in financial services with a high quality firm. He is sincerely interested in becoming a Best Buddy while also exploring helping out with a one-on-one relationship with SPRED, special religious education, and as a volunteer coach with Special Olympics.

His late uncle, Father William (Will) Prospero, a dynamic Jesuit priest, played a huge role in his formative years. Father Will was diagnosed in 2014 with an aggressive form of cancer and died the same year at the age of 49. This is the same age I was when cancer raised its ugly head and when my friend Mike Cary passed on. In every life there is an end, and much uncertainty. This is magnified when premature death occurs.

A disabled individual, like our Maggie, is considered impoverished so long as her personal assets are less than $2,000. I have heard the horror stories of government benefits being frozen, denied, or required to be paid back when this modest figure is exceeded—even slightly.

Numerous situations occur in which special needs individuals become the unanticipated beneficiaries of an estate or other well-meaning gift. At times, cash from Grandma might have to be returned to avoid tripping the $2,000 limit and jeopardizing government benefits and services.

Such inheritances and gifts should instead be directed to an **irrevocable special needs trust** for the sole benefit of the disabled individual. This trust is a vehicle uniquely designed to receive gifts and bequests earmarked for the disabled person's well-being. It can accept assets from various sources, including from grandparents and other family members.

Your next critical step is choosing a **trustee** to manage the trust. This trustee has absolute discretion over when and how to spend the money and is legally responsible for managing funds in the trust and spending those funds appropriately.

The ideal trustee should possess investment knowledge to administer this account. This is not a job for an amateur. One could hire a professional to act as trustee, such as a bank, a trust company, or an attorney. Alternatively, a local community (pooled) trust may be less expensive and not require substantial minimums.

Many attorneys who handle special needs issues counsel against naming the same person to serve as both trustee and guardian. For one, these are two different roles with different responsibilities. I have heard it said that good trustees must think with their heads, while good guardians think with their hearts. In our case, Cathy and I have named Matt Miler, a partner with McCarthy Grittinger Financial Group, as trustee if I am not able. Matt is a top-notch financial, investment, and tax professional, still in his mid-thirties, whom we trust explicitly. He knows Maggie and our family, and Cathy has great respect for him.

Before the widespread adoption of special needs trusts, a common strategy was to disinherit a disabled family member so the government would take care of the loved one without diminishing the estate.

A new law came into existence in late 2014, Achieving a Better Life Experience Act, that offers a mechanism for a) protecting a disabled individual, b) getting around the $2,000 asset maximum, while c) still qualifying for government benefits. This law expands on the section 529 tax-advantaged plans used for college funding, now with provisions to save and care for disabled individuals. The 529 ABLE, though still needing to be established by individual states, is attractive as an addition to—or a replacement for—a special needs trust. Keep in mind that tax laws are continually changing. Stay alert and informed, because this new 529 ABLE law holds promise.

Because life is unpredictable and health often fails prematurely, strategies to protect vulnerable family members must be a priority. Act sooner rather than later to put these important safeguards in place because there may not be a later, as in the sudden death at 49 of our friend Mike Cary. Both his family and ours were fortunate in having plans already in place to deal with the unexpected when it occurred. I was a fortunate survivor whose plan did not have to be implemented. We had been proactive. Planning allowed one less worry as we dealt with treatment, healing, and the gift of a future together. I wish no less for every family. Planning is key.

CHAPTER 11

AUNT CASSIE & COUSIN BRIAN

"Angels descending, bring from above, echoes of mercy,
whispers of love."

Fanny J. Crosby

I was very close to my mom's only sister, my Aunt Cassie. Cassie was also my godmother, a relationship she took seriously and carried out in exemplary fashion. The role of godmother defined her philosophy of life. To her, a child was a gift from God, and a mother was a dispenser of love. Aunt Cassie's focus in life was her four blue-eyed, blond, curly-haired children. It was her unlimited capacity, courage, and strength to care for and love her youngest child that especially defined her as Mother, with a capital "M."

Her son, Brian, started life with a very difficult birth. My cousin's diagnosis was a rare chromosomal disorder known as Trisomy 8 Mosaic. Most babies die at birth from this but for some reason we were blessed to have Brian for 33 years. His sister, Mimi, remembers her mother saying that the physicians were fascinated by Brian's case, and it was written about in medical journals. Mimi believes it was a miracle that her brother lived as long as he did.

Brian endured a string of hospitalizations related to Crohn's disease and assorted other health problems. As a young boy, he wore an eye patch that gave him the look of a pirate. Later, he required thick eyeglasses. Brian grew into a well-mannered, nicely dressed young man, quick with a handshake and a genuinely warm greeting. Cathy and I learned firsthand from Aunt Cassie how to love and care for our own special child.

When I introduced my bride-to-be to my family, Aunt Cassie took to her right away and graciously opened her lovely home to host a bridal shower for Cathy. I think she respected Cathy for, among other reasons, being a nurse and working at a children's hospital. Cassie had spent countless hours in hospitals and observed angel nurses helping to care for her stricken son.

During our first couple of years of marriage before Maggie arrived, we took Brian into our home occasionally to provide a weekend respite for Aunt Cassie and Uncle Dan. Those special needs parents welcomed a break and quick getaway, secure in the knowledge that their son was in good hands. They drove Brian from their home in Chicago to our Milwaukee home, an hour-and-a-half away.

Brian's bladder didn't always empty, making him prone to urinary tract infections that could be serious and even deadly. I distinctly remember standing outside our bathroom door listening, making sure my cousin urinated sufficiently. To guard against infection he needed to be catheterized each day, something Cathy was qualified to handle. Brian was at that time in his early twenties.

Cassie lamented to Cathy that his medical needs limited his housing and care options. I recall all the medications Brian had to take. And I learned that Brian needed his rest. He took more naps and slept longer than I expected. Our Maggie also needs her sleep and cannot be over-scheduled without becoming irritable and cranky.

To make Brian's stay enjoyable, we planned his favorite activities—eating at an authentic, old-fashioned diner and going to the movies. We saw the 1983 hit, *Trading Places,* starring Eddie Murphy, Dan Ackroyd, and Jamie Lee Curtis. I will never forget

Brian's reaction when actress Jamie Lee bared her breasts in a memorable scene. Like any young man, he was excited to see this attractive woman, but Brian went further by loudly demonstrating his approval. Cousin Brian had been raised on a steady diet of Disney movies, not this adult fare. I am thankful it was dark in the movie theater.

Aging was a difficult adjustment for Brian. He became increasingly aware of his siblings and cousins moving on in life and leaving him behind. Brian surprised his family when he took exception to his cousin Mary Joyce being charged with watching him, very much aware Mary Joyce was a few years younger than he was. My sister Nancy grew up with Brian, and they were very close, but when Nancy announced her engagement Brian was adamant in his displeasure over this news. He went so far as to say he would object at the wedding ceremony. Brian knew that his favorite cousin would be moving on and his relationship with her would never be the same.

Brian spent the last year of his life at a fully supported and licensed living center run by the non-profit Trinity Services Inc. of New Lenox, Illinois. This Intermediate Care Facility for the Developmentally Disabled (ICF/DD) provided Brian with his own bedroom and storage space. There he also received necessary nursing services. The staff giggled whenever his sister Mimi visited because he usually asked her how "that damn baby" of hers was. Brian was somewhat jealous of baby Cassie, his niece and godchild. His brother Dan appreciated the staff at Trinity treating Brian like family, despite him residing there less than a year. Cousin Brian's multiple health problems sadly caught up with him. He died suddenly of an infection that overpowered him.

Brian's father, my Uncle Dan, was a hard-working attorney and a good provider for his family, but he could not defeat cancer. The following year Cassie was stricken with the same disease. She survived only a short six months after her diagnosis.

I felt honored that Cassie, through her children, had asked me to deliver the reflections at her church funeral service. She also instructed that I read *A Parable for Mothers* by Temple Bailey. Written in 1933, it remains a delightful tribute to moms—a simple, earthly story seasoned with a powerful, heavenly meaning. Cassie's intent to all of us was to celebrate her life, but embedded in the words of the parable was a message directed to her children and grandchildren that her departure was okay, her work was complete, and we should be assured she now rests peacefully in heaven.

I was at work when I learned of the passing of my beloved aunt and godmother. Filled with sadness, I returned home and immediately felt her presence there. In our front hall hangs a beautiful work of art she crafted for us of the Madonna with Child. Looking at this piece I had a vision of Cassie with Brian cradled in her arms. On another wall in our home hangs "An Old Irish Blessing" she made in needlepoint. "May the road rise to meet you, May the wind be always at your back." I cherish this. I learned from her daughter Mimi that Cassie thought of her needlepoint as a good tranquilizer to cope with the many challenges she faced with Brian.

All of us—especially mothers of special needs children—can use a destresser. Cathy's is meditation, yoga, painting, walking, tai chi, and gardening. Cathy believes her stress has lessened and I heartily concur. She has suggested I consider meditation, too. Being a typical guy, I've resisted but admit it wouldn't hurt to at least give it a try.

As father to Maggie, I have come around of late to believing I should embrace the wisdom and power of serenity. Theologian Reinhold Niebuhr's simple 1941 "Serenity Prayer" speaks volumes:

> *God grant me the serenity to accept the things I cannot change: courage to change the things I can; and wisdom to know the difference.*

Dictionaries define serenity as calmness or tranquility. All parents or caregivers of a special needs individual could use more serenity and peace in their often chaotic lives.

As Maggie's parent, one example from my own life of chaotic surprises began one morning when Maggie and I had breakfast at John's Sandwich Shop, her favorite family restaurant. She has taken to calling herself a John's fanatic. If I wake her up and let her know we are headed to John's, she jumps out of bed and is more highly motivated than usual to get dressed, toileted, take her medicine, and get on with her day. This encounter happened on a Labor Day Monday, which Maggie refers to as a paid holiday.

She ordered her standard fare, "An omelet with ham, bacon, and cheese, and grapefruit to drink, please." Adding every time, "Try not to burn it." Maybe due to drinking the grapefruit juice too quickly, she gagged and ended up vomiting her meal onto the plate. I'd like to think I had the Serenity Prayer top of mind, because I remained remarkably calm as I cleaned her up and made no big deal of the incident—which, after all, was beyond her control. Maggie also remained calm. She even apologized, which I assured her was unnecessary. These incidents happen and I know will happen again.

Lately, as a result of my annual physical, my doctor has me monitoring my own blood pressure, which on occasion is high. One avenue to better control this important health indicator is to remain more serene. Cathy has counseled me not to fixate on that which I can't control such as the fortunes of the stock market, weather, traffic jams, technology, sports, or politics. I am happy and relieved to report my blood pressure has returned to normal.

Aunt Cassie cherished the poem "Heaven's Very Special Child." It resonated with her as mother to Brian. She made it a point to familiarize Cathy and me with it, believing it could help ease our path. Cassie also incorporated it into Brian's moving funeral service.

"Heaven's Very Special Child" has been widely circulated and reprinted countless times over many decades. Long identified as "author unknown," more recently it has been rightly credited to Edna Massimilla. The author's inspiration was her daughter Ruth, who lived with severe disabilities until her death at age 43.

Edna's poem tells the poignant story of a meeting held in heaven to find suitable parents for the important mission of caring for a special child, who will need much love and be known as handicapped. These parents will not realize the value of their gift from heaven right away, but will eventually be rewarded with "stronger faith and richer love."

I have tried unsuccessfully to discover where the term "special" came into use in the now widely accepted phrase "special needs" which replaces the term "mentally retarded" and even "handicapped." It could well be that this poem, with its sensitive description of a special child, was helpful in changing mindsets.

In searching for the definition of "special needs" I gained much information from a site hosted by *Parenting Magazine* and from Terri Mauro, expert in children with special needs. She observed, "Special needs is an umbrella underneath which a staggering array of diagnoses can be wedged."

Mauro states that although "special needs" might seem like a tragic designation due to a host of things your child *can't* do, parents "may find their child's challenges make triumphs sweeter, and that weakness is often accompanied by amazing strengths."

CHAPTER 12

SWEET KATIE—WHEN I GROW UP

Kathleen Helen, the first-born child of Tom and Julie Hackett, was welcomed into the world in 1969. Named after both sets of grandmothers, Katie, as she came to be called, was born at Blytheville Air Force Base in Arkansas while her father served there as an officer.

Like many doctors of that era, the Hacketts' young obstetrician counseled the anguished new parents to not take their newborn home but place her in an institution. He stated with certainty that infants like Katie would never develop mentally past the age of three. His stern advice was to give up their daughter now, before they became attached to her. Julie, who'd carried this child for nine months, countered that they were already attached.

While discussing Katie, her mother gave me a copy of "Welcome to Holland," a one-page essay about taking into your life a child with Down syndrome or a disability. Emily Perl Kingsley authored this groundbreaking essay in 1987 about nurturing a child with a disability, written from her experience as the mother of Jason, then a 13-year-old Down syndrome son. Kingsley was at the time counseling families of newborns with Down syndrome, looking to inspire these shaken parents to think bigger and encourage them to help fulfill each child's full potential.

This copyrighted essay is widely available and readily found online. Written from the perspective of parents expecting a child,

"Welcome to Holland" tells the story of the excitement and anticipation surrounding a planned dream trip to Italy. Instead, upon the
birth of a child with a lifelong disability such as Down syndrome,
they are told, "Welcome to Holland." Having landed in Holland
and not Italy as expected, the shocked parents are understandably
confused and dismayed at this unwelcome detour.

The author suggests the tremendous popularity of "Welcome
to Holland" comes from its theme of an unexpected development
changing a long-held dream and having to adapt one's original
plan to reality. The point of the story is that it's okay to be disappointed on missing out on the wonders of Italy, but take the time
to reflect on all the lovely things Holland has to offer. Putting aside
the disappointment makes it possible to appreciate that life with a
special needs child—despite being very different—can be equally
wonderful. "It's just a different place," writes this special mom.

Speaking about her surprising smash hit of a story, Kingsley
adds, "It was the fact that raising Jason turned out to be a special
kind of reward and job (not, perhaps what I had expected—but
rewarding just the same) that I was inspired to come up with
'Welcome to Holland'."

We also have much to learn from devoted parents such as
Julie and Tom Hackett about life and living with a special needs
child. This intelligent couple has been immersed in a laboratory
for 47 years, having tried, tested, considered, and experimented
with dozens of ideas, problems, therapies, surgeries, counseling,
and medications—all to help their sweet daughter, Katie, fulfill
her potential. Like scientists, they too experienced successes and
failures, hopes and disappointments. They learned through trial
and error. One could even say they earned a doctorate in Life with
Katie. Still, they would be the first to admit they have more to try
and much to learn.

I asked Tom and Julie if they had any accumulated wisdom
to pass on to young parents of a special needs child today. "Pace
yourselves" they said, as life with a special child is a marathon,

not a sprint. Regular children grow up, mature, and eventually leave the nest at 18, when they are considered an adult capable of independence. Not so with the cognitively disabled, like Katie, like Maggie, who grow up, surpass 18, but never become indcpendent. In some respects, parenting is permanent childhood. It is different. It's tulips and windmills.

Katie has accomplished much in her life in spite of her disability. She is quite literate and has held gainful employment, most recently a position at a deli. She's competed in Special Olympics in swimming and has dozens of medals to show for it. She gained an appreciation for art by participating in special needs art programming, and several art pieces of her own creation adorn her bedroom.

When her brothers started piano lessons, their perceptive older sister expressed a desire to do the same. She learned enough to play some basic pieces, but her progress, especially compared with her more naturally gifted younger siblings, was slow and uneven. In retrospect, Mom and Dad look at the piano in the living room and wish they had continued Katie's lessons, at least somewhat longer than they did.

Because I have always enjoyed bicycling, as a dad I looked forward to teaching Maggie this rite of childhood passage. Our younger children, Martha and Jack, quickly learned to ride a two-wheeler on their own, spending at most a couple of hours practicing alone in the driveway. I don't even recall helping them, and no training wheels were involved. They just did it.

When Maggie was in middle school, I was determined to teach her to ride a "big kid's bike" like the other neighborhood children. This proved challenging, taking many hours of patient effort. We started on a small bike with training wheels to get her comfortable, then progressed to her own bike. Many nights followed of taking Maggie and her bike to the church parking lot, enduring a sore back from holding both of them upright as she struggled to maintain her balance. In this, Cathy thought Maggie would never be able to ride a bike. I think I kept at it because biking was something I liked. It was also one effort for which I mustered much patience. Well, I am proud to say we did it. Maggie eventually learned to bike on her own, and her parents learned an important lesson.

As Maggie aged and her neurological condition started to affect her balance, she lost her ability to ride a two-wheel bike. I like to think our family learned to adapt. We purchased a tandem bike, on which she sat behind me and pedaled, and for a number of years the two of us rode through the neighborhood, on the parkways, and along the bike paths. A year or two ago, Maggie's anxiety became an issue, and she became afraid to get on the tandem. In her words it was "too tippy." I then realized her fear was too great and reluctantly sold the tandem.

Life goes on, so we purchased an adult tricycle for our Maggie. This three-wheeler does provide her with stability and is not tippy. We take it out of the garage when the Wisconsin weather permits, and Maggie pedals a mile to the local custard stand or into the village, sometimes stopping at the farmer's market. I walk or jog along beside her while she offers running commentaries about other bike riders. On a recent ride we encountered the "basket lady," who had a basket mounted on the front of her bike. Then there was "Speedy Gonzales," a young guy tucked into the racing position who blew past us. All this provides our girl with needed exercise, as well as a sense of ownership in managing her own bike. More important, Maggie considers herself a biker.

Unfortunately, Katie Hackett has developed some serious psychological issues and now refuses to put on her swim suit. She is no longer swimming. Tom and Julie Hackett are avid skiers and, remarkably, Katie learned to ski. This let them enjoy family ski vacations. One memorable trip took them to Winter Park outside Denver, in the Rocky Mountains of Colorado, where a willing Katie became part of this resort's Adaptive Ski program. Its instructors have training in helping the blind, the one-legged, and the Katies of the world learn to ski using special adaptive equipment—and ample patience.

One day Tom and Julie were shocked to find their special daughter calling to them from the top of an 11,000- foot elevation. The ski lift brought her up to the summit but how would she be able to get down? With the instructor by her side, Katie managed quite well by learning to traverse the hill instead of barreling down it like the young guns were doing. At the end of the day, Mom and Dad were thrilled to find their daughter safely waiting for them at the lodge, a big smile on her face and her favorite beverage, Diet Coke, in hand.

Skiing proved a mixed blessing for the Hacketts. Because Katie wanted to ski, it meant either Tom or Julie staying with her on the more gentle beginner slopes. Chalk up the inconvenience to one of the minor sacrifices necessary to include Katie in certain family activities. Maggie also takes us longer to walk to the store or church with her, or even to finish a meal, so family members learn to account for this extra time and plan ahead.

Maggie's friend from summer camp, day programs, and Special Olympics is Jessie, aka Jessica Lynn, and Jess to her dad. She is a 32-year-old woman from a loving family. Cathy and I feel privileged to know Jessie's remarkable parents, Brian and Sue Lanser, and to have grown close to both. Jessie has gotten to be more comfortable with me, but it has taken years. Just recently she floored me by proclaiming, "I like you." Wow!

Despite her considerable cognitive disability, the more I get to know Jessie and learn her accomplishments, the more intrigued I become. Whenever she and Maggie share a ride to day programming I often ask Jessie how she is doing. The only response I have ever gotten from her on those days is when she pipes up: "going swimming." Jessie loves to swim. But like everything in her life, learning how proved a monumental—but not insurmountable—challenge. Sue shared with me how she discovered a special needs swimming program and enrolled her daughter in it when she was young.

The point I want to emphasize is that Jessie required—and still requires—continuous, repetitive work to acquire basic skills, such as the ability to swim. But Sue persevered, refusing to give up on Jessie, as evidenced by her investing in 15 years of swim lessons for her disabled daughter. Jessie went on to earn her Red Cross card for swimming proficiency and now thoroughly enjoys this activity, as well as deriving its healthful benefits. Jessie swims at the local Y as a part of its day camp and year-round at the family vacation spot in Door County. She also enjoys the local community pool during the summer months, often with Jean, her devoted caregiver and companion.

Perhaps I can compare conquering the challenge of swimming for Maggie, Jessie, Katie, and others to the challenge for most of us of running a 26.2-mile marathon. The fact is many recreational runners are fully capable of running this long distance if they put in the necessary training. This takes time. Not even naturally gifted athletes can tackle the marathon without the requisite preparation. For ordinary runners, being able to complete 26.2 miles could well take up to two years of continuous training to gradually build up to this ultimate goal. I completed marathons in 1980, 1982, and 1984, yet as far as running goes I would describe myself as average and ordinary. Maggie was born in 1985, and this parental responsibility put an end to my long-distance pursuits because of less time to train.

For those saddled with an intellectual disability, learning to swim, ski, play the piano, or ride a bike is the equivalent for most people of learning to run a marathon. It can be done but will take much more time and patience than most of us are willing to devote. Our Martha learned to walk before she was nine months old. Maggie was two years old. Sue Lanser was afraid Jessie would never walk. As it was, she used a child-sized walker until she managed to walk independently at age eight. Had it not been for the encouragement Jessie received in school, coupled with supportive care at home, it is likely she would never have learned to walk.

All her life Katie Hackett has told her parents that she was going to do this or that "when I grow up"—a phrase she most often stated throughout the years about moving into an apartment on her own. Two years ago, now middle-aged at 45 and conceivably "all grown up," Katie took the big step of moving into a group home with three other special needs women and a live-in caregiver, five miles from Mom and Dad. This experiment is working better than expected for all involved. Mom and dad are pleased their daughter is accepting her independence from them and handling this major life transition so well. Her psychological issues even seem lessened in this new environment, an added plus for all of them.

Making housing arrangements for our Maggie is the number one planning matter that Cathy and I must still address. While our younger children were growing up at home, I thought the best living arrangement for Maggie was at home with us. Now that our youngest child, Jack, is off to college, we would otherwise be empty nesters. Cathy, to her credit, keeps pressing me to think seriously about housing for Maggie independent of us.

Activists for the disabled community strongly recommend that a special needs child leave the nest and move to independent housing in the age range of 22 to 30. Their thinking is that learning independence beyond this age requires too many adjustments of the child. Clearly, Maggie is already set in her ways and routines. It is more difficult for a special needs individual to be abruptly pulled out of the home she knows in the event of a sudden death or disability of her caregiver parents.

I readily admit this part of my journey scares me. Having Maggie live outside the comfort and security of our home life after 30-plus years troubles me. In my role as father protector, I worry about her being abused, hurt, or neglected. As Tom and Julie Hackett advised me, do not expect the care at a group home to be as good as what you can offer in your own home. At home, she has both a mom and a dad to look after her. Nobody knows your child as well as you do. Still, in the right setting, a loved one can be happy and secure.

Joy, Maggie's classmate through middle and high school, had her first experience with group housing that did not work out so well. Her diet wasn't as good as she was accustomed to at home, and she rapidly gained 30 pounds, which caused the onset of diabetes. Mom and Dad brought Joy back to their home, where she has since shed the excess weight, looks great again, and has returned to good health. It seems a common occurrence for housing to start on a trial basis, but you won't know until you try. Despite the challenges it is better to explore options that might work for your special child.

CHAPTER 13

ERMA ON MOTHERS

Patience is not my strong suit—just ask Cathy. But patience is an absolute necessity when dealing with Maggie. To be honest, I would have to describe myself as impatient. I suspect this lack of patience is something of a guy thing. It is definitely a character flaw.

Our Maggie operates at two speeds: slow and deliberate—or stopped cold. Hurrying Maggie, if foolishly attempted, is guaranteed to be counterproductive. I have been known to bellow phrases such as "let's go," "hurry up," or "move it, now." No matter the urgency or volume of my command, the result is always the same. Our girl responds by coming to a complete stop.

You might think I was a slow learner, failing to learn the lesson of patience after many years of no success with impatience. In voicing my frustration with Maggie's slowness, Cathy admonishes me with the well-known truth: "Insanity is trying the same thing again and again, and expecting a different result."

St. Augustine, an intellectual in the early church, put it this way: "Patience is the companion of wisdom."

Although a slow learner, I am making progress, primarily by listening to and learning from Cathy, spending more quality time with Maggie as her caregiver, and following the guidance and professional help of a psychologist who has prepared a behavior intervention plan.

In many respects Maggie is like a young child, and we must employ age-appropriate child psychology. A prime example is her medication regime, which must occur four times a day. In the past, this could be challenging. Thankfully, it is now for the most part a non-event. We use a plastic spoon and applesauce to ease down the multiple pills and capsules. My previous method, which, unsurprisingly, did not work, was to aim the spoon into her mouth while yelling "open up."

Cathy, on the other hand, uses a calm and patient voice to say to Maggie, "Tell me when you are ready." At this, Maggie opens up and says "Awhh." Favorite companion to Maggie is a special education major in college Danielle, or Danie, who has even higher expectations, along with the requisite patience. She simply hands Maggie the spoon and our daughter promptly downs her medicine.

Maggie frequently refers to her Danie by her last name, O'Neil. The other day she broke me up by referring to her caregiver as Shaquille, as in Shaquille O'Neal. The seven-foot 325-pound former star NBA basketball player is now a TV analyst and ad pitchman. I suspect Maggie doesn't know a thing about him but grooves his name: Shaquille O'Neal.

Experience has taught me perseverance and patience go hand-in-hand in dealing with special needs children. To attend art class held on the lower level of the West Milwaukee Donna Lexa Art Center, Maggie and I always take the stairs instead of the elevator. For one thing, she can use the exercise. For another, she sees the elevator as being used for those, as she puts it, "with handicaps," such as her art companions Janet and Jane, who use wheelchairs. In Maggie's world it has always been easier for her to climb up stairs, not descend them, and going down has been a slow step-at-a-time operation. After a couple of years of trying to get her to alternate feet every other step, I am proud to say we have succeeded. She now looks forward to walking down the stairs, at an appropriate speed.

As a husband and father, I like to think I have grown to more fully appreciate the demanding role of the mother of young children. I don't recall much wailing from our children that called for Dad, but the cry of Mom rang in my ears plenty of times. I readily admit the parental equity is unfairly gender biased. To be a mother of a special needs child—such as Cathy is to Maggie, Diane is to twins Nikki and Jenni, Kristen is to Jacob, Sue is to Jessie, Julie is to Katie, or Aunt Cassie was to Brian—is often an unbearable role. Yet moms persevere. Our Maggie is still apt to loudly call out "Mom" a couple of times in the average day. Maggie, although an adult, has not outgrown being demanding of her mother—and probably never will.

From my reading, observation, and discussions with mothers of special needs children, I frequently hear them express a general feeling of being overwhelmed.

A dictionary definition of *overwhelm* is:
1. To pour down upon and cover up or bury
2. To make helpless, as with greater force or deep emotion; overcome; crush; overpower.

What comes to my mind is the feeling of drowning.

Counterpoint to that feeling is this inspiring thought: "Instead of asking to lighten the load, I ask for stronger shoulders."

I was drawn to purchase the book *Journey with Jeff* because of the cover: a photograph of a young boy sitting cross-legged, wearing a bow tie, vest, and best Sunday clothes, and sporting a radiant smile. I was hooked by this beautiful child with the distinctive facial features of Down syndrome. The book's subtitle, *Inspiration for Caregivers of People with Special Needs,* persuaded me to learn more about Jeff and his life journey.

The book is a love story of a devoted mother and her firstborn, a son, and his precious 27 years of life. I came away from reading the book marveling at Jeff's mom, Sybil Reisch, the book's author.

As Sybil recounts in *Journey,* by far the most difficult and challenging episodes in Jeff's life were the scores of frightening seizures he suffered over many years. As parents, they felt helpless and blindsided whenever these occurred.

According to a medical dictionary, a seizure occurs after an episode of abnormal electrical activity in the brain. The term *seizure* often refers to a convulsion during which an individual convulses or shakes as muscles involuntarily and repeatedly contract. If seizures continue after treatment, the condition is called epilepsy. Seizures lasting up to 20 minutes deprive the brain of oxygen and can cause significant brain damage.

We are fortunate that Maggie never, to the best of our knowledge, has had a seizure. The various doctors who saw her through the years always inquired whether we noted any seizure activity, because many special needs children do experience this problem. Seizures can be so mild as to involve nothing more than staring spells.

In her intensely personal account, Sybil opens up about how blindsided she was when Jeff once again and without warning seized and fell down during a church service. Mom writes, "I was so sick of those seizures that I burst into tears."

The seizures seemed unending. In one instance, Jeff fell and shattered some glass in their home, cutting himself badly. Mom honestly admits this was the final straw.

"I was still feeling stretched, totally helpless, and unsettled. Jeff should not have to live through these mean-spirited seizures! I was so frustrated I contemplated piling Jeff and me into the car and ending these devastating attacks by crashing into the bridge support down the road from our house."

Sybil Reisch felt so overwhelmed she seriously contemplated ending the lives of her son and herself. But she summoned the strength to persevere and reached out to a counselor friend with whom she felt comfortable sharing her grief.

"You've come so far, you can't stop now," he counseled.

Writer Erma Bombeck (1927-1996) the popular syndicated columnist, was the same general age as my Aunt Cassie. Described as an American original who used humor to address the human condition, Bombeck often spoke to what it is to be a mother. Two examples from her column *At Wit's End* give a flavor of her basic philosophy. "If you can laugh at it, you can live with it," and this gem, "A child needs your love most when he deserves it least."

Two of Bombeck's hundreds of columns speak particularly eloquently to motherhood and special moms. In *When God Created Mothers,* an angel is having to work "overtime" to create the almost impossible, a creature to be known as a mother. Commiserating, the Lord says to the angel, "Have you read the specs on this order?"

The multitude of design characteristics this mother must have include: "a kiss that can cure anything, and six pairs of hands."

The angel cannot believe the requirement for six pairs of hands. "It's not the hands that are causing me problems, God remarked, it's the three pairs of eyes that mothers have to have."

Later the angel remarks that the model for mothers is too soft. "But tough!" says God excitedly. "You can imagine what this mother can do or endure."

When God Created Mothers was appropriately first published and often reprinted on Mother's Day to honor and celebrate mothers.

The Special Mother column hits particularly close to home, asking: "Have you ever wondered how mothers of disabled children were chosen?" Once again, Bombeck has God up above working in conjunction with angels as they select which mothers to pair with which newborn.

Smiling, God instructs the angel, "Give her a handicapped child." The angel is curious about the choice of this particular mother-to-be, so God explains. "You see, the child I'm going to give her has her own world. She has to make her live in her world and that's not going to be easy," adding further justification:

"Yes, here is a woman whom I will bless with a child less than perfect. She doesn't realize it yet, but she is to be envied. She will never consider a step ordinary. When her child says Momma for the first time, she will be present at a miracle, and will know it!"

Cathy introduced me to Sherry Boas, an adoptive mother of four children, including a daughter born with Down syndrome, Teresa. Sherry authored a series of novels in which the protagonist, Lily, is a grown woman with Down syndrome who unpredictably heals and transforms the lives of others whom she encounters.

Inspiration for these highly acclaimed novels is Teresa, now 14 years old. While tucking Teresa into bed one evening, Sherry imagined herself as an elderly woman and wondered what the world would be like had this precious child not come into her life. The whole point of each book, she says, "is to look at what is the value of one life and what one life can mean to everyone else in the world, even a life that is judged by the world as less perfect or less important."

Wishing to learn more, I came across a 2014 blog post by Boas on *CatholicMom.com*. A devout Catholic, this Phoenix area special needs parent offers hope and gratitude that brings to mind Kingsley's *Welcome to Holland*.

Sherry Boas's touching blog piece, titled "Life's Surprises as a Special Needs Parent," notes the understandably natural tendency of parents of special needs children to focus on all the heart-wrenching things that won't happen. When she looks at her daughter with Down syndrome, the author readily admits what won't happen, but goes further turning it around to show the amazing things that *will* happen for those of us who love a special kid. Although apparent that Teresa will never grow up to be an accountant, brain surgeon, or engineer, because she can't add or count and lacks the intellectual capacity to be a professional, Boas wants us to focus instead on the positive: what Teresa *can* do.

She observes, "Yes, she can't count, but you will never be able to begin to count the number of hugs she will give you at just the moments you need them."

Again, "While she will never contribute to the healing of anyone's brain, she can help heal your heart with that sweet smile of hers."

Saying that Teresa will never be an engineer, her mom adds, "but she can sure build bridges," observing how her young daughter has the innate ability to bring people together and foster healing. This is the underlying hope-filled theme of the Lily series.

CHAPTER 14

IT'S A WONDERFUL LIFE

"The reason angels can fly is because they take themselves lightly."
G.K.Chesterton

N ancy and Larry Maloney were newlyweds living in Milwaukee, excited to welcome their firstborn into the world, a daughter they named Shawn. The young doctor who delivered the child noted some physical abnormalities and stated ominously that something was wrong. He admitted to being over his head, not having delivered a baby who was, at that time, commonly referred to as Mongoloid. The year was 1967, and the recommendation to these anguished parents was to institutionalize their infant. Instead, they brought baby Shawn home.

Almost three years later, a red-haired son arrived whom they named Tim. The medical consensus was even more dire for Tim. Like his big sister, Shawn, he was born with what would become known as Down syndrome. According to the doctors, Tim's condition was much more severe than Shawn's. He faced an extremely bleak future.

Nancy recalls crying to her sister about what all this meant and what they should do. But once the nurses brought Tim to her and she held her child in a maternal embrace, absolutely no doubt remained about bringing this struggling baby home, too, and loving him just as they loved Shawn.

It is estimated that a child with Down syndrome accounts for one in every eight hundred to a thousand births. This congenital condition results from a defect that occurs because of an extra chromosome. Individuals with Down syndrome are small in stature, display distinguishing physical features, and exhibit varying forms of mental retardation.

Larry Maloney said they do not personally know of other families who have more than one child with Down syndrome. However, thousands of families have adopted Down syndrome children, many times multiples.

Newspaper columnist and Fox news commentator George Will and his first wife faced the same painful dilemma in 1972 when their eldest child, Jonathan, was born. As Will publicly shared in his *Washington Post* column, the doctor's first question was whether they intended to take their child home. Similar to the Maloneys, the Wills responded that Jon was their child and taking him home is what they thought parents did with newborns.

In the late 1960s and early seventies, the life expectancy of individuals with Down syndrome was about 20 years. Increases in longevity can be attributed to the early intervention, nurturing, stimulation, and care these children receive from loving families in their own homes.

The lesson here is that an environment of constancy and higher expectations is largely responsible for the children who were labeled at birth with low expectations now growing into middle-aged adults who are leading full, happy, and productive lives. Losers in life's lottery, these adults are nonetheless winners in the game of life.

Fast forward to today for the unpromising starts at birth of this trio of offspring. Jon Will takes the Washington D.C. subway system independently to his job as a clubhouse attendant for the Washington Nationals major league baseball team. This is a dream job for the baseball-loving Jon. It doesn't hurt that his Pulitzer prize-winning dad owns a minority stake in the ball club.

George Will, in his 2012 *Washington Post* column celebrating Jon's 40th birthday, discussed the reaction by the Nationals' players to his son: "Major leaguers, all of whom understand what it is to be gifted, have been uniformly welcoming to Jon, who is not."

The Maloney siblings Shawn and Tim have likewise not let Down syndrome define them, each one leading a remarkable life. Larry and Nancy are extraordinary parents, although they would say with genuine humility that they have done nothing special. They feel truly blessed with their children and couldn't fathom life without them. Nancy notes that although she will never have grandchildren, "Life is good."

Shawn and Tim live happily with their parents at their comfortable suburban Milwaukee home, with no near-term plans from any of this quartet to live anywhere else. The "kids' rooms" are filled with scores of medals and ribbons from participating over the past 40 years in Special Olympics. It is safe to say the Maloneys' social and family lives have been totally consumed with Special Olympics and its extraordinary power.

Both of the Maloney offspring are valued long-time employees at McDonalds, serving as fry cooks during the four-hour lunch shift. Due to some natural sibling rivalries, they work at different yet close locations of this fast-food giant, which Maggie—her ear often picking up new and interesting sounds—refers to as Mickey Ds. Mom and Dad dutifully transport these uniformed job-holders to their respective Golden Arches.

In addition to each other, Shawn and Tim have many friends from among their circle of Special Olympics teammates. Shawn is quick to point out her relationship with her boyfriend, John, which has lasted 25 years. John, three years Shawn's senior, is also a Special Olympian and veteran McDonald's employee at yet a third location. John is a true gentleman, a decent man, and one of my favorite people. He is also Tim's close friend and regular roommate at the State summer games. One year, at the conclusion of the Fourth of July parade, I heard a fellow refer to John as "his guy." I quipped that I thought *I* was "his guy." John informed me, correctly, "I have a lot of guys."

Tim also has someone special in his life, his long-time girl-friend Deb who is 15 years Tim's senior. In the beauty of this remarkable community age differences are not a big deal. This winsome foursome enjoys attending dances. John has some great dance moves reminiscent of John Travolta in the movie *Saturday Night Fever*. Having been an observer at many Special Olympics dances, I enjoy watching all these nice people exhibiting much freedom, movement, and smiles on the dance floor.

The doctors who'd been so negative at Tim's birth would be shocked to learn that he has developed into an accomplished leader and productive employee, who excels at multiple sports in Special Olympics. Tim being Tim is not only a decades-long McDonald's employee, but was recognized as the 2011 Employee of the Year for his valuable and meritorious service. His award came with a check for $500, so Tim splurged it on renting a limo and treating his good friends to a night on the town. As a gifted athlete, he has competed and excelled in track, basketball, bowling, and golf, with countless medals to attest to his competence and skill.

President Obama early in his first term appeared on the *Tonight Show* with Jay Leno and was asked if he had tried out the bowling alley in the White House. Apparently trying to be funny, and making fun of his own bowling ineptitude and pedestrian 125 average, the President said he bowled "like a Special Olympian." Obviously he is politically astute and did not mean to ridicule Special Olympians, but this ill-advised quip landed President Obama in hot water.

As to be expected, the White House Public Relations staff went into crisis mode. The embarrassed President put in a call while aboard Air Force One to Special Olympics Chairman Timothy Shriver, son of the founder of Special Olympics, the late Eunice Kennedy Shriver. The President's sincere and heartfelt apology was accepted by Shriver, who appeared the next day on *Good*

Morning America to address the controversy, saying: "I think it's important to see that words hurt and words do matter. And these words, that in some respect can be seen as humiliating or a put-down to people with special needs, do cause pain and do result in stereotypes."

The Milwaukee media searched for a local Special Olympics bowler to get a reaction to the President's faux pas. Up popped one Tim Maloney, a then 38-year-old who maintained a 165 bowling average any politician would envy. Tim was asked how he felt about the President's remark and was pressed as to whether he was angry. Hoping to elicit a controversy, the reporter was clearly disappointed when Tim said he was not angry and the comments didn't bother him at all. The interview was picked up by the *Fox News* affiliate in Dallas. An online post shows a smiling Tim with a bowling ball in hand and the alley behind him. He did have some solid advice for the President to bring his average score closer to this Special Olympian's 165: "He [the President] needs to practice more."

Tim, a veteran of 30 years of rolling the lanes, offered the following tips: "Focus, take his time, relax, and keep your eyes on the alley."

Of all his multiple sports interests, Tim says he enjoys bowling the most. "I stay around my dad and my friends and loved ones." Tim has now moved up to the number two bowler on a team with his dad and friends. Tim rolled a high game of 264 and a series of 615. The President wouldn't stand a chance. Bowling is a family affair for the Maloneys; Dad Larry sports a 190 average, Mom Nancy a not-too-shoddy 160, and sister Shawn a respectable 125.

Shawn is a true sweetheart. For evidence, there is the Special Olympics basketball game in which the contest got a little heated over some disputed foul calls by the officials. During a timeout, Shawn, all 4 feet 10 inches of her, approached the targeted referee. Sensing he could use a hug, she proceeded to give him one. This act of kindness and ultimate sportsmanship was well-received by all who saw it, calmed the tense situation, and, as expected, brought a big smile from the referee. Had someone captured this poignant scene on video, it would have been a viral hit.

As you may know, medical evidence exists that hugging is good for our health. It has been shown to lower blood pressure and reduce stress. For its healing properties some folks refer to it as the hug drug. Lately, I have taken a cue from Shawn. Now, whenever I raise my voice or get into a row with Maggie, I ask for a hug—and get it. No doubt it is effective therapy for both of us. In fact, hugging works equally well in my role as a husband after a cross word or spat with my wife, Cathy.

As the late Love doctor, Leo Buscaglia, put it, "Everybody needs a hug. It changes your metabolism."

CHAPTER 15

OLIVIA—A PROFILE IN COURAGE

I became acquainted with Olivia in 2011 when she joined the Tosa Special Olympic track team and became one of Maggie's teammates. A 20-year-old sprinter, strong, fast, and powerful, Olivia stood out. With her innate athletic ability, personal drive, coaching and training, Olivia found early success in the 100- and 200-meter dashes. This fueled her to dream big and to reach for higher goals.

Early in the life of Special Olympics, concern was widespread that special athletes would embarrass themselves and be ridiculed. That concern couldn't be further from the truth. Anyone who has ever witnessed a Special Olympic competition knows this fear is belied by reality. To see the likes of Olivia compete is to be inspired and awestruck. Olivia runs like the wind. I love to watch her.

For the past dozen years, the McCarthy family has had the pleasure of hosting a post-season Special Olympics track party for the Tosa team in the backyard of our home. This is a fun time that brings together the entire track team and their families and coaches. Everybody brings a dish to pass, and we serve sub sandwiches and beverages. A good time is had by all. Track coaches Kay and Eileen do a splendid job of individually recognizing and highlighting the positive achievements of each athlete.

Our backyard party is where I first met Olivia's devoted parents,

Judy and Dan Quigley, who adopted their daughter at age three from an orphanage in China. Only after they brought their young child into their home and life did they learn of her intellectual disability. Olivia was diagnosed with autism and OCD: obsessive compulsive disorder. OCD is characterized by upsetting thoughts and fears (obsessions) that lead the individual to engage in repetitive behaviors (compulsions). OCD can be accompanied by eating and other anxiety disorders, or by depression. Olivia's challenge is depression, which several times led to her hospitalization.

As we are coming to learn, the human brain is much more complex than experts previously thought. Mental health specialists have a vast amount of work to do to unlock these myriad mysteries. Our Maggie's unreasonable fears and anxieties, such as separation from her mom, cause her to seek constant reassurance. When stressed, she is likely to lose control and act out inappropriately, such as by shouting repetitive obscenities. This occasional antisocial behavior holds our girl back from participating in group activities and in the community.

As for Olivia, the medical community told the Quigleys not to have high expectations for their daughter's future. Various specialists were quite sure she would never live independently or hold a regular job. These well-meaning professionals had no way to measure the drive and spirit in Olivia, and they underestimated the abundant love, nurturing, and resolve of the Quigleys.

Fast forward to today. Olivia is living on her own with a spaniel named Oliver. Numerous research studies have shown that a pet, such as Oliver the dog, can help its owner cope emotionally, reduce stress and anxiety, and even lower blood pressure, making for a happier and more well-adjusted life.

Olivia's having gone through Project SEARCH, a comprehensive workplace immersion program, helped her find a full-time position in the Nutrition and Food Services Department of Children's Hospital of Wisconsin. Her manager, Ashley Cludy, noted with pride how Olivia started as an intern at the hospital three years ago, worked her way into a full-time position, and went on to receive a promotion.

Olivia also discovered the unique power that is Special Olympics. Success proved a magical elixir and she quickly excelled. Similar to the uplifting story of the remarkable Cindy Bentley, competing and winning gave Olivia a real sense of accomplishment. As she herself observed, "My depression goes down, then it goes up. Special Olympics makes me positive. My coaches and family lift my spirit."

Olivia soon learned that along with annual regional and state events, Special Olympics holds national competitions, as well as its pinnacle, the World Games, every four years. This determined young woman is highly goal-focused. At our backyard party she told me and others within earshot of her quest to reach her dream: winning a medal on the World Games stage.

Olivia's Special Olympic coach is Kay Fronk. Some 10 years ago, Kay and her husband, Steve, found themselves empty nesters. Despite having no direct relationship to a Special Olympian, they decided to give of their hearts and volunteer their time as coaches. Kay coached track; Steve, basketball. Kay, a wonderful woman, is an accomplished recreational runner still highly competitive in her age group. Now a doting grandmother, she continues to dedicate herself to helping lift others like Olivia.

Kay is a good friend of Coach Eileen, and together these two fine women serve as head track coaches. As mentioned, Maggie has a keen sense of character in being attracted to kind and decent people like Kay and Eileen. In her unique style, Maggie has taken to referring to these two coaches as one—Kayleen.

At the 2014 Special Olympics held in Trenton, New Jersey, Olivia was excited to compete and medal nationally. Her high-level Special Olympics competition experience bolstered her self-esteem, so much so that she now rightly identifies herself as a top athlete. Building on that 2014 success, Coach Kay was proud and happy to nominate Olivia to represent Wisconsin and the United States at the World Games, scheduled for July 2015 in Los Angeles.

Olivia was absolutely thrilled to be headed to the World Games, a beautiful dream coming true. With the big event still six months away, she was devastated to learn alarming news: a diagnosis of stage four breast cancer. A highly aggressive invasive cancer, it would require months of intensive chemotherapy to combat and hopefully shrink the tumors. Follow-up surgery would be scheduled for that summer. What a punch in the gut to learn this 24-year-old athlete I had come to know, admire, and care about was facing such an insidious life-threatening disease. I felt terrible that Olivia's quest for a medal had been cruelly derailed.

You can understand my amazement when track season kicked off at the end of March and Olivia showed up. Wearing a bandana on her head to hide the effects of her chemo treatments, she was determined to compete to fulfill her dream. I approached Olivia and inquired how she was doing. She told me she felt very tired and only that morning had been sick to her stomach. She admitted to being quite scared by the mystery and uncertainty surrounding her cancer. I shared with her that I am a fortunate fourth-stage cancer survivor, reminding her that Coach Kay had also beaten back this ugly disease. Olivia lowered her voice and said she hoped she too would survive. With a lump in my throat, I replied I hoped and prayed the same thing.

Her mom told me that Olivia had passionately informed all her doctors, "You cannot interfere with the World Games. I have a chance to medal and you cannot interfere with that. I'm not missing this opportunity."

"The doctors wanted to do my surgery in July," Olivia added. "I said NO, I'm not doing it. Because I'm gonna go to the World Games with cancer or not. Nothing is stopping me from going."

Speaking of her star athlete, Coach Kay came to realize it "would have killed her" to miss the 2015 World Games.

The regional Special Olympics qualifying track event was

held the first Saturday in May. I was with Maggie and the other race walkers in a different area, but heard that Olivia had tripped and fallen hard that morning while running the 200-meter dash. According to Coach Kay, Olivia was a "bloody mess," with cuts and scrapes on her knees and legs. Medics had to attend to this injured athlete.

But Olivia enthusiastically embraced the concept of a team and what it is to be a teammate. Despite being banged up, bloody, and suffering from the ill-effects of cancer treatment, Olivia was determined not to let her team down. She resolutely went on to anchor the 4 by 100 relay event that afternoon that qualified for State.

In addition, as a Wisconsin representative to the World Games, Olivia was showcased at the State Summer Games held the next month. She would share the stage at the opening ceremony with Vince Vitrano, a board member of Special Olympics Wisconsin and a popular anchor and media personality on Milwaukee television.

A native of our hometown of Wauwatosa, Vitrano was often seen interacting with our athletes prior to the Fourth of July Wauwatosa parade. His wife's Uncle Roger was a Special Olympian. A long-time Special Olympics supporter, Vince's commitment has grown even more over the years. As he says, and I know it to be true, "The athletes and their families are so welcoming, so thankful, and so inspiring that I found myself wanting to be around them."

The Thursday night opening ceremony of the Summer Games is memorable. Over the loudspeaker, 1,000 uniformed athletes from every part of Wisconsin are introduced by team as they parade into the stadium. Upon entering the field, the athletes are met by dozens of law enforcement officers from around the state, who have come expressly to show support for the disabled Special Olympian heroes. It is quite a spectacle as the athletes go through a lineup of officers flanking both sides. They are given enthusiastic high-fives and hearty encouragement. Family and friends in the stands cheer their favorites.

The local fire department stages quite a production of hoisting a giant American flag from a fire truck. The assemblage sings a spirited version of the national anthem, hats off and hands over hearts. I swell with emotion listening to Maggie sing the anthem. The Olympic flame is lit, the oath is recited, and the games are officially begun. The athletes are fully charged up and ready to go.

Through the years, we have been addressed by luminaries, including members of the beloved Green Bay Packers, media celebrities, a lieutenant governor and national Special Olympics leaders. But in my admittedly biased opinion, the 2015 opening ceremony was the most memorable of them all. That's because its master of ceremonies was Olivia Quigley, representing all the athletes, her Wauwatosa team, and the State of Wisconsin, acting in tandem with emcee Vince Vitrano from NBC television affiliate WTMJ4. Having an athlete upfront and center stage was inspiring and altogether fitting.

Earlier that day in the dorm, Olivia had shown me her script, her lines highlighted in yellow. Our young woman was a mixture of excitement and nervousness in anticipation of taking the stage and occupying the limelight. She told me she had prepared and rehearsed for hours, determined to get it right.

Although Vitrano is a consummate professional, Special Olympian Olivia Quigley stole the show. Wearing a bandana, she stated the obvious during her speech: that she could not and would not hide the fact she was dealing with cancer and as a result had no hair. She was there to tell the assembled masses she would be heading to Los Angeles in six weeks to represent them at the World Games—no matter what.

Part of the Walt Disney Company, ESPN was the official media partner of the Special Olympics World Games L.A. 2015. With 7,000 athletes from 177 countries competing in 25 sports, it is the largest sporting and humanitarian event in the world. ESPN wanted to be part of it. They provided hours of coverage and powerful and moving features on participants.

As a veteran reporter for ESPN, Marty Smith covers a wide variety of college and pro sports. His highlight feature story on Olivia Quigley was titled "Outrunning Autism… and Cancer." The day leading up to the Games he sat down on a bench and conducted a one-on-one interview with Olivia.

Smith admits to having been around many high-profile athletes in the wide world of sports. Yet to him, Olivia was a true star in that world. "She stole my heart within minutes. I was floored. Humbled. Amazed. Honored. Inspired."

Smith drew a contrast between the humble Special Olympian with the soft voice and bandana and the great variety of people he has met, observed, and reported on over the years. "But you don't see true innate grace very often. And when you see it, you know it. You feel it. You're taken by it. And Olivia has it."

She also had the usual reaction to chemo. To be effective, chemotherapy treatment pushes one's body and mind to the very limits. Olivia admits to a fear of needles, is constantly fatigued, her stomach hurts, and she gets sick. The port that delivers the chemo burns. Yet Olivia knows that without these powerful drugs she would not survive. She is a fiercely determined cancer patient with a strong will to do whatever it takes to live. "I'm gonna push through it. I just remind myself I can do it."

Olivia had actually postponed a round of chemotherapy treatments in order to travel to L.A., determined to fulfill her quest. This feel-good Hollywood story, complete with much drama, was about to be played out. Prior to the 100-meter sprint final, Olivia felt extremely fatigued and in pain. Her Team USA coach, watching her warm up, observed, "I didn't think there was any way she'd make it."

Olivia's mom, Judy, was equally nervous that running this race and fulfilling a dream wouldn't happen for her girl. "Her coaches said she was very tired."

One song speaks to Olivia's inspiring journey, the mega 1982 hit "Eye of the Tiger" by Survivor. It was a theme song of the character Rocky Balboa in the Rocky series. The song's lyrics tell of someone training to overcome hardships—"Risin' up to the challenge." Both coaches and parents noticed a distinct change in Olivia's demeanor: at the starting line, in lane 7, wearing bib number 913, with a bald head, Olivia seemed to possess the eye of the tiger.

A young woman, Olivia's taste in music is more in line with 21st century pop stars. She is a huge fan of Katy Perry, who wrote, performed the music video, and sings the song "Roar." These lines from its chorus could have been written expressly for Olivia:

> I got the eye of the tiger, a fighter
> 'Cause I am a champion
> And you're gonna hear me roar.

Here is how sportswriter Marty Smith reported the tense moments before Olivia's race of a lifetime. Referring to parents and coaches he said, "Both noticed a look in Olivia's eye, a transformation of sorts, and then, a slight grin. This was the moment for which Olivia spent years training. It was a defining moment, and she was convinced she could further impact the world; she had already impacted it just being here."

Never one to give up, a fearless Olivia seemed to roar and explode at the sound of the starter gun. She rocketed down the lane and won by a comfortable margin. Take that, cancer! Mission accomplished. The gold medal was hers.

Watching this race unfold, her mom was so nervous she didn't breathe the entire 16.80 seconds it took for her daughter to triumphantly cross the finish line. Judy admitted to being more than happily surprised by the result. She knew Olivia was fast but didn't know how her stamina could possibly hold up. A proud father, Dan Quigley, suggested that anyone who knew Olivia should not have had any doubts about the outcome. According to Dan, "The bigger the occasion, the better she does. There is no hesitation for her. She is calm. We learn from that."

Olivia had succeeded in an improbable, once-in-a-lifetime opportunity against long odds and a formidable cancer to overcome its effects and realize her dream. In doing so she personified all that was great about sports and Special Olympics. Basking in the glow of victory, Olivia seemed to realize it was about much more than her gold medal. In a post-race interview she said, "I was so tired in the beginning. I tried so hard in that race." She explained eloquently, "I wanted to dedicate this gold medal to everybody who's struggling for their lives with breast cancer and also for breast cancer survivors."

Olivia had made her mark. In a touching demonstration of support, her USA teammates were seen wearing matching American flag bandanas. She was treated as a national celebrity and profiled in *USA Today* and on ESPN. Police officers who were on hand and involved with Special Olympics were observed to be particularly moved by her courage. All were drawn to her.

As might be expected, Olivia has a strong—might I say special—bond with her mother, calling Judy "my rock star" and "the best mom in the world."

Judy Quigley's love and admiration for her daughter shines brightly, too. "We're really proud of her. Because, through all this cancer, she's continued to work. She's very proud of that. That's so much courage. She's one of the most courageous women I've ever met. I don't have the courage she does."

Olivia's improbable run and celebrity status only gets better. In December 2015 Olivia Quigley was one of 25 women athletes to be named by espnW for its inaugural IMPACT 25 honor. In February 2016, Olivia traveled to the bright lights of New York City with her parents to participate in the gala ceremony. There they were treated royally, with a red carpet, and even backstage passes to Disney's production of the *Lion King*. To top it off, our very special Special Olympic athlete was awarded with the first-ever Pegasus Award of Inspiration. This inaugural award recognized Olivia's perseverance and accomplishment in the face of a battle royal with an aggressive breast cancer.

Olivia still faces much uncertainty. A long and difficult road lies ahead of her. She must endure another year of chemotherapy, a twice-a-day course of radiation treatments and additional surgery. It would be a big mistake however, to count Olivia out. This spring she is back at track practice, raring to go for another season of Special Olympics competition.

It is a cruel fact that cancer could take Olivia's young life, but it will never defeat her indomitable spirit. She has overcome extreme odds. Olivia is a winner and a profile in courage who will fight on because she is a champion in every sense of the word.

CHAPTER 16

A SPORTS FANATIC LOOKS AT FORTY

Doug Pommerening met me at the door of the comfortable suburban home he shares with his devoted mother, Sandy. He had donned a Milwaukee Brewers t-shirt, Wisconsin Badgers socks, and a Green Bay Packers hoodie. Life for Doug revolves around his love of sports and his dear mom.

I had come to know, like, and respect Doug, or Dougie, as many of his friends refer to him. He is a stalwart member of the Wauwatosa Special Olympics soccer team. Maggie and Doug have been part of Team Tosa at the Special Olympics State summer games over the years.

Both his late father and maternal grandfather fostered in Doug a true love of sports. His father started a baseball card collection that Doug still has today. His grandfather cherished his special needs grandson, and after he retired made it a point to phone Doug every day. Whenever he could, he took the boy to see the powerhouse Nebraska football team play in Lincoln. Sadly, both his father and grandfather passed away in 1999 when Doug was 25. He greatly misses these men in his life but maintains their spirit through the passion for sports they instilled in him.

Doug has a part-time job bagging groceries at Sendik's in the quiet village of Elm Grove where he resides. Although the original grocery store was bought out eight years ago, Doug was one of only a handful of store employees asked to stay on. This young man with a winning smile had made himself so much a fixture of Sendik's through the years that if Doug had not kept his job, loyal customers might have revolted. He is now so associated with the store that it is not uncommon for people to greet him from all over the greater Milwaukee community. Fortunately, he is able to get to and from work each weekday by walking the mile to the shopping center. His mom, Sandy, has asked well-meaning neighborhood folks to not offer her disabled son a ride, because he needs the exercise that walking to work provides.

I asked Doug what he does with his earnings, which he supplements by being the "go to" guy for neighborhood snow shoveling and lawn cutting. He turned to Mom for the answer. According to Sandy, Doug must be one of Barnes & Noble's best customers. He regularly purchases sports-related books and magazines, such as *Sports Illustrated* and *ESPN*. Although Doug finished school having attained only a fourth-grade reading level, he is remarkable in his ability to devour the subject material that so fascinates him. He also has an ever-expanding collection of team sports apparel—even a man cave sports room in the basement of his home to warehouse all his "stuff." Doug not only loves reading as well as watching and attending sporting events but also is an active and dedicated participant. He is no armchair athlete.

 Like many thousands of individuals with an intellectual disability, Doug has had his life immeasurably enriched by actively participating in the power that is Special Olympics. In addition to soccer, Doug particularly enjoys bowling, along with basketball and golf.

Sandy, is an intelligent and astute mother, who is so grateful for the fabulous opportunities Special Olympics provides. She says, "Life just wouldn't be the same without this organization."

Sandy points out, this national (now international) nonprofit organization is one big, welcoming fraternity. In this respect, it is like a family connection. Despite job changes that meant relocating the family multiple times, in each new community they found

Special Olympics. This lifeline afforded Doug opportunities to compete in athletics, be part of a team, forge friendships, and find social outlets. As a parent, Sandy also found instant support networks and was befriended by other moms and dads who know what it is to love and live with a special needs child. Sandy counts this support as a major blessing.

The highlight of Doug's vaunted career as a Special Olympian was his being selected to represent his country and the State of Wisconsin as a soccer player at the 2003 World Games. Like the Olympics itself, this major event is held every four years. The 2003 games were truly special in being hosted in Dublin, Ireland, the first time the World Games were staged outside of the United States.

At the World Games, ceremonies and pageantry are done in a big way. The opening ceremony was held at Croke Park in the heart of Dublin. The spectacular was attended by 75,000, including Doug's mom and 10 members of his extended family, who'd traveled all the way to Ireland to demonstrate their love and support for their special relative. They were entertained by no less than Irish music legends U2 and superstar Bono. Sandy especially enjoyed the phenomenal Irish dancers from Riverdance, the largest troupe ever assembled to perform.

The USA team was one of the last to enter the stadium. Because the family's anticipation of spotting Doug was excruciating, one can understand Sandy's panic when her son did not immediately march in with his team. Doug had experienced some anxiety from all the excitement surrounding the opening, made a quick trip to the bathroom, and then feeling fine somehow managed to catch up with his group. When Doug finally appeared, Mom was greatly relieved and his family all excited to see their hero.

He went on to play in five soccer games and scored two goals, one with his nondominant left foot. He was understandably proud of this accomplishment, which offered memories to last a lifetime for him and his family.

What impresses me so much about Doug is his enthusiasm as a star fundraiser for Special Olympics. For the past few years he has willingly leapt into an icy Wisconsin lake in the middle of winter as part of "Freezin for a Reason." Popularly referred to as the Polar Plunge, this bizarre activity is a winter fundraiser to support Special Olympics. Doug has no reluctance in asking for sponsorships, so much so that his mother cringes at his boldness. For example, when he phones me he asks for a pledge in his distinctive high-pitched voice without even bothering to identify himself, whereas Sandy laughs that Doug frequently calls her and actually identifies himself as Doug. Because I fit the "too chicken to plunge" category, I am only too happy to monetarily support Doug in this worthy cause.

Doug's partner plunger is Jim Haas, his devoted and long-time veteran soccer coach. He is a dedicated volunteer and a prime example of what makes Special Olympics tick. Jim enjoys "getting into character." A full-sized grandfather, he takes his polar plunge wearing a pink tutu. Photos testify that this image is not a pretty sight, but the team does whatever it takes to raise money for its beloved Special Olympics. The dynamic duo of "Dougie and the tutu guy" have raised thousands over the years to make possible the activities of Special Olympics. This colorful duo has been recognized with a plaque for their outstanding fundraising efforts.

Coach Jim has taken a liking to our Maggie. On one memorable bus ride back from the State summer games, Maggie kept busy with her sketchbook and pencils. Noticing this, Jim asked Maggie if she would draw a picture of him. She immediately took to the task and produced a humorous head likeness that we all enjoyed. Jim told Maggie he would put it in a place of honor on his refrigerator. I understand it is still there today.

Rumor has it that Coach Jim is also Santa Claus, making his appearance at the annual Special Olympics Christmas party. A true believer in Santa, the big guy in the red suit called Maggie by name to come forward and be his helper. He asked our excited daughter to ring the bell while he led the festive group of partygoers in a spirited rendition of the holiday classic, "Rudolph the Red Nosed Reindeer." Our Maggie can be seen on video next to Santa beaming while she vigorously rings the bell. It doesn't get much better than having Santa himself pay attention to you. Coach Santa brings the spirit of everyday giving to Special Olympics.

Our man Doug is set to soon turn the "Big 40." Like all athletes, age has caught up with him. No longer as fast a runner as he was in his prime, he was moved to a less competitive soccer team. And he is now 40 pounds above his playing weight at age 29 in the World Games. Fortunately, Special Olympics offers plenty of athletic opportunities for aging and less able athletes, including bowling, bocce ball, golf, and race walking. There also are wheelchair events.

I played a memorable round of golf with my buddy Dougie at a charitable golf outing for the benefit of Life Navigators. Our foursome started with Tim and his dad, Larry Maloney, and I was excited to be teeing it up with my friends the Maloney men. When Dougie somehow caught wind of this golf event, he called me and basically invited himself to fill out our group. As it turned out, he was a pleasure to play with, a true gentleman and a fair golfer, to boot. Nobody had a better time on the course than did Doug. His spirit was infectious. I am glad to have included Tim and Doug, and look forward to bringing back this fearsome foursome in future years.

Sandy, a widowed single mom, still in good health, is a grandmother in her seventies and must plan for the future for herself and her disabled son. Her other son, Brad, Doug's older brother, lives 80 miles away in Madison, Wisconsin, with his wife and two extremely active young boys. Doug is fortunate to have his big brother in his life. Although one never knows what the future holds, Sandy has given serious thought to someday relocating herself and Doug to Madison. She could sell her house and downsize to a no-maintenance condo. Most important is that the move would put them closer to Brad and family.

As I write this, Doug phones and leaves a voice message eager to know when *our* book will be available so he can go to Barnes & Noble in the mall and purchase a copy.

This reminds me of a day some years ago when our three children were young and I had recently published a book on personal finance. Often taking the three kids out of the house for a couple of hours on weekends to give Mom a needed break, one particular Sunday afternoon in inclement weather we were kicking around at the mall. I ventured into the bookstore with children in tow, as I like to peruse the shelves. Walking through the aisles, young Jack, then four or five, discovered a single copy of my finance book on a bottom shelf.

Excited, he said "Look, Dad, your book!"

At this, Maggie piped up, "Let's buy it!"

I will admit I thought about it until 10-year-old Martha, the voice of reason, said: "Why would we buy it? We have a whole garage full of books at home." Indeed we did.

CHAPTER 17

PROTECTING TOMORROW FOR YOUR LOVED ONES

A critical rite of passage in preparing your special child for transition to adulthood is the guardianship process. A guardian is a person who guards, protects, or takes care of another person. Think of the concept as that of a "guardian angel." The state has an interest in protecting citizens and minors who cannot protect themselves, including the cognitively disabled, the elderly, and those who have been determined incompetent. The individual or individuals who become guardians of others are placed legally in control of them and their affairs. When Maggie reached age 18, Cathy and I had to go through a formal guardianship process to be legally named her caretakers.

The teacher and administrators in her high school special needs program insisted we take this step with Maggie. Incredibly, the procedure required an administrative judge—a total stranger—to grant us the authority to care for our firstborn child.

The administrative hearing was held in our home. The court-appointed attorney interviewing Maggie asked if she was okay with her mom and dad making decisions for her. She quickly responded in a confident voice, "Oh, no! I don't want that."

Surprised, the attorney probed further. Was she able to take the bus and go on her own to the shopping mall. "Yeah, sure I could."

Cathy and I were listening from the adjoining room and found their conversation amusing. Our Maggie sounded so convincing, yet we knew she was playing this guy. Not until he asked her address and she offered her phone number was her capacity brought to light.

Next, we appeared in front of a judge at the Milwaukee County Courthouse. I was not thrilled with his demeanor or the surrounding atmosphere. After all, this was my baby girl we were talking about. In retrospect, this attitude was probably on my side as a man and a father.

We worked with a total of three attorneys on the guardianship petition at a not insignificant cost. I wonder what other families do that lack the legal contacts and financial resources to establish a guardianship.

A too-often overlooked estate planning matter is the need to provide care for minor children—those under the age of 18—by naming guardians in a will. As a financial planner, I have always been confounded by parents who purchase insurance on their own lives to protect the family but do not draw up a will naming guardians for their minor children.

The seriousness of this lack of planning is exemplified by a tragic accident I know of in which young parents were killed by a drunk driver who crossed the median and hit their car head-on. Miraculously, the couple's two young children—a two-year-old boy and a baby girl barely two months old—were buckled up in the back seat and survived this deadly crash with only minor injuries. The tragedy for these orphaned children continued for some time after the accident with a nasty fight over legal guardianship. Motivation for the suit may be partly attributable to the funds made available from life insurance and accident settlement proceeds. Had the parents drawn up a will to name a guardian for their minor children, this legal anguish could have been minimized.

Take any kind of poll of the parents of special needs adult children, and their number one concern, by far, is what the future holds for their loved one. This is especially chilling once they and their spouse are unable to care for their disabled child.

Jessie's father, Brian Lanser, is a highly intelligent attorney trained to be prepared and to deal with contingencies. His greatest fear, as he expressed it to me, is what will happen to his vulnerable 32-year-old dependent daughter after he and his wife, Sue, are no longer alive to care for her—or alive but incapable of doing so. "Our family is great and will make sure that Jess is well taken care of when we are gone. However, it is still a worry."

Brian's own father died of a heart attack. Because of that loss, this disciplined 60-year-old father, husband, and grandfather has adhered to an exercise regimen for the last four years to maximize his good health. He does yoga and a mix of cardio and weight training, mainly treadmill or elliptical, and core work with a personal trainer. Brian admits to the difficulty of meeting his weekly goals because of work and family obligations. Nonetheless, he has lost considerable weight and is in great shape. He explains that his reasons for taking care of himself and his health are: "Not only so that I can be here longer for Jess, but also so that I am physically able to do the work of caring for her while I am still here."

Life is all about planning for uncertainty and dealing with change. In our own estate planning documents, Cathy and I have named Maggie's younger siblings, Martha and Jack, as successor guardians for her in the event she outlives us. We are fortunate in that our other two children truly love their older sister, and are willing, competent, and capable of serving as Maggie's guardians if and when needed.

Having dependent adult children with special needs means planning for the time when because of your own age, infirmity, or death you are no longer able to be the parental primary caregiver. Deb, the older girlfriend of Special Olympics bowling champion Tim Maloney, is now a senior citizen herself. Sixty-two can no longer be thought of as middle age when no individuals of twice this age are walking about. Deb's mom and caregiver, Shirley, is a robust 89. Shirley's stated wish is that she outlive Deb by one day.

From my many discussions with friends and acquaintances in researching this book, I appreciate that most parents echo Shirley's hope of outliving their special needs children. Nancy Maloney, who still refers to Tim and Shawn, now middle-aged, as "the kids," exhibits an understandable tendency that runs counter to the thinking of conventional parents. My maternal grandmother, who lived to be 100, told me she felt it was not the natural order of life that she had outlived her daughter, my mom Peggy, who lost out to cancer at age 63.

For Nancy and Larry, a major concern at their stage of life is if they cannot care for Tim and Shawn, they have no other children to do so. The Maloney family is a tight-knit foursome. It will be particularly traumatic for the survivors when the first of them passes on. Because Nancy would never wish to separate Tim and Shawn from each other, the Maloneys planned wisely and named successor guardians for their disabled middle-aged children. Plans even reflect a thought for the "kids" to stay in the comfort and familiarity of their own house with some outside care.

Like a lot of men, as well as fathers of special needs children, I assume Cathy will in all probability outlive me and be there to care for our Maggie. Of course, there is no certainty about any of these assumptions. My father and my uncles outlived their spouses. But Cathy is six years younger than I am, healthy, and takes excellent care of herself. Genes are also on Cathy's side. Her widowed 89-year-old mother is still living independently.

Another Wauwatosa Special Olympian I know, Mark, was born an only child with Down syndrome. He became an orphan in 2013 at age 54 when his widowed mother, Marjorie, died at age 89. I got to know Mark through his participation in swimming and bowling and by his being good friends with many of the team's athletes.

His mother, a wonderful woman, was a nurse. She and her late husband, Don, a Lutheran pastor, provided Mark with a lifetime of love, care, and support. Marjorie was active in many volunteer capacities with Special Olympics, receiving a well-deserved 40-year service award for her efforts.

To plan ahead for Mark's future, Marjorie met with Life Navigators, a social service agency serving the disabled. As a loving and protective mom, she sought the peace of mind that comes from knowing that this respected agency would be there for her son when she was gone. And it was.

Today, Life Navigators, originally ARC, the Association of Retarded Citizens, is Mark's guardian. This agency has been licensed by the State of Wisconsin since 1977 as a corporate guardian for persons with disabilities. Their social workers and caring staff assist Mark by coordinating his medical, residential, recreational, and other needs, and by making important life decisions for him. Their goal is to help Mark live as his mother fervently wished, Happy—Healthy—Safe, the three securities in that organization's tag line.

After Marjorie's death, Life Navigators put into place her son's transition. Mark was moved to a new, more suitable, and proximate residence and reconnected with his support network—his church, bowling team, and friends. These days he is seen out and about, smiling at community events and sporting a haircut from his favorite barber. To culminate his successful life change, Mark celebrated—with the help of Life Navigators—his 55th birthday surrounded by 30 friends, including Tim and Shawn Maloney.

A recent summer also marked the 40th birthday for Maggie's track teammate and a personal Special Olympics favorite, Brad Westfall. Maggie knows his name but insists on calling him Brad Pitt—probably because she fancies pairing those distinctive one-syllable sounds. A nice picture of Maggie and Brad shows them standing arm-in-arm at his milestone birthday celebration. Though Brad doesn't talk much, he is always ready with a smile, genuinely happy to see us. His party was held at Leff's Lucky Town, a popular local watering hole where Brad has worked for almost

20 years, ever since he finished high school. I contend that Brad actually runs the place. He does a good job of stocking the coolers and cleaning up around the busy bar and restaurant. He landed this perfect position for him through a family connection with the owner. He either walks or rides his bike the short distance to work.

Brad is the youngest in a family of five, close to both his brother, Robert, and sister, Julie. His parents, Bob and Polly, are terrific people. Now in their seventies and having dealt with some health issues, they must confront the future for Brad. Fortunately, his sister is ready, able, and more than willing to have her dear brother live with her when the time arrives.

As it so happened, Bob passed away suddenly this very year. The grieving family asked if I would share this loss with the Wauwatosa Special Olympics community, and I obliged. At the church funeral service for Bob, Brad sat in the front row pew with his dear mother. I witnessed him tenderly put his arm on her shoulder to comfort her.

Weeks later, I came across a smiling Brad, beer in hand, with mom Polly and sister Julie at halftime of a Marquette College basketball game. It was good to visit and observe this trio holding up so well. The Westfall family is going to be all right.

All of these families have found solutions appropriate for their special needs children. What I find significant is that each planned ahead for the time when they could no longer be protector, caregiver, and advocate. The key for the well-being of the special needs child is to be proactive in ensuring there is always a guardian angel in the loved one's future.

CHAPTER 18

THE KENNEDY FAMILY SAGA AND SPECIAL OLYMPICS

As father to Maggie as well as an Irish-American long-fascinated with the famous Kennedy clan, I am particularly interested in three family members: Joseph P. Kennedy Sr., the controversial father and patriarch, his eldest daughter, Rosemary, sometimes referred to as the forgotten Kennedy, and one of her younger sisters, Eunice Kennedy Shriver, founder of Special Olympics.

While visiting the JFK Presidential Library and Museum in Boston, I was drawn to a wall-sized picture of the entire 11-member Kennedy family. Taken in London in 1938 before the outbreak of war when Joe Sr. was made U.S. Ambassador to England, the photo shows an attractive and smiling group. A buoyant-looking father and mother sit in the middle of their brood of nine children, who are lined up by age. I was particularly interested in their eldest daughter, Rosemary. At 20, she was a fashionable young woman who clearly took after her mother and namesake, Rose. Father to these nine, Joseph P. Kennedy, spoke ruefully late in life about having eight bright, shining lights and one dull bulb, his reference to their third child, Rosemary.

Unlike older brothers Joe Jr. and Jack, both of whom attended prestigious boarding schools and followed in their father's footsteps to Harvard, young Rosemary struggled mightily in school, despite special academic help and constant attention spearheaded and funded by her bewildered father. It was perplexing to the family why this child was slow—or, in the cruel vernacular of that time, "dim-witted." Only later would the family refer to her as being mentally retarded. Rosemary grew into a beautiful, vivacious young woman, but fell farther and farther behind her gifted, ambitious siblings. As she entered her late teen years, Rosemary regressed mentally and exhibited alarming mood swings, anger, and acting out. Her father expressed real concerns about her erratic behavior and for her safety.

As a take-charge father, Joe always assumed the parental lead, consulting with the best doctors and coordinating medical care for all his children. This was especially the case for son Jack, future U.S. President, who suffered bouts of grave illness throughout his life. Joe's search for answers to help Rosemary led him eventually to prominent physicians, who offered the miracle cure of a promising new neurosurgical procedure.

In 1941 at the age of 23, Rosemary—apparently without her mother's knowledge or consent—underwent an invasive lobotomy surgery that cut into the frontal lobes of her brain. This radical surgery went terribly wrong, leaving Rosemary severely disabled, permanently incapacitated, and requiring of round-the-clock custodial care for the rest of her long life. Rosemary was sent by her father a thousand miles west of home to rural Jefferson, Wisconsin, where she resided in virtual seclusion for the remainder of her life. She was well-cared for by Catholic nuns of the Sisters of St. Francis of Assisi at the convent of St. Coletta.

It is tempting to fault her father for allowing what is now seen as barbaric experimentation to be performed on his challenged daughter. In his defense, lobotomies—though always controversial—were then widely considered mainstream. The introduction of antipsychotic drugs soon came to the fore as a more viable and humane treatment alternative.

With our own Maggie, because many of her challenges revolve

around her mental state, the mood-altering drugs she takes are prescribed by a psychiatrist. This treatment does make her life and ours easier. My late cousin Brian also acted out, showing serious anger management issues as he matured and came to realize how life was different for him than for his siblings.

Many tragedies confronted the Kennedy family. Among the most well documented are the combat death in WWII of son Joe Jr., the loss of daughter Kit in an airplane crash, and the assassinations of our sitting President John F. Kennedy as well as presidential candidate Robert F. Kennedy. Rosemary's botched lobotomy can be viewed as the first of these major family tragedies.

From this sad tale, Joe Sr. and, more notably, his daughter Eunice helped fuel a movement that brought heightened awareness and acceptance of individuals living with intellectual disabilities. It culminated in the founding of the worldwide phenomenon of Special Olympics.

Joe Sr. fulfilled the role of provider extremely well. He built a tremendous fortune that placed him among the wealthiest of all Americans. There is no doubt he dearly loved his children and perhaps none more so than his first daughter, Rosemary. Yet, even with all his money, influence, and power, he could not find a way to "fix" his daughter. He didn't know how to confront the challenge of her differences. Today, compared to the 1940s, it is likely he would have taken a more enlightened approach to accepting and openly caring for his mentally retarded and mentally ill child, whereas in that era 65 years ago, keeping someone like Rosemary hidden away was common practice. As it was, Joe Sr. was shattered by having to live with his decision to allow what turned out to be a horrific procedure. For the rest of his life, although he regularly checked up on her and provided financially for her care, he never visited his firstborn daughter.

Joe Kennedy was a very generous philanthropist, especially to Catholic charities. He bestowed millions through the Joseph P. Kennedy Jr. Foundation, named in memory of his first child, to take up the cause of the mentally retarded as his family's special mission. He recognized how great was the need and wanted the foundation to take the initiative of holding a National Conference on Mental Retardation. Wisely he steered the energy of his driven daughter Eunice by naming her to head the Foundation.

Once JFK became president in 1960, the federal government became a major force for action on the issue of mental retardation. As President Kennedy would say in promoting the greater acceptance and heightened visibility for this cause: "We must provide for the retarded the same opportunity for full social development that is the birthright of every American child."

Eunice Kennedy went on to marry Sargent Shriver and have five children. She possessed a steely determination and a strong sense of mission. It is fair to say that no single individual is more responsible for championing the great cause of intellectually disabled children and adults than Eunice Kennedy Shriver. In 1962 she started Camp Shriver at their Maryland home and brought together 35 disabled individuals for the experience. As head of the Kennedy Foundation, Eunice was instrumental in also providing grants for similar camps across the country. These camps were the seeds of what grew to become the colossus that is today Special Olympics.

Eunice is widely considered the founder of Special Olympics, and rightly so. Additionally, a 24-year-old physical education teacher working with disabled children in the Chicago Park District deserves honorable mention for actually kick-starting the movement. Anne McGlone Burke received a Kennedy Foundation grant in the summer of 1968 that brought 1,500 disabled athletes to compete where the Chicago Bears play football, at Soldier Field on the shores of Lake Michigan.

Anne McGlone Burke is a remarkable woman and long-time advocate for the disabled community. She discovered after struggling in school that she was herself dyslexic and operating with a learning disability. Yet this teacher, later the mother of an autistic son and adoptive mother of a cocaine baby, went on to become a respected attorney. Currently, she serves as an Illinois Supreme Court justice. Anne is proud, rightly, of her role as a catalyst in birthing Special Olympics.

In reading *Fully Alive*, the 2014 memoir by Timothy Shriver, Eunice's son, this very special athletic event was initially to be called the National Olympics for the Retarded. According to Tim, Eunice was responsible, thankfully, for changing that designation to its present name Special Olympics. But there is an interesting side note to this story.

Avery Brundage, a prominent Chicagoan, was the powerful president, some critics would say emperor, of the International Olympic Committee (IOC). Reportedly, he took umbrage at this nascent disability organization using the word "Olympics." Just weeks before its kickoff, with all its materials printed and public relations in place identifying the event as Special Olympics, Anne McGlone received an ominous letter from Brundage. In it he threatened all sorts of legal action unless they removed the word "Olympics" from the name. A heartbroken McGlone realized this action would derail, or at least seriously delay, the long-planned event. Fortunately, she and Special Olympics had a powerful ally in their corner who was not intimidated by Brundage's bullying or the IOC. Richard J. Daley, mayor of Chicago, came to the rescue. Daley would employ the "Chicago way" of getting worthwhile things done.

As related in *Fully Alive*, Daley phoned Brundage in McGlone's presence. Confirming that Brundage was indeed serious about following through with his threat for the use of the word *Olympics*, the mayor counterpunched. The historic downtown Chicago LaSalle hotel where the Special Olympics athletes were scheduled to stay was coincidentally owned by Brundage. Playing hardball, Daley implied the LaSalle had fire code violations. He told Brundage, "I'm afraid you know what that means."

Having made his point, Daley hung up the phone, smiled at

the young woman in his office, and assured her, "You go along. You'll have no more problems from Brundage. I'll tell Eunice. The Olympics people think 'Special Olympics' is a fine name."

Growing up in Chicago, I was a proud member of a Daley Democrat family. Mayor Daley stopped by the wakes for each of my grandfathers in 1970 to pay his respects. I am happy, though not surprised, to hear how Daley saved the day for the first of many Special Olympics.

Presidential candidate Robert F. Kennedy, JFK's younger brother, had been assassinated on June 5, a mere six weeks before the Chicago Special Olympics. Undeterred, the Kennedy family and Eunice went forward, albeit with a heavy heart. U.S. Olympic hero and gold medal decathlete Rafer Johnson, an ardent supporter of RFK, was with him at the political event when he was gunned down in a Los Angeles hotel. In fact, it was Rafer Johnson who helped subdue and wrestle the gun away from the assassin Sirhan Sirhan.

Rafer was understandably shaken by this tragic killing, following as it did the senseless shooting earlier the same year of Martin Luther King. He reportedly went into a deep despair, holing up in his California home. He did take a phone call from the sister of his murdered friend. Eunice asked him to please come to Chicago. According to Rafer, "I had no expectations. I had only just enough energy to say 'yes' and show up." The event greatly helped in his healing process, and Rafer Johnson, Olympic legend, became inspired to play a major role in Special Olympics.

The earth shook in Chicago the summer of 1968, and the world would never be the same for those with intellectual disabilities. From this signal event, history was made. Special Olympics was born. As Special Olympics Chairman Timothy Shriver recounts in his book, "On July 20, 1968, for the first time in history, people with intellectual disabilities were celebrated as great individuals by others who discovered their gifts in the joy of sports."

Rafer Johnson, reflecting on that July day, said, "Everywhere you turned, you saw an experience no one had ever seen before. No one had seen these people. No one had ever seen their exhilaration. It was so simple, but it was amazing."

Eunice was said to be particularly close to her older sister Rosemary. Clearly, this special relationship played a major part in her fierce and effective advocacy. In 1969, while her husband was ambassador to France, she led the international expansion of Special Olympics that resulted in robust growth in the 1970s and eighties.

In 1984 President Ronald Reagan presented the Presidential Medal of Freedom to Eunice Shriver for her tireless work on behalf of those with intellectual disabilities. She is the first woman whose portrait appears on a U.S. coin—a commemorative Special Olympics silver dollar issued in 1995 with the powerful inscription: "As we hope for the best in them, hope is reborn in us."

I had the distinct pleasure of meeting Sister Margaret Ann Recker and discussing with this gentle woman the 30 years she dutifully lived with and cared for Rosemary Kennedy at St. Coletta. Nearing 90 years of age and living at the St. Francis convent in Milwaukee, this good woman is now in need of care herself. At our meeting she was accompanied by Kim Bell, a wonderful nurse and caregiver, who wheeled Sister Margaret Ann, a colorful shawl resting on her lap, into a room for us to talk. With me was my friend Father Larry Sepich, a retired priest from the Archdiocese of Milwaukee who had gotten to know Sister Margaret Ann over the years through his convent ministry. He was aware of this good and simple woman's caring devotion to Rosemary Kennedy. As a means of introduction, I told Sister that my daughter's name is also Margaret. I shared with her a picture on my phone of Maggie. Sister remarked on Maggie's prominent smile dimples. Irish folklore has it that dimples are formed when the angels kiss you.

Although she lives in the memory unit at the care facility for the retired sisters, Sister Margaret Ann was engaged and seemed to enjoy reminiscing about Rosemary, Eunice, and the Kennedy family—a constant smile on her face. Sister admitted she had initially turned down the position of caring for Rosemary when offered by her superior, feeling she was unworthy. But as she described her life's work as a joyful caregiver, her face lit up.

In *Fully Alive,* Tim Shriver poignantly recounts that after the death of his aunt, Sister Margaret Ann confided to him how she grew to love Rosemary. Sister felt loved in return, and this affection changed her life. Meeting and talking with Sister, I knew this love story to be true.

According to Sister Margaret Ann, all the Kennedy family was very good to her, although she developed a very close relationship with Eunice. Eunice called often to inquire about Rosemary, and to also ask about Sister Margaret Ann. She made regular visits and celebrated special occasions, such as birthdays, with them both. Sister Margaret Ann cannot say enough good things about Eunice, adding simply, "She was the best."

Despite her failing memory, Sister was able to quickly name all of Eunice and Sargent Shriver's five children. As for son, Timothy, the current Chair of Special Olympics, she referred to him as a great guy, always interested in her work and her calling, and appreciative of the care his aunt Rosemary received. Sister also fondly recalled Maria Shriver, a dynamo like her mother and a dedicated Special Olympics volunteer and Board member.

I was not familiar with Anthony Shriver until Sister mentioned him. I came to learn he is the Chair of Best Buddies and founded it in 1989 while in college. This growing international nonprofit has as its mission to foster one-to-one relationships and friendships between people with and without intellectual disabilities.

Our Maggie recently enrolled in Best Buddies and is excited to be a part of it. Cathy is the one, once again, who took the initiative for our daughter. Years earlier, we did have some involvement with this volunteer movement, but we found it disorganized and largely ineffective. But this time around, we were gratified to see trained staff coordinating and creating good fits and matches between clients and volunteers.

Maggie's best buddy Liza is no doubt another angel coming on the scene. We could not be happier with this warm, personable, and patient young woman and her budding relationship with Maggie. It came as no surprise to learn that Liza's mother was that special breed, a special education teacher. Liza, age 25, is from Appleton, Wisconsin, now working in a corporate position in downtown Milwaukee. Maggie and Liza (Liza with a Z) are headed to a Best Buddies-sponsored bowling and pizza party in a week. After that these new friends will see a movie.

Rosemary Kennedy died of natural causes at age 86 in January 2005 at a hospital in Fort Atkinson, Wisconsin, close to St. Coletta. At her bedside were her four living Kennedy siblings, sisters Eunice, Jean, Patricia, and brother Ted. Sister Margaret Ann was there also, keeping vigil. Rosemary is buried in Brookline, Massachusetts, where she was born, alongside her mother and father.

A strong case can be made that Rosemary's life did have meaning in that she helped spur a movement that made life better for millions of disabled individuals worldwide. "Her role was so powerful," writes Tim Shriver, "she deserves our gratitude." Credit should be given, he says, to his aunt Rosemary as "the true inspiration for his family's love of service."

Eunice Kennedy Shriver died in 2009 at age 88. At her eulogy, her surviving brother, now the late Senator Ted Kennedy, described Eunice as "a living center of power" who "set out to change the world and did." He went on to say how his sister founded the movement that became Special Olympics, "the largest movement for acceptance and inclusion for people with intellectual disabilities in the history of the world. Her work transformed the lives of hundreds of millions of people across the globe, and they in turn are her living legacy."

Eunice's legacy lives on, reminding us of the power of one to change the world for the better.

CHAPTER 19

MONICA "DUFF"—IN A HAPPY PLACE

I find many parallels between the lives of the late Rosemary Kennedy and Monica Duffey. Both women were part of large, energetic, Irish Catholic families of nine children. Rosemary was the third child: Monica, the fourth. In both cases, oxygen deprivation at birth delivery caused brain damage and the resulting developmental disability.

Monica is a longtime resident—referred to as a client—at St. Coletta in Jefferson, Wisconsin; where Rosemary quietly lived out her life for 59 years. I have seen the Kennedy cottage on the grounds of St. Coletta where Rosemary resided and was cared for by Sister Margaret Ann and another sister.

St. Coletta began as a school for girls. Early in the 1900s the school began accepting developmentally disabled students. In 1931, The St. Coletta Institute for Backward Youth was renamed St. Coletta School for Exceptional Children. This progressive name change was due in part to one resident's observation that "We don't walk backward." That comment sounds like a wise observation our own Maggie might have made.

I came to know about Monica by forging a friendship with her brother and oldest sibling, Joseph Patrick Duffey. Interestingly, his given name of Joseph P. is the same as that of Rosemary's father and eldest sibling Joseph P. Kennedy Jr. As I got to know Joe Duffey better, I also learned more about Monica. My Cathy was a high school friend of Joe's brother Tom and also knew of his special sister, Monica.

Joe is an attorney. Each of us served in lay leadership positions at our parish church in Wauwatosa. From this connection, I discovered Joe had served on the St. Coletta board of directors and was a past chairman. Over several breakfast meetings with him, I learned more about Monica, St. Coletta, and what it was like growing up in the Duffey family with a special child and sister.

Monica was born in 1959, smack in the middle position of this large family. The nine Duffey children arrived over a span of just 14 years. Her loving parents, Joanne, a speech therapist, and Tom, also an attorney, attempted valiantly to accommodate her special needs, seeking out any venues to help her. They enrolled Monica at Milwaukee County Curative Care Network, which provides therapy services for children with developmental delays. With this help, she learned to walk by age four. Our Maggie also benefitted from the Curative Birth-To-Three program for early intervention. Monica then attended a special education school in Milwaukee associated with St. Coletta. The younger Duffey children rapidly surpassed their middle sister in ability. Because she was unable to keep pace, after careful consideration and much anguish, mom and dad decided it was best for their 13-year-old daughter to move 35 miles from home to St. Coletta. Her father shared with me how truly difficult was this decision.

Predictably, as it turned out, this major move lacked neither heartache nor anxious moments over the decades. Tom recalled how, in 1972, residents were housed on the top floors of an old facility, with poor lighting, narrow hallways, and creaky wooden stairs. He still thanks God there was never a fire. Once, without notice, Monica was about to be relocated to a home in a remote community. Tom hustled back from a trip out-of-state to look after his daughter during the move. All in all, despite the occasional blips, the experience of Monica living at St. Coletta over the past 40-plus years was positive.

I had the pleasure of meeting with members of the Duffey

family, including Monica, on a recent Sunday afternoon. On her biweekly visits home she has her own bedroom. She also makes it home to celebrate her birthday and for a week at Christmas. Monica especially enjoys the Christmas holiday and all that surrounds it.

Monica is very particular about her routines. Her sisters Maureen and Ann described for me, smiling, how they take their sister shopping to Target and Walmart, as she loves to walk the aisles and examine the merchandise. One can easily see, feel, and sense the shared love of the tight-knit Duffey family.

From my discussion with the family I learned that life with Monica has had both triumphs and travails. Now 55, gray-haired and bespectacled, she has experienced some health issues. Her siblings shared that Monica can be sly, will seek special favors, and with St. Coletta's three separate dining rooms, has been known to double dip at meal times. The family admits to spoiling their sister with special treats, but now pay more attention to her diet because she has put on weight.

Joe told me his special sister has developed an encyclopedic knowledge of music, old TV sitcoms, and commercials popular in the 1960s, seventies, and eighties. Amazingly, she can recall lyrics, jingles, and characters from that period, and CDs of music from that era fill her bedroom at the group home. On the wall hangs a small framed saying: "Angels protect me here." I am reminded of this observation from Scottish philosopher and historian Thomas Carlyle: "Music is well said to be the speech of angels."

Music also fills an important role in Maggie's life. Some time ago Jack and Martha put together a playlist of some 200 favorite songs on her iPod shuffle, and music plays softly as background in her room 24/7. It seems to comfort her.

Once at an airport while traveling with her dad, Monica used the women's restroom so Tom quickly ducked into the men's room. He then stood patiently outside the bathroom waiting for Monica. When she didn't appear he asked a woman to see if his daughter was still inside. To his alarm, she was gone. After some frantic minutes he heard over the loudspeaker that a confused and apparently lost young woman was in the baggage area. Greatly relieved, he hurried downstairs to retrieve his special daughter.

As father to Maggie, I can readily relate to Tom, including bathroom logistics and adventures when away from home. I have learned to look for family bathrooms in areas such as airports and malls. One time when Maggie was with me at the Milwaukee Public Museum for a Halloween party, I was distracted for a few moments, and when I turned around she was nowhere in sight. Panicked, I talked to the security people, who made sure she didn't somehow get outside. After about 10 harrowing minutes, I discovered Maggie. She had entered a darkened room and taken a seat for the showing of a movie.

Another time, our entire family headed to the lakefront with friends to catch the Fourth of July fireworks. It was getting dark and hundreds of spectators were milling about. Suddenly we realized Maggie, then just ten years old, was gone. Cathy and I and our friends conducted an anxious search for our girl. I had a lump in my throat and my heart was racing. Knowing Maggie loves playgrounds and swing sets, we searched and found her on the swings in the adjoining park.

Around the same time, I took Maggie to a circus parade held downtown on a summer weekend. We parked in a structure adjoining the office building where I was employed at the time, took the elevator down to the lobby, and got off. That is, I got off. When the doors closed behind me with Maggie still inside, I panicked. Thinking she could well be trapped in the elevator, I became terrified that I wouldn't be able to get to her and she might end up on any of the building's 25 floors. Thankfully, after what seemed like minutes but was probably seconds, the elevator doors opened again, my Maggie safe inside. I put my arms tightly around her, and my heart restarted. Since then, I always hold her hand around elevators, even though as Maggie has aged, she no longer moves as fast as she used to, runs away, or is inclined to go off on her own.

I learned from the Duffey family that Monica loves the water and swimming. She regularly uses St. Coletta's pool. When the Duffey family escaped the Wisconsin winters in Florida, Monica relished making a splash in the pool while there. Her sisters told me Monica is a champion diver and would retrieve pennies from the bottom of the pool to show off her talent. Determined, she regularly accomplished this feat, causing her family members to marvel over how long she would stay submerged, and at the same time feel mild concern about it.

Her brother and her father credit their mom, Joanne, for making sure Monica was central to this large and talented family. Joanne taught her children to involve this special sister in family activities. In this she was like another devoted mother, Rose Kennedy, who counseled her other children to include Rosemary. There is the story of Rose persuading her son Jack to take his younger sister with him to a school dance. According to the future president, Rosemary had fun and "was just like all the rest."

Because Monica was "different," at times she acted up and embarrassed her brothers and sisters in interactions outside the Duffey household. Joe tells how his sister still confounds strangers, especially young people, by her demanding an answer to her query, "Who are you?"

Joanne had successfully raised her children and taught them important life lessons before she passed away from leukemia in 2009. At her moving funeral service, son Joe eulogized his mother's devotion and caring for all her brood and her special attention to Monica, for whom she was a strong advocate. Joe also shared with the mourners his mother's instructions to all the children when they were growing up that when people stared or seemed disturbed by Monica's behavior, to remember: "It is their problem, not your problem."

Tom said losing their mother hit Monica extremely hard. The

Duffey family decided to not include Monica in the funeral service, reasoning it would be too emotional for her. Instead, after the
burial, the family members went to Jefferson to console Monica.
When they arrived her immediate question was, "Where is Mom?"

To this day, Monica frequently holds in her hands certain family photos that she stores in her bedside drawer. She handles these
so often, the family needs to replace these cherished images on a
regular basis. I shudder to think how our Maggie would cope with
the loss of her mother, Cathy.

In yet another interesting Duffey connection to the Kennedy
family saga, when Monica's father, Tom, attended Rosemary's
funeral service at St. Coletta, Senator Ted Kennedy led the singing. Tom, a retired labor attorney, remains very sharp at age 88. He
told me he was a friend of Dan Shannon, who is mentioned in Tim
Shriver's book, *Fully Alive*. Shannon was a Chicago Park District
official and powerful union leader who supported initiatives that
evolved into Special Olympics. This large, strong, gruff former
Notre Dame All-American football player was moved almost to
tears by watching an eye-opening production put on by intellectually disabled children. The power to foster change could be felt in
Dan Shannon's words of commitment to help the fledgling movement. "I'll do anything you ever want. Anything for these people.
Just ask me."

In Jefferson, Wisconsin, Monica resides contentedly and se-
curely in one of St. Coletta's controlled group homes. The modest
yet comfortable home is located on a quiet cul-de-sac. Monica's
weekdays are spent at Excel Center, St. Coletta's own daycare facility located close by on the main campus. There, she participates
in activities that include cooking, a variety of classes, and even
some contracted work. Three important areas of her care at St.
Coletta's are coordinated and supervised: housing, transportation,
and day programming.

One factor that always interests me is the happiness of special
needs individuals. Joe Duffey satisfies my curiosity by telling me

about the drive back to Jefferson after Monica's regular visits to her father's house. Having enjoyed her time with the family, she has been known to wear out her welcome by the end of a visit. During the 45-minute commute, she is usually reserved and quiet, lovingly holding the hand of her brother while in the car, and listening to popular oldies on the radio. As they approach her St. Coletta home, Joe sees a complete change come over her. "Duff," as she is affectionately called by her housemates, is welcomed back with open arms and warm hugs. There is no doubt this is Monica's home and where she is most happy.

CHAPTER 20

MARIBETH: BLESSED WITH MISERICORDIA

Maribeth has lived the last forty years of her life at Misericordia in Chicago. She is the sibling of my good friends, the brothers Jim and David Omastiak. I am very familiar with Misericordia, a nonprofit residential facility serving over 600 children and adults with intellectual disabilities, many with physical disabilities as well. I grew up in this neighborhood on the far north side of Chicago, and my youngest sister, Sheila, was employed there, and my friend and client, the late Carol Barrett, volunteered many hours there.

Before becoming the site of Misericordia in 1976, this forty-acre parcel was the home of Angel Guardian Orphanage (AGO). The Catholic Archdiocese of Chicago repurposed this property and donated it to Misericordia. In my formative years in the later half of the 1960s, I frequently played basketball at AGO in their spacious new gymnasium, swam in their indoor pool, and played football and baseball on their grass fields. As a kid, I foolishly thought the disadvantaged residents of AGO "had it made" living with these sports facilities.

Misericordia is Latin for "heart of mercy." This community of care has been a godsend for Maribeth and for the large and loving Omastiak family. Maribeth is the youngest of eight children, all of whom grew up on the south side of Chicago, the daughter of a hardworking father, Jim Sr., and an extremely busy stay-at-home mother, Marge. David describes his father as the perfect provider, one who toiled at two jobs his entire life to take care of his large family of three sons and five daughters—but, he obviously had a special connection with his youngest. He was known for spending quality time with Maribeth and taking her for long walks in the neighborhood. Marge, like countless other mothers, was the heroic and consummate caregiver devoted to her youngest child and determined to make life better for her.

Maribeth is now 50 years of age. Her oldest brother, Jim, my good friend from college, is frankly amazed that his special needs "baby" sister has survived this long, owing to countless seizures, hospitalizations, falls, and massive doses of medicine. She wears a white bicycle helmet to protect her head from seizure-related falls. Credit for her longevity is due to the love of her family and the quality of care she receives at Misericordia. By reaching middle age, Maribeth has outlived both her parents. Her sister Susan and brother Mike reside nearby in Chicago and serve as her legal guardians. Maribeth remains a close part of the Omastiak family.

When Maribeth was a child, the medical establishment advocated the use of patterning for treating children with brain damage. Patterning required Maribeth to be placed on a table, with up to five family members or neighbors holding her arms and legs while her head was manipulated according to a series of movements meant to stimulate brain development, and this was done four times every day over a couple of years. Patterning has long been discredited as ineffective, outmoded, and unwarranted, which is why most people today have never heard of it. At the time, these exercises were strongly encouraged to improve neurological impairment of affected children. In fact, dire health consequences were implied and adequacy of parents questioned if they did not make arrangements to have their child undergo patterning.

The Omastiak family was more than willing to go down any road to help their disabled daughter and youngest child. But it is not difficult to understand these many hours of exercises for Maribeth remained an indelible part of her seven siblings' childhood memories. They couldn't help but be affected by their disabled sister.

Maribeth never attended traditional school. Instead, she was an early resident at Misericordia, entering that facility at the age of 11. The Omastiaks struggled mightily with the heart-wrenching decision to move their child out of their home, as did the Duffey family with Monica.

My friend Jim believes his special needs sister is happy, in her unique way. Music manages to lift her spirits. From an early age she had a boom box and could push the buttons and listen to the Beatles or Neil Diamond. I asked several members of the family what it is that makes Maribeth particularly happy, and in chorus they responded the Beatles song "Help." At family get-togethers, her sisters, who—like their mom—possess excellent voices, hold Maribeth around the waist to keep her from falling, then parade her from room to room, singing a spirited version of her signature theme song:

> Help!
> Help! I need somebody,
> Help! Not just anybody,
> Help! You know I need someone,
> Help!

Maribeth cannot sing, but somehow is able to call out "Help."

Her days at Misericordia are full, with therapy sessions and art and music classes. A highlight occurred last year when Maribeth was named Prom Queen for the annual Misericordia resident ball.

Another resident of the Chicago Misericordia community is Lauren Axelrod, the daughter of David Axelrod, the close personal friend of President Obama who served as his campaign strategist and White House political adviser. David and Susan's firstborn, Lauren, now 34, suffers from a disability associated with epileptic seizures. The seizures started for the child at age seven months. According to her father, "We didn't realize this would define her whole life, that she would have thousands of these afterward and that they would eat away at her brain."

Supporting their love for their daughter, the Axelrods have used their high profile to increase awareness and fund research to help the three million Americans suffering with what they describe as "terrorism of the brain." To combat this scourge they initiated Citizens United for Research in Epilepsy, known by the hopeful acronym CURE.

According to Lauren's mom Susan, by the year 2000, "I thought we were about to lose her." The seizures became unrelenting and seemed unstoppable. Her doctors had no solutions, and worse, did not hold out much, if any, hope. The Axelrods were at the end of their rope. Then, through CURE, Susan learned of a new anti-convulsive drug. "The first day we started on the medication, her seizures subsided. It has been almost nine years, and she hasn't had a seizure since. This drug won't work for everyone, but it has been a magic bullet for Lauren. She is blooming." Parents never want to give up hope.

David Axelrod was not spinning a tale in offering an observation about his wife, Susan: "As a parent of a child with a chronic illness and special needs, I know there's no force on earth as powerful as a mother's love." I too know this firsthand. The force of love is equally true of countless mothers of special needs children.

I cannot talk about Misericordia without mentioning its dynamic and irrepressible leader, Sister Rosemary Connelly. As a young religious, she dreamed of finding a loving environment for her nephew who was cognitively disabled. David Omastiak refers to her as a modern-day saint. This religious nun, a member of the Sisters of Mercy, has built, nurtured, pleaded, prayed, and guided this caring institution, Misericordia, over the past 45 years. Sister Rosemary was named 2014 Chicagoan of the Year, a well-deserved recognition for her leadership in caregiving as well as in the phenomenal growth and success of Misericordia. In accepting this award, Sister refers to her calling and her mission as "a wonderful journey." She adds, "It has been one of the greatest gifts of my life."

As Sister shares the mission of Misericordia and refers to residents such as Maribeth and Lauren, she says: "We believe, we accept, we love each person and we are better people because they have touched our lives."

The Misericordia residential campus model goes against the national trend. The prevailing notion, as Sister Rosemary describes it, is that "big is bad and all persons with disabilities, no matter how disabled they are, should be living in houses in neighborhoods, preferably with four or less people."

Today's emphasis is definitely on these smaller group homes. Sister is on record strongly disagreeing with this rigid "right way, the only way" attitude by bureaucrats and government officials. Personally, I believe a campus or some type of larger residential setting would be a better fit for our Maggie. I wholeheartedly agree with Sister's contention that "Families know their most vulnerable member better than anyone else," therefore families deserve choice.

Reflecting on the life of Maribeth, I am struck by this quote from Sister Rosemary Connelly speaking for the residents in Misericordia's care. "Each one is unique, a gift to us today, a loving and loved person made by God with a purpose in life—no matter how wrapped in mystery that purpose is."

CHAPTER 21

NAUGHTY KATHY— MAKING THE PUZZLE PIECES FIT

My good friend Dennis Russell has four sisters, one of whom lives strong despite being born with a developmental disability. I had the pleasure of meeting Kathy Russell on a number of occasions. Her love for her siblings and extended family is apparent, as is their abundant love for her. Dennis describes her great spirit and how Kathy always sees the best in others. He describes her alternately as a jewel, a gift, a blessing. Dennis's daughter Shannon remarks how her beloved Aunt Kathy has shaped the Russell family in a good way.

Now 64 years young, Kathy lives independently and comfortably in a 35-unit apartment complex in the small town of Montgomery, Minnesota, some 45 miles south of Minneapolis. One of her sisters lives less than a mile away with her husband. They keep an eye on Kathy and are there for her. Small town life has been great for Kathy. She can walk anywhere she needs to go, and everyone knows her. She has made herself a special part of the fabric of Montgomery.

Kathy is extremely close to her younger sister Jane (Janie), who lives in Milwaukee, less than five hours away. Janie is 11 months younger than Kathy—what we refer to as Irish twins. Being so close in age, Kathy and Janie, the two youngest in the Russell family, have had their lives inextricably linked in positive ways for both. Perhaps the best testament to that link is Janie's having chosen a career as a special education teacher.

Life is good for Kathy. She is very happy, loves her family, adores her many nieces and nephews, and now is a grand-aunt. Dennis says, "She is healthy as a horse." What amazes us all is that Kathy is not on any medications. Like the Russell family, Cathy and I feel fortunate that our Maggie is also physically healthy, with a sound heart and lungs.

The Russell siblings were told by their parents that their special sister had contracted a virus while in the womb. This produced a very high fever at birth, resulting in Kathy's brain damage. Like many accounts from that era half a century ago, the Russells were advised by medical personnel it would be best to institutionalize her. In Wisconsin that meant to place their infant in the Colonies. Recall that Cindy Bentley was sent to Southern Colony in Union Grove, Wisconsin. The doctors foresaw a very poor quality of life for tiny Kathy. Maureen, speaking of her parents' decision, "Thank goodness they did not."

Dennis credits his late parents for how well Kathy has done in life. He recognizes that parenting had to be challenging for them. But seeing how happy and content their special child turned out, they succeeded wonderfully. Not only did his parents raise Dennis and his four sisters, including Kathy with her special needs, they also tragically lost another son, Michael. He died suddenly at the tender age of five from the horror that is spinal meningitis. With all their painful experiences, the Russell family courageously persevered.

Growing up, young Kathy apparently was a handful. She was described as mischievous, into everything, devilish. Although she is no longer hyperactive and grew into a well-adjusted, delightful adult, she does possess a quirky personality streak that has stayed with her. So much so, in fact, her niece Shannon playfully refers to her favorite aunt as being "naughty."

Somehow Kathy acquired a credit card, and without the family's knowledge proceeded to load up on all the Winnie the Pooh stuffed animals she could find at the Disney store. Another time she was clever enough to use the ATM for cash withdrawals, with negative consequences, before the rest of the family knew what was taking place. She also booked a photoshoot at Glamour Studios, explaining that everyone else had graduation photos except her. Janie suggests all this was Kathy gamely trying to keep pace with her brother and sisters.

Back in the 1950s and sixties, there wasn't much in the way of opportunities, special education, or social agencies for the Kathys of the world. Nonetheless, Mom and Dad sought out every venue they could find to help their special needs daughter aspire to be all that she could be. At 18, Kathy was an early pioneer in the August 1970 second International Special Olympics Summer Games held in Chicago. Along with Mom and Dad, she and her three sisters trooped the 100 miles from Milwaukee to Soldier Field to root for their Olympic athlete. Kathy competed bravely in two track events, a 50-yard dash and a relay. She came home with a gold medal.

Maureen recalls, "It was so exciting. It was her time to shine." Kathy was very proud of that medal. However, soon after she relocated to Minnesota a fire in her building caused the loss of this medal along with other cherished personal items.

When Kathy was young, her mom took her to Easter Seals where she received speech and physical therapy. Maureen and Janie remember practicing therapies with her every day as part of their collective "homework." According to Janie, Kathy attended special education classes in the Wauwatosa public school system until age 19. One of the reasons the family remained in the community of Wauwatosa was because of its excellent programming for special needs.

It is common for parents of special needs children to seek out the best educational opportunities they can find. This might involve moving into a better school district. Sometimes, this involves moving across county or even state lines. Kathy was mainstreamed in junior high. She couldn't read the textbooks, but would come home and tell the family what she learned in her classes from lectures and movies. At the appropriate age, she moved on to high school and attended the very same Wauwatosa school as our own Maggie did. While in high school, Kathy attended classes held in a house on the high school property, learning living skills such as shopping, cleaning, and cooking, along with the academics of reading, money skills, and math. Janie, as a special needs educator herself, feels the education her sister received was exemplary and instrumental to her ability to live independently.

Mom always insisted that Kathy's siblings include their special sister. Dennis acknowledges how this could have been awkward at times, such as when his sister Janie was required to take Kathy with her to local school dances. But instead of scarring Janie, Dennis suggests that this sibling duty actually went a long way to making her the confident, accomplished adult and dedicated teacher she grew to be.

Kathy always worked, holding a variety of jobs. After graduating from high school, she became a client of Goodwill Industries, which assisted her in finding jobs and receiving on-the-job training. She did quite well working at area restaurants bussing tables and washing dishes. Heinemann's, a once popular Milwaukee family restaurant, loved her and employed her for many years. Currently, she is employed four hours a week helping to clean at a local drug store. She loves it there and feels an important part of the store. Kathy finds dignity in work that keeps her busy and involved in the community.

Kathy, like Maggie, possesses the simple goodness of a young child. Kathy is partial to Winnie the Pooh, whereas Maggie is fond of her American Girl dolls. Kathy also loves M&Ms and has been known to hide a stash away. Our Maggie prefers peanut M&Ms.

What really stands out in my mind about Kathy is her ability with jigsaw puzzles. She must have done a thousand over the years, and gives them away as gifts. As a Christmas present, Kathy gave one of her completed special puzzles to our Maggie. She put it on a board, wrapped it in plastic, and signed and dated her work. It is really a touching gift, as well as quite a work of art, its 600 pieces depicting adorable, frolicking puppies. Maggie thinks it is cute, and she plans to give one of her own works of art to Kathy for her next birthday, along with M&Ms for her sweet tooth.

According to Shannon, her Aunt Kathy is proficient at assembling puzzles and likes the challenge of assembling those consisting of 1,000 pieces. Shannon and her siblings made the error once of purchasing used puzzles from thrift stores because they were inexpensive—something they will never do again. The used puzzles were missing pieces, which proved upsetting to the puzzle master.

For her large, extended family, Kathy is the puzzle piece that completes the Russell family mosaic. A gift that keeps on giving, she is an angel who has enriched their lives and taught them all that love is what is really important.

CHAPTER 22

THE GIFT THEY WERE GIVEN

"Angels have no philosophy but love."
Terri Guillemets

Maggie turned 30 the month before her sister's wedding day, so Martha wrote and distributed *Thirty Reasons Why My Sister Maggie is the Best Ever* to mark and celebrate her major life milestone. To illustrate how deeply Martha loves her older sister, here are a select ten of the 30 reasons that explain their special sister relationship:

1. She audibly says things that everyone else is thinking but wouldn't dare say. Like yelling, "Excuse me, where's my salad?" at a restaurant.

   This reminds me of one Christmas with the whole family staying in downtown Chicago. We all piled into a taxi for the short ride to Navy Pier. The cab driver was barreling down the city street at a dangerous rate of speed. At this, Maggie yelled at him from the back seat, "Hey, slow down." He did. Thanks Mag.

2. She cherishes her American Girl doll collection, but isn't too uptight about it. When her doll Samantha (Sammie) lost a plastic leg, Maggie nonchalantly explained, "Oh, you know, she lost it."

3. In middle school my "Spanish class name" was Margarita. She thought that was ridiculous. It should obviously be

"Martharita." So that is what she referred to me as for about a year.

4. She asks babies and dogs the same question, "Can you talk?"
5. Sometimes she pants like a dog for no apparent reason. Except that she knows I will burst out laughing.
6. Speaking of Disney, there's no happier place on earth for people like Maggie. Although she's afraid of many of the rides because of balance issues, the $100/day admission price to sit on a park bench, munch popcorn, and watch the characters float by is somehow all worth it when you see how happy it makes her.
7. If she heard me recite any of this aloud, she'd say, "Stop imitating me." She takes pride in her one-liners and doesn't like a copycat.
8. She calls me her "Fashion Consultant," which is her sneaky way of saying, "Get over here and help me pick out what to wear, now!"
9. She'll casually drop "It's true" at the end of completely false statements. She does it with such conviction you wouldn't dare correct her.
10. If you ask her where her grandpas are, she'll say, "Heaven. Up in the clouds. Just sleeping on beds in the clouds. They took a giant escalator to get there." I believe this to be true. If anyone knows how to get to heaven, it's my sister Maggie.

At the age of 21, Jordan Spieth took the world of golf by storm, winning the prestigious 2015 Masters in record-breaking fashion. Polite, poised, and mature beyond his years, the significance of his back story revolves around his 14-year-old sister Ellie. Spieth hails as his key inspiration his sister Ellie, who has a neurological disorder linked to severe autism. It is clear her special needs journey has served as a touchstone for her now famous older brother's life. According to Spieth, "Being Ellie's brother humbles me every day of my life."

When Spieth became immortalized in the sport of golf by winning the coveted green jacket as Masters champion, he had this to say: "How has she shaped my upbringing? Well, she's the most special part of my family. She's the funniest part of our family."

Our own Martha would concur, believing Maggie is the most special part of the McCarthy family and—with her distinctive brand of humor—the funniest.

Ellie has made the Spieth family stay grounded and recognize the right priorities. Before the pressure-packed final Sunday round that won his championship, Jordan received this reminder from his father: "The Masters might be the greatest game in sports, but it is still a game." His mother, Chris, tellingly pointed out that her oldest son "wouldn't be at the Masters if he didn't grow up with Ellie."

Speaking as the mother of both a special needs child and a celebrated pro golfer, Chris also observed, "Jordan realizes this isn't real life at the Masters. Trying to sit around and have dinner when his sister doesn't want to eat when everybody else is eating and has a fit, that's real life."

Other touching examples exist of the natural bond between top athletes and disabled siblings. There is a heartwarming story from the Sochi Winter Olympic Games about Canadian freestyle skiing gold medal winner Alex Bilodeau and his brother, Frederic. Like Jordan Spieth, Alex Bilodeau might never have stepped on to the top step of the podium without the example of his brother and biggest supporter, who lives large despite cerebral palsy. Bilodeau stood on the dais and immediately paid tribute to Frederic, saying, "He's my everyday inspiration."

Another example is Chicagoan Mary Anne Ehlert and her sister Marcia. I first met Ehlert at a financial planning conference. I was intrigued by her *Protected Tomorrows^R* practice, centered on planning for special needs families. Interested in learning more, I purchased her 2009 book, *The Gift I Was Given*. Subsequently, I engaged her to give a presentation to our firm's clients and guests on the topic of Planning for Families with Special Needs.

Ehlert dedicates her book to Marcia, to whom she credits her own mission in life of serving the disabled. She says, "Marcia was my teacher and my life's inspiration." Born with cerebral palsy, Marcia was one of six children and said to possess a one-of-a-kind laugh. Sadly, she passed away at age 39.

Ehlert was devastated by her younger sister's death. Looking back, she came to realize Marcia was truly a gift to her, hence the title of her book, *The Gift I Was Given*. Musing about who she would have become without her special sister, Ehlert said: "She changed my life forever. The experience and wisdom Marcia was able to impart to me at a relatively young age prepared me for life."

I marvel at the maturity of young Jordan Spieth and seek a reason for the genuine goodness and humbleness of my friends Jim and David Omastiak, Joe Duffey, and Dennis Russell. Each of my friends is successful in life, appreciative of what he has, and is a good father, husband, and family man. I have come to believe what they all have in common is being blessed with the gift of a special sibling making a positive impact on their lives. Like Ehlert with Marcia, and Spieth with Ellie, each of my friends was gifted with siblings Maribeth Omastiak, Monica Duffey, and Kathy Russell. I hope and pray that siblings Martha and Jack are truly blessed to have Maggie as their sister. I honestly believe they are.

Returning to the world of golf, one of my favorite professional golfers is the major champion Ernie Els. He is known as "The Big Easy" for his fluid golf swing. Els is also becoming known for his efforts to combat autism. In 2008 Els announced the autism diagnosis of his son to the public, especially to the world of golf, by placing the "Autism Speaks" logo on his golf bag. Autism Speaks is a research and advocacy group founded in 2005 by Bob Wright, then Vice Chairman of General Electric, and his wife, Suzanne, after their grandson Christian was diagnosed with autism. In 2009 the Ernie Els Autism Foundation was established to raise awareness of and fund research for addressing the growing incidence of this disabling condition.

Els young son Ben is profoundly impacted by autism. Following the boy's diagnosis, Els and his wife, Liezl, decided to use their high-profile status and financial resources to help their son and the hundreds of thousands of others hit hard by autism. Speaking from the heart, Els said this of his son: "He's a very friendly, very happy, very shy kid. The more loving attention he gets and the smiles that he sees, the better."

As Ben reached school age, the Els family relocated to Jupiter, Florida, for more effective treatment and education for their special needs son at the Renaissance Learning Center, a nonprofit charter school. They simultaneously launched the Els Center for Excellence, whose stated goal is to break par and find answers and solutions to help those people on the autism spectrum reach their full potential. The Els Center aims to be a hub of education and a top resource for information. Its goal is to offer best practices on a global scale.

Autism remains a medical mystery, but—as Ernie recognizes—it is becoming alarmingly more common. A known fact is that an autism diagnosis is much more common for boys than for girls. The reason for this gender disparity is still puzzling, although when girls are affected, such as Ellie Spieth, the disability tends to be more severe.

Evan Eichler, a geneticist and researcher at the University of Washington, believes about 500 genes are connected to autism, and these genes fit about a dozen different pathways. His research is focused on identifying effective treatments and therapies for these different subtypes. According to Eichler, "It's going to be really important to know which pathway your child is in. I would put money on it that not all drugs and not all behavioral treatments will work the same, depending on the basis for how that child developed autism."

Researchers such as Eichler are valiantly seeking to unlock the mystery of the acceleration in autism diagnoses. There are no definitive explanations, but a combination of improved diagnoses and environmental factors seems to be involved. The consensus view is that autism is likely to be caused by a number of different developmental brain disorders. It is thought to have a genetic predisposition, coupled with environmental triggers. What is not in doubt is the tremendous cost autism extracts for behavioral intervention, special education, and adult residential placements.

The son of celebrity Jenny McCarthy (no relation), Evan, was diagnosed with autism in 2005. In the decade since, she has been loud and vocal in her belief that childhood vaccines for measles, mumps, and whooping cough have somehow led to autism for her son—and others—and have thereby contributed to the spike in diagnoses. I find it important to say that Jenny McCarthy's controversial anti-vaccine stance has been widely discredited. The public health establishment warns that avoiding vaccinations in children is unwise and dangerous.

In a 2015 *Medscape* article about celebrities who speak out about illness, Jeffrey A. Lieberman, Chairman of Psychiatry at Columbia University, harshly criticized McCarthy for her views on vaccines, thimerosal, and autism: "She has no idea what she is talking about."

An opposing viewpoint along the lines of Jenny McCarthy is offered by no less than Robert F. Kennedy Jr., son of Ethel and the slain RFK, nephew of Rosemary Kennedy and Eunice Kennedy Shriver, and cousin of Timothy Shriver. He authored the book *Thimerosal: Let The Science Speak,* and produced a film that takes aim at the pharmaceutical industry and a supposed link between autism and the use of the mercury-based preservative thimerosal in vaccines given to millions of children. The supposition is this preservative is a contributing factor in the decade-long rise in autism spectrum disorder. Further research will help illuminate better answers.

CHAPTER 23

PLANNING PAYS OFF

F inancial independence can be defined as the ability to live a comfortable and secure lifestyle without relying on income from employment. The major financial objective for most of us is to reach financial independence by a certain time in life—which is commonly associated with retirement. Parents of special needs children are further challenged by having offspring who are likely to remain dependent into adulthood. As a consequence, it is paramount that we begin preparing early for financial security in retirement.

Now that I'm 65, Cathy and I are fortunate in being financially independent and secure in retirement. This freedom allows us to spend more quality time with Maggie and make life happier and healthier for our daughter. As a veteran financial planner and investment advisor, I know firsthand that planning pays off. As both a planner and special needs parent, I hope to shine a light on a path forward for others.

Procrastination and inertia are two of the biggest obstacles to success, both in life and finances. Being proactive is the number one habit of *The Seven Habits of Highly Effective People*, according to the late Steven Covey, author of that groundbreaking perennial bestseller.

What is called for is a bias toward taking action. James Stowers is founder and chairman of the mutual fund firm American Century.

His philosophy for success is to just get started. According to Stowers, "The best time to plant an oak was 20 years ago. The second best time is now."

Often, planning does not come naturally. As an unfortunate result, too many people put off until tomorrow that which is better tackled today. Noting this propensity, British actor Sir John Harvey once quipped, "The nicest thing about not planning is that failure comes as a complete surprise, rather than being preceded by periods of worry and depression."

Planning deals with overcoming the uncertainty inherent in the future. Uncertainty is heightened when a family member has special needs. The act of planning or strategizing about the future provides the planner with a sense of exerting some control over that uncertainty.

Life planning is a movement within the financial planning community that I fully embrace. It balances the management of one's personal finances with the hopes, dreams, and values that go into making a happy and productive life.

My personal life plan revolves around Maggie, including being a better father and husband. As a 65-year-old male, according to the life expectancy tables, I should remain breathing for another 18 years, to age 83. Naturally, I would like to round this up and plan on being around for the next 20 years to 85.

Time does indeed fly. It was over 21 years ago when I made the big leap of starting my own financial planning and investment advisory firm. Maggie was a young girl of 10. If I manage to live 20 years to the year 2035, I would see Maggie turn 50.

So my plan, hope, and dream is to live each day of the next 20 years as happily and healthfully as possible. Although there is only so much control we have over how long we live, we can improve the odds. At Cathy's suggestion I watch my diet, moderate my alcohol intake, joined a health club, exercise regularly, and use a personal trainer. Importantly, I see my personal physician annually.

Above all, I look for avenues that will help Cathy and me make the best possible life for our special needs daughter.

The first part of any financial plan is to identify your own current status or condition. I recommend that you put together a **net worth statement**. This most basic of personal finance statements is simple to construct and interpret. A net worth statement, also referred to as a statement of financial condition, can be thought of as a snapshot of your financial condition on any given date. It accounts for both your assets and your debts and yields a figure representing the difference. Put simply, what you *own* minus what you *owe* equals what you are worth. Your net worth is synonymous with your retirement nest egg. For estate planning purposes, add in any life insurance and you'll arrive at an **estate value**.

Another essential financial document is the **income statement**. If the net worth statement represents a snapshot of your financial condition, the income statement is like a motion picture. The top section identifies the income that flowed in during the year. The middle section pinpoints the outgo or expense items for the year. All serious planners need to get a handle on where their money is spent.

The third section of the income statement tells the story. The difference between inflows and outflows equals net income. In business the net income is the bottom line, and if positive, the business has a profit and is operating in the black.

Having a positive bottom line is equally important to an individual. If income exceeds outgo, you are living within your means. Surplus dollars are available for savings and investment purposes. This sum can be converted into an asset in your drive to build your net worth. As comedian Art Buck told us, "If you're only making ends meet, you're running in circles."

No one can hope to enjoy real financial independence unless expenditures are kept well within the limits of income. Think in terms of a spending plan and resist the popular urge to overspend.

Earmark a generous portion of your earned income for the purchase of assets that appreciate in value. Note that investing is not the purchase of cars, boats, or jewelry.

It is reasonable to target a savings rate in the range of 10 to 25 percent of gross pay. Substantial money put aside regularly can provide handsomely for the future. The real key to wealth accumulation is compounded savings.

According to *The Wealthy Barber*, "Wealth beyond your wildest dreams is possible if you follow the golden rule: Invest 10 percent of all you make for long-term growth. If you follow that one simple guideline, some day you'll be very rich."

The foundation of your long-term wealth-building effort depends on your developing a systematic savings program. Thomas Edison said, "We all make mistakes in life, but saving money is never one of them."

PYF stands for "pay yourself first." It suggests a saving mindset. That is, if exercised conscientiously, PYF programs us to save even before we meet the monthly mortgage payment. The secret of financial independence is not brilliance, luck, or some complicated strategy, but rather common-sense discipline to save a part of what you earn and put it to work for you.

A prime example of paying yourself first is to participate in a retirement plan with your employer, such as a 401K. You could elect to put 10 percent of each and every paycheck into this tax-advantaged retirement accumulation vehicle.

You can also readily put your PYF savings program on automatic pilot to an IRA, Roth, or taxable account. Say you plan to save and invest $5,000 annually. You arrange to have 1/12 of that goal, or $416.67, debited each and every month from your bank account and automatically directed to a diversified investment portfolio.

Another common-sense method is to target a rate at which you begin to save and modestly increase that rate each year going forward to retirement.

Follow a simple yet effective financial plan. Save diligently, invest wisely, and systematically pay down debt. Every dollar you save and every dollar you pay off debt adds a dollar to your net worth. Combine this with the powerful multiplier of compound growth, and your net worth will grow dramatically over the years, helping to assure financial independence and long-term retirement security.

CHAPTER 24

KEEP IT SIMPLE SILLY

Many of us are familiar with the KISS acronym for Keep It Simple, Stupid. I am a big believer in the power of simplicity. It is especially beneficial that parents of special needs children have a clear, straightforward pathway for addressing the personal financial anxiety we face and the confusing investment environment that faces us. As the father of an intellectually disabled child, I am sensitive about referring to anyone as "stupid"—even a discomfort with books titled for "dummies."

A frequent word in Maggie's vocabulary is to refer to someone or something as "silly." Occasionally, I am on the receiving end of that label myself. Maggie was with me when I was headed to the ATM drive-thru at our local bank. Although our girl has absolutely no interest or concern about money, Maggie inquired whether I needed money. Was I out of it? She wondered (incorrectly) if Mom had taken it all. I asked her if she needed any money. Her succinct reply: "Don't be silly."

So I would like to have KISS stand for *Keep It Simple, Silly*—at least in this book. My personal friend and trusted editor Jan Lennon suggested *Keep Investing Simple and Sane*. Either way, when it comes to investment behavior, it is always silly season out there, and we would all be much better off practicing good sense and simplicity.

The most successful investor in modern times, billionaire Warren Buffett, is quick to admit he owes his phenomenal investment and financial success to common sense. My friend and investment advisor Matt Miler likes to tell investment clients that Buffett will also add, "Investing is simple, but it is not easy." This is due to the psychological (emotional) aspects of investing, which tends to make the simple more difficult than it need be.

Fortunately, common sense is an enduring democratic quality. "Common sense," said 19th-century poet and essayist Ralph Waldo Emerson, "is genius dressed in working clothes."

In this single chapter, I take on the challenge of distilling my long professional career as an investment advisor to a simple, common-sense investment approach. I call it the KISS Method, and it consists of just seven steps.

1. KEEP IT SIMPLE

First, accept the fact that most people experience a constant and unrelenting urge to over-complicate matters. This pull comes from within your own mind and is reinforced by external forces. Individuals are hard-wired to believe investment success must really be much more difficult than it is.

My good friend Carl Unis, who has a soft spot for our Maggie, is a PGA golf professional whose highlight was playing in the 1967 U.S. Open golf tournament. He regularly instructs his students on the golf swing that "less is more." I contend the same wisdom holds true in investing.

2. EXERCISE PATIENCE

Similar to the virtue of loving a special needs individual, patience is a necessary trait when it comes to investing. It helps to think of investing as a long-distance race and to pattern your own actions after a marathoner, not a sprinter.

Irving Kahn, a disciple of legendary investor Benjamin Graham—also Warren Buffett's mentor—was a disciplined and successful investor in his own right. Kahn died in his home of natural causes in 2015 at 109. According to him, the most important quality an investor can possess is patience. "You gain much more by slow investing…than on fast investing, which is nothing more than gambling." To the end of his extraordinarily long life, Kahn preached patience, labeling widespread rapid trading as "crazy."

3. USE EXCLUSIVELY MUTUAL FUNDS

Former SEC commissioner Arthur Levitt has been quoted as saying, "In the fullness of time, the mutual fund will come to be regarded among the greatest financial innovations of the modern era."

By making an investment in a mutual fund, ordinary investors gain access to professional money managers to whom they entrust the difficult and perplexing buy-sell-hold decisions. But the greatest benefit of mutual fund investing is that investors achieve instant and continuous diversification from the first dollar invested.

Warren Buffett and mutual fund industry icon and Vanguard founder John Bogle, along with countless other knowledgeable and successful investors, fully support the view that mutual funds offer a simple, common-sense way to invest.

4. BE COST CONSCIOUS

It is a simple matter of investment math that any money you expend on investment costs directly reduces both your current yields and your overall returns. Costs really do matter. A major reason for the popularity of passive indexing is due to their low-cost advantage. As John Bogle reminds us, "Never forget that costs, like weeds, impede the garden's growth."

Once derided by the investment establishment as a radical, Bogle has lived long enough to see his thinking on razor-thin cost, passive investing (indexing), and a return to investment basics become widely accepted as mainstream truths.

5. DIVERSIFY, DIVERSIFY, DIVERSIFY

Legendary investor John Templeton advised anyone who would listen to diversify, diversify, diversify. Diversification is the proven best defense against risk. In keeping with a common-sense theme, this protection to limit loss cannot be overemphasized. To not diversify is to speculate.

6. INVEST IN A MIX OF BOTH GROWTH AND INCOME

To be a successful investor over the long term dictates allocating your funds among stocks (aka equities) for the growth and superior return potential they offer and fixed income (aka bonds) for current income and to reduce risk and dampen volatility.

The essence of successful investing is to maximize or push up return on the one hand and, at the same time, minimize or push down risk or volatility on the other. Studies have shown that more than 90 percent of investment performance is a direct function of how individuals decide how much and in what instrument to put their assets. Hence, asset allocation is where your focus and attention should be. For most investors the emphasis should be on stocks for growth.

I suggest keeping it simple by considering the same balanced approach typically followed by pension and institutional investors. Institutional investment plans have a fiduciary responsibility to take a prudent approach. Therefore, it is very common to see portfolios of 60 percent stocks balanced with 40 percent in bonds and cash, popularly known as 60/40.

Peter L. Bernstein (1919-2009) was an American financial historian, economist, and educator, known for presenting investment concepts to the public in understandable terms. *Money* magazine once said Peter Bernstein may have known more about investing than anyone alive. In Bernstein's considered opinion, the ideal 60/40 mix for an allocation represents the center of gravity, "a good compromise for the long-run average balance between maximizing return and minimizing risk."

7. SIMPLE SOLUTIONS

Nobel Prize winner in economics Daniel Kahneman told a group of financial advisors that "we would all be better off if we made fewer financial decisions." Following Kahneman's simplicity theme, I have narrowed the vast universe of investment choices to just two specific mutual funds for your consideration. Each of these spotlighted funds neatly fit the KISS criteria.

In my opinion, the best and least complicated investment vehicle to be found might be the Vanguard Star (VGSTX) mutual fund. I can say with confidence it is an easy and inexpensive way to derive the benefits of broad-based diversification and the optimum 60/40 allocation split recommended by Peter Bernstein, and it is widely followed in institutional portfolios.

The T. Rowe Price fund group sports a similar offering: the T. Rowe Price Personal Balanced (TRPBX) fund. Like Vanguard Star, this balanced fund takes a middle-of-the-road or all-weather approach, with a moderate allocation of 60/40.

Fund-tracker *Morningstar* says this about T. Rowe Price Personal Balanced: "Investors face the often inevitable task of selecting good investments, putting together a diversified group of holdings, and re-jiggering their portfolios regularly to ensure no one piece of the portfolio comes to dominate. There's the option of doing all that on your own, of course, but this offering does all the work for you."

For the vast majority of individuals, an overwhelming and frustrating puzzle is how to invest their 401K, IRA, and other retirement accounts given the perplexing choices and bewildering maze of possibilities. The fact is, most plan participants are rank amateurs, not at all suited to making investing decisions. Consequently, they do a lousy job at solving this vitally important task of establishing retirement security.

The solution, using my KISS method, is to make one clear decision to pick a target retirement fund that neatly corresponds to your age and planning horizon. Fortunately, Vanguard, T. Rowe

Price, and Fidelity recognized the value of so-called target funds for retirement accounts and were among the first to make them available.

Specifically, the Vanguard Target Retirement 2025 (VTTVX), T. Rowe Price Retirement 2025 (TRRHX), and Fidelity Freedom 2025 (FFTWX) offerings have been professionally designed to work well for an investor planning on retiring at or near 2025. For example, if you were born in 1960 you will turn 65 in the year 2025. In my case I am using a 2020 target that is closer to age 70. Either way, any of these age-appropriate funds would be a smart choice. Additional fund choices for you target the years 2015, 2020, 2030, 2035, 2040, 2045, and 2050, as well.

The beauty of target funds is that you can make one simple decision and know your retirement investing is on track as well as on target. These funds are unique in that the asset allocation mix is adjusted as you age to reflect an increasingly more conservative low-risk composition that favors more bonds and fewer stocks. This reallocation is often called your glide path, putting your investing on automatic pilot.

Resist the urge to monitor your investments too closely or switch your target date fund. As the Vanguard Group says in a print ad targeted to retirement plan savers, "Sometimes, the best way to manage your retirement fund is to ignore it."

In an opinion piece in *The Wall Street Journal,* Robert L. Reynolds, vice chairman of Fidelity Investments, built a strong case for what he refers to as "lifecycle" or "asset allocation" investment strategies, including target date funds, because these "offer the greatest chance for retirement savers to accumulate the largest possible nest eggs while reducing risk and volatility as retirement age approaches."

My KISS seven-step method offers a useful roadmap to help you navigate the oftentimes rocky road to financial independence and retirement security. As our Maggie might say, "Don't be silly."

CHAPTER 25

A DAD'S JOURNEY WITH JILLIAN

Maggie is a regular and dedicated thrift store shopper. She believes anything can be found in her favorite small shop in our local St. Jude church basement. And indeed it can, because one day last summer Cathy brought a book home she found there for only 50 cents titled *An Uncomplicated Life*. She correctly assumed I would find it of interest because of its subtitle, *A Father's Memoir of His Exceptional Daughter*.

What a rare and welcome surprise it was to experience this parallel perspective of a father and his special needs daughter. I read it eagerly, grateful this brand new "used" hardcover book found its way into my hands.

The author, Paul Daugherty, is a veteran sports writer for the *Cincinnati Enquirer* and the proud father of a truly exceptional daughter, Jillian, born October 17, 1989 with Down syndrome. Of her uncomplicated life, her dad writes, "The junk that clutters our day—anger, anxiety, jealousy, finances, cynicism, guile, agendas—has no place in her world."

Reading this well-written, highly personal memoir, both inspiring and humorous, I could readily relate from the perspective of a father who loves and lives with his own daughter challenged with an intellectual disability and who desperately wants the best for her. As Paul Daugherty tells us, "I love Jillian with a part of me no one can touch." He goes on with this honest admission: "But the limitations imposed by Jillian's needs are never fully reconciled."

At one point early in his daughter's life, he wished: "If I hugged Jillian hard enough, maybe the Down syndrome would go away." Like me, Paul readily admits that certain frustrations regularly boil over. Also like me, he is often impatient and frustrated.

It is no secret that mothers bear the brunt of child-raising, and raising a child with special needs is often exhausting. Paul lauds Jillian's devoted mom, Kerry, as the Rock of Gibraltar in their parenting partnership. I can definitely say the same rock-solid character and determination is true of Maggie's mom, Cathy, who—like Kerry—immersed herself in a maternal mission to shape a better world and the best Maggie possible.

An Uncomplicated Life is a heart-tugging read, a true love story told by an imperfect father with the talent of an award-winning journalist about his favorite subject, his exceptional daughter. It reveals the triumph of the human spirit, of hopes, dreams, and the importance of never giving up. The book deftly traces the often emotional journey of Jillian—and her parents—as she works her way through life.

When she was only months old, baby Jills was hospitalized for 11 days with a life-threatening build-up of thick mucus in her lungs. She could barely breathe. Ultimately overcoming this condition foreshadowed her ability to not only survive, but thrive—and beyond all expectations.

Daugherty's readers follow each milestone in Jillian's uncomplicated life as she works her way around the neighborhood, enters school, and meets Ryan, the love of her life. She goes on to graduate from high school, face the new frontier of college, and celebrate her 21st birthday with a beer and a party. She leaves home to live independently, and becomes engaged to marry Ryan.

In my opinion, the most valuable piece of advice offered to all of us, in particular to educators, by this professional journalist and special needs father is to not look at the Down syndrome—the ready-made stereotype of almond-eyes, diminutive stature, even loving personality— *but rather to see* the person for what she is and can become. Jillian constantly fought to be seen for who she is, not judged for what she looks like. A classic example of such misjudgment by a teacher was to tell the Daughertys their young daughter was incapable of learning because of her disability.

Jillian's vibrant approach to life and her boundless capacity for joy have much to teach everyone about living better. As her biographer-father writes, "Having a child with a disability is like having a life coach you didn't ask for."

Similar to our experience with Maggie, Jillian also has guardian angels enter her life to give her a lift up. Her first angel was her speech therapist, Martha, who came to her rescue at the age of three and spent the next decade opening the child's world by developing her ability to talk and communicate. Dad credits therapist Martha with giving his darling Jillian the true gift of a voice.

Our Maggie also benefited greatly from early intervention speech therapy. In fact, it was an area where she made great strides, beginning as a very young child. Therapists wanted Maggie to be able to communicate her needs without reverting to crying or grunting, so she was taught some simple sign language. Rather than fussing, when she wanted to eat, Maggie was taught to place her hands to her mouth. Cathy and I always got a kick out of Maggie's tapping the fingers of her hands together to signify "more." She even signed for more while her mouth was still full.

Our other daughter, Martha, recalls that Maggie did not speak much as a young girl but grew to talk so constantly that now it is often difficult to quiet her. Martha remembers how one day Maggie came home from summer camp wearing an arts and crafts project from that day, a paper and feather headdress that had "Chief Running Mouth" printed across her forehead. According to Martha, "Not totally PC, but absolutely spot-on."

Jillian's speech, though continuing to sound stunted and immature, is nonetheless part of her personal charm. As a young adult she underscores a point in conversation with "zackly," wants to live independently in her own "partment," and has learned (with much effort) to "wide bike" (ride a bike).

A takeaway from *Uncomplicated* is that we, as parents of special needs children, need to set the bar for our expectations higher, even though such a course requires great patience and is rarely easy or without obstacles.

Reading *An Uncomplicated Life* brought back vivid memories of Maggie's own school years. In many ways Jillian's father is critical of the special education his daughter received, expecting more, unwilling to settle for the status quo.

Once a special needs child like Jillian or Maggie enters school, we parents become deluged with a flood of acronyms from school officials. The cornerstone of a child's special education is the Individualized Education Program, or IEP. If your child receives special education services, an IEP is mandated by federal law—a legal document spelling out your child's learning needs, the services the school will provide, and how your child's progress will be measured. This vital document is for students from preschool age three to post high-school transition age 22. Each IEP is created by a process that involves parents and school officials as parts of a team approach. It is designed to address unique learning issues and specific educational goals. An important part of the plan is how modifications and accommodations shall be tailored to the unique needs of the special needs student and how the disability will affect a student's learning.

Jillian's parents, Kerry and Paul, fought the good fight with the school establishment to get the best education possible for their special needs daughter. For her part, Jillian simply loved school, just as she loved her life in general. Her enthusiasm was such that she never allowed herself a bad day.

Even with all this support going for her, learning remained a monumental challenge. According to her dad, "Homework was a nightly bang at a wall." He became frustrated when homework assignments weren't modified as they should have been. In Jillian's

16 years of education her dad never could figure out whether many of her teachers viewed his daughter as a burden or as an opportunity for professional growth and enrichment.

Daugherty takes particular aim at the special education establishment in his chapter titled, "The Battleground of Dreams." He sensed the prevailing attitude was one of expecting parents to settle for their child's merely getting along. Looking back, he now feels Jillian's education was stunted, with educators looking to take the easiest path instead of being interested in reaching for a more challenging route.

Still, another angel entering Jillian's life was Nancy, her third grade teacher. A caring educator, Nancy realized Jillian was capable of learning, but in a different way from other students. Learning and grasping would never be fast or easy for this child. She could learn—just in slow motion. Nancy admired this young girl's resolve and determination to learn. So she became a strong advocate for her and a lifelong friend, believing that too many special education teachers pigeonhole kids like Jillian, holding low expectations for them and consequently setting goals too easily reached.

Paul Daugherty describes IEP meetings as feeling like the constant push-pull of a divorce settlement—without the divorce. He sees the IEP document itself as 12 pages of "coma-inducing" vaguely defined goals. And in some IEP meetings, he writes, the assembled saw Jillian "as an itch they'd rather not scratch."

From our own perspective of sitting through many IEP meetings, Cathy would tell you it all sounded wonderful but rarely delivered on its promise. The Daughertys found the IEP was rarely revised or updated and was frequently a waste of paper. In fact, Cathy discovered that Maggie's IEP in high school was almost identical to that of another student in her class. So much for an individualized plan. I suspect it is mostly boilerplate language that serves to pass muster with bureaucrats.

Cathy reminded me of a parent-teacher conference she attended, solo, with Maggie's regular education fourth grade art teacher. She was devastated to find no evidence whatsoever that our girl was part of this class or classroom. No artwork on the walls, nothing. To make matters worse, the teacher shortchanged her conference time. He implied that because Maggie was "Special Ed," she was therefore not his responsibility. Leaving that conference in tears she was met in the hall by the principal. Cathy expressed her disappointment at this teacher's attitude. The principal did say she would have a word and offered empathy. In his book, Paul states he never once attended an IEP in which any educator at the table even had a special needs student.

Kerry Daugherty notes that in intermediate school Jillian did not have a secured locker like the other students. When this slight was brought to the attention of the school officials, they revealed their assumption that Jillian was incapable of mastering the combination. With some extra help, Jillian did learn to operate her locker and felt like everyone else. In her high school years she was frequently pulled out of the regular classroom and assigned to the resource room, where little actual learning activity took place, so she couldn't help but feel excluded.

Cathy, too, frequently crossed swords with the special education teacher in Maggie's high school. She never seemed open to any of Cathy's suggestions, although nobody knows Maggie as well as her mom. We elected to not attend Maggie's high school graduation, knowing for the most part our girl had been warehoused. Graduation therefore was not a cause for celebration, as it had been from middle school with a caring teacher. This was an easy call for us, as the date of graduation coincided with the Special Olympics State games. Maggie had qualified to compete and felt a true part of her team.

Perhaps the most important takeaway from *An Uncomplicated Life* is the need to persuade the educational establishment, and yourself, that just because a student is intellectually challenged doesn't mean he or she cannot or will not learn. Kerry, on her blog, recommends that special needs parents inform themselves of educational rights, cautioning that it will become a necessity. She also suggests coming prepared for the IEP meetings. Knowing how intimidating the IEP process can be for families, the Association for the Rights of Citizens with handicaps (ARCh) in neighboring Waukesha County, offers as a valuable advocacy service sitting in on these meetings with bewildered parents.

Jillian did succeed, as evidenced by her being the first student with Down syndrome to graduate from Loveland High School as a fully included "normal" student. Credit goes to mom Kerry for "19 years of heavy lifting" and to Jillian herself for never having stopped trying. Her proud father writes, "It was a perfect intersection of effort and courage."

When Jillian turned 21, her paternal grandfather traveled 1,000 miles from Florida to attend her birthday celebration. Paul describes his father as generally practicing a form of "absentee love" regarding his grandchildren, although he was clearly moved by this important occasion.

He implored his journalist son, "Write about this," adding, "People need to know how this works." He was not only pleasantly surprised but actually amazed that his granddaughter with Down syndrome was the source of such an abundant outpouring of affection for her coming-of-age birthday party, and that his intellectually challenged own flesh and blood managed to graduate from high school, attend college, live independently, take public transportation, manage a basketball team, and became engaged to be married!

As for her proud father, witnessing the crowd happily celebrating this landmark birthday, he gushes, "A wonder of Jillian is the joy she inspires in others. Her disability enables."

CHAPTER 26

LIFE GOES ON WITH AN EXTRA CHROMOSOME

"All God's angels come to us disguised."
James Russell Lowell

Siblings Shawn and Tim Maloney and their friend John Pyter are three amazing people. I have come to view this trio as a single unit, for their lives are so woven together.

Shawn, a bespectacled social dynamo, tells all within earshot that Tim is *her* brother and John is *her* boyfriend. She is very possessive of John and can be a bossy big sister to Tim. When I became acquainted with the two young men, I actually thought they were related because I saw them together so often.

Some years ago at State, rain caused many game delays. Having time to kill, Tim, John, my Maggie and I, and Brandon, a large fellow with autism, decided to trek across campus to find the University bookstore. As Maggie tramped across the rain-soaked field her shoe came off and became stuck in the mud. She broke out laughing, finding this a lot funnier than I did.

Brandon does not speak, but holds up one finger when he wants your attention, and at this moment he desperately wanted to shop. After we solved Maggie's shoe problem, Brandon eventually got his way. When we were ready to leave the bookstore, I couldn't find Tim and John anywhere. I kept looking up and down aisles but did not see them. I didn't panic, because of all the athletes this pair was the most responsible and independent. Still, their disappearance was a mystery because the store is not that big. Finally, I happened to literally trip over them. They were crouched on the floor, engrossed looking at magazines.

Tim and John seem to communicate with each other on another level. They also find humor in everyday life, which is a delightful dynamic to observe.

Shawn, Tim, and John accomplish a high quality of life living with an extra 23rd chromosome, indicative of Down syndrome. All three individuals of this fine group are decent, honest, and likeable people from loving families, living strong, full, and active social lives. This winsome trio is imbued with all that is great about Special Olympics as competitive athletes, teammates, and very special friends.

One Friday night at the State summer games, the annual dance had just wrapped up. Alone in my dorm room doing some work on this book about Maggie, I left the door open in case I was needed. Around 9 pm Shawn, flanked by brother and boyfriend, came to the door and politely asked if they could come in. We all sat down and had a far-reaching, 45-minute conversation.

Cathy had previously introduced me to TED talks as well as a piece on the art of storytelling. What I learned can be summed up by this quote: "The single most powerful way to connect with another person is to tell them a personal story or to listen to them tell one." Connection is especially compelling for those of us who have a deep conversation with special needs individuals—often ignored, marginalized, or made to feel invisible. We tend to treat special needs individuals as children, when in fact John, 52, Shawn, 49, and Tim, 46, are all at an age in which they could well be grandparents. They have deep feelings and a wealth of life experiences, like everyone else, albeit seen through a different prism.

When these three friends seated themselves in my dorm room that post-dance evening, I learned of Shawn's sincere interest in having her beautiful, quarter-of-a-century love story with John told—and spotlighted. Shawn's mom, Nancy, notes her special daughter's love affair has consumed her adult life and knows no bounds. I honestly don't know if there could be a couple more in love than Shawn and John. Although this couple lives apart, they are otherwise inseparable, sitting together and holding hands on bus rides, eating together, dancing together, and showing public displays of affection. Shawn's brother Tim told me when they are not physically together they spend hours on the phone, carrying on a commentary even while watching a favorite television show, such as *Dancing with the Stars*. As Shawn tells it, her relationship with John started as a casual friendship, but evolved into a serious boyfriend-girlfriend thing. Shawn shared that John was the first man she ever kissed. When her dad, Larry, originally heard Shawn make this claim, he countered he thought he had been the first. Shawn promptly corrected her dad: John's was the first romantic kiss, not a quick peck on the cheek.

Although age catches up with us all, the aging process is cruelly accelerated for many of those living with Down syndrome. According to the *WebMD* website, people with Down syndrome experience premature aging, with the result that Alzheimer-like disease is three- to five-times more common than in the general population. I recently asked John how work and life in general were going. He has always been a good conversationalist, expressive and quite knowledgeable in a wide variety of subject areas. So I was alarmed when this basic question drew a blank from him. Noticing this, Tim, perceptive and sensitive, mentioned that his good friend has memory problems. I had earlier been made aware of John's condition: however, I was taken aback by observing firsthand how much this good fellow had declined in the past year.

John's dear 92-year-old mother, Esther, discussed with me recently her son's memory decline, which led him to retire from his long-term job at McDonald's. I first got to know this wonderful, gentle woman when she was the "lunch room lady" at Maggie's high school. Esther told me her quest in life is to be there for John, a major concern at her age. She shared with me the tough news that her daughter has terminal cancer. Thus she feels most responsible for taking care of John.

On a couple of occasions over the three days of the games, John made impromptu and impassioned diatribes in public on the meaning of the Special Olympics oath and the importance of attitude and giving your all in competition. John did perform well in his race-walking event Saturday morning. Although outmatched, he persevered and won a silver medal. John has always exhibited good sportsmanship and makes it a point to shake hands with his fellow competitors and congratulate them. I am quite taken by his regularly acknowledging me, as his coach, for his own success. I am honored, privileged, and humbled by this fine gentleman's vocal appreciation. Some of us fear this could be John's last medal. For any athlete, the dream is to go out at the top of one's game.

In my dorm room the evening of our intense four-way conversation, fun-loving Tim, who also has a deep and serious side, asked if I was familiar with the actor Chris Burke. I wasn't. I don't usually discuss Down syndrome in the company of these special athletes, but Tim wanted me to know that Chris Burke, who lives with Down syndrome, starred in the TV series *Life Goes On,* which aired from 1989 to 1993. Tim also noted that Chris Burke's character, Corky, appeared in an episode in which he marries a woman who also has Down syndrome. It occurred to me Tim was thinking of the heavy-duty subject of marriage, not only for his sister and the love of her life, but also for himself and his own long-time girlfriend, Deb. Tim had brought to State three framed photos of Deb and him that he displayed on his dorm room's desk. He told me Chris Burke also had written a book: *A Special Kind of Hero* (1991), co-authored by JoBeth McDaniel. According to Tim, not only is Chris a famous actor but also is lead singer in a band. Tim later loaned me his own well-worn copy of the book to read. Although I was vaguely familiar with that ground-breaking TV series, Tim piqued my interest to learn more, so I promptly read this book cover to cover.

Chris Burke was born in 1965, five years earlier than Tim Maloney. They have in common being determined, intelligent, sociable, happy, and successful, as well as being handsome, fair-skinned redheads of Irish descent. Like the voice of his hero, Chris, Tim's voice is slightly throaty and gravely, typical with Down syndrome. Tim is probably the better athlete, while Chris's talents shine in performance and music. Growing up, each participated in Boy Scouts. Tim's dad, Larry, was his scoutmaster. Today, there are troops that accommodate scouts with special needs.

A rather humorous story appears in Chris Burke's book of him gallantly trying to be a good scout by assisting an elderly woman cross a busy Manhattan street. This startled woman feared she was being mugged and frantically waved her cane and screamed at Chris. He couldn't comprehend how his good deed could be mistaken.

Larry Maloney shared with me how the book reminded him of how much Chris Burke's pioneering accomplishments and related celebrity status encouraged and inspired his son Tim. I learned from Tim that he had met Chris Burke some dozen years earlier when his idol was keynote speaker at a Wisconsin Down syndrome event. Tim got to shake hands with his hero and came away with an autographed picture as a remembrance.

Like Tim Maloney's parents, Chris's parents were advised to institutionalize their son at birth, because the prevailing expectation assumed his quality of life would be poor. Their pediatrician, a family friend, was blunt about it, telling the Burkes, "Put him in an institution. Forget you ever had him. It will be the best thing for you and your family."

Oprah had Chris and his now widowed mother, Marian, on her show to talk about where are they now. Marian said the best decision they ever made in her long life was to ignore this cold advice. Looking at her son, she called him "the joy of her life."

Chris referred to his mom as beautiful, and the TV cameras caught a shot of deep love on his beaming face.

Chris grew up in New York, the youngest of four children. The loving and close-knit Burke family nurtured him and spurred his development. He was raised to be strong and independent. Nevertheless, as I learned from *A Special Kind of Hero*, it's no surprise that life for Chris was not without significant challenges. His local educational options were limited, so he had to leave home to attend special education schools. One time an emotionally disturbed fellow student played a cruel trick on a naïve Chris, telling him to close his eyes and open his mouth, as he had a surprise in store. The boy then shoved an evergreen branch down his throat. Chris forgave this boy, looking to him as a wayward friend, but in the coming weeks he began coughing up blood. The evergreen was deeply lodged, causing a serious medical emergency. A small piece actually began to grow in his lungs. For a while, doctors thought this baffling condition was somehow related to his syndrome.

Another time when Chris was out on his own in New York City and did not make it home at the expected hour, his mother and father grew increasingly anxious about their special teenager. His policeman father was alarmed when another officer came to the door to assure them their son would be all right after being hit by a car. He'd stepped off a curb as a cabbie ran a red light. Eventually apprehended, the offending cabdriver had fled the scene at high speed the wrong way down a one-way street, explaining that he panicked, believing he'd killed this innocent pedestrian. Chris was fine, other than being shaken up with bumps and bruises, and being taken by ambulance to the hospital for observation. To this day he is hesitant to ride in cabs and avoids that particular busy intersection.

Emily Perl Kingsley, introduced earlier as the author of the epic poem *Welcome to Holland,* recommended Chris for a role in the ABC television movie *Desperate.* Although that series was not picked up, Chris did gain notice by ABC network executives because he "lit up the screen." The TV series *Life Goes On* was written with Chris in mind. He played the lead character, Charles "Corky" Thatcher. The show earned high marks for covering uncharted territory and for a realistic portrayal of an individual with Down syndrome. Playing Corky, Chris "stole the nation's heart." It propelled him, then 23 years old, to fame. A common line in Corky's dialogue was, *"Life goes on. I have feelings."* For Tim, Shawn, and John, too, life goes on. They share the same deep feelings reflected in Corky's storyline.

Many of us think Hollywood is all glamour, but from reading this book I learned how hard Chris worked on his craft. He took acting lessons, toiled to learn and deliver his lines, and put in the necessary hard work and effort demanded by the grind of a weekly TV series. Chris also won a recurring role in the feel-good TV hit *Touched by an Angel,* in which he played Taylor, an angel with Down syndrome.

Chris Burke's character was not merely an oddity. And it was more than a revolutionary TV role. It represented a breakthrough sociological phenomenon needing to happen. A lot rode on his performance—not just for himself but also for countless others. In a way Chris's role was similar to Jackie Robinson's breaking the color barrier in major league baseball. Chris needed to fulfill his dream by succeeding to be worthy of his book's title, *A Special Kind of Hero*. Chris is all that and more to Tim Maloney and many others.

Chris Burke and Tim Maloney are each big fans of country music. I have observed that many Special Olympians share this taste in music, including Jillian Daugherty. Chris says, "I like country music because it tells a story. I like it because they sing their hearts out. And it's honest."

Maggie can instantly identify a country music song on the radio. And like Maggie and Chris Burke, I too am fond of country music, finding the best of songs spark in me an emotional charge. A prime example is the moving ballad "I Loved Her First," about a father giving away his daughter in marriage. As father to Martha and Maggie, this line in particular speaks the truth to me: "I know the love of a father runs deep."

This past summer as father of the bride for Martha's wedding, I recited the lyrics to this country song as my talk at the reception. I stood directly behind my son-in-law, Matt, and reminded him in all seriousness, as the song says, "But I loved her first and I held her first / And she still means the world to me / Just so you know."

As the lyrics also tell us, I always knew and prayed this day would come—but I knew it would happen for only one of my precious daughters. On the other side of our family's table at the reception sat Maggie. I also know my eldest is highly unlikely to ever find her own "Matt," and that makes me sad.

The episode of *Life Goes On* that Tim Maloney specifically referenced, in which Chris as Corky marries a young woman with Down syndrome, brings the whole weighty topic of marriage to the forefront. As disclosed in the book about Chris, many people inquired of his parents whether their son would ever marry. Nancy Maloney has told me Shawn has talked about marrying John many times over the years of their courtship. These conversations must be difficult, even heart-wrenching. After all, when two people love each other, it is natural and even expected in our society that the next step is to join together as husband and wife. Chris's folks had a number of concerns about marriage when it came to their young-est son. His mom was direct: "I don't think it's the ideal situation." I believe Nancy and Larry would have similar thoughts.

I empathize for Shawn and John in their inability to express their true love for each other through marriage, but I understand it is not the best fit for them.

As I mentioned earlier, adults with Down syndrome tend to age more quickly than the general population. Chris Burke, now 50, no longer performs with his band. Also, he is retiring after more than 20 years as a Goodwill Ambassador and staff member with the National Down Syndrome Society (NDSS)in New York.

He wrote, "I don't want to leave but my heart is telling me I have to. I will miss all of you and will say, well, Life Goes On!"

A legitimate claim has been made by some that Chris Burke has had as great an influence on how those with disabilities are positively viewed as did the great Helen Keller.

Her life story, told in the play and in the movie, *The Miracle Worker*, remains an inspiration to us all, especially in the realm of special education. A favorite quote attributed to Helen Keller is: "When one door closes, another opens. But we often look so regretfully upon the closed door that we don't see the one that has opened for us."

I have come to believe from knowing Shawn, Tim, and John, and now being exposed to Chris, there must be something truly special in that extra 23rd chromosome to celebrate. For each possesses the special ability to love and be loved, to dream big dreams, and to bring joy and expressive love to those who choose the privilege of getting to know any one of them.

CHAPTER 27

SISTER EDNA HAD A DREAM

Maggie is our family's connection to Milwaukee's St. Ann Center for Intergenerational Care, as well as to the Center's dynamic president and leader, Sister Edna Lonergan. A member of the Sisters of St. Francis of Assisi, Sister Edna is the founder and face of St. Ann Center. A wonderful study in contrasts, Sister is both gentle in demeanor yet rock firm; smart and stylish yet humble and reserved; soft spoken yet resolute; and deeply religious yet worldly and astute. Over the past 30-plus years, she founded, nurtured, and faithfully built St. Ann Center into an award-winning institution. With a proven care model and a noble mission, it meets the needs of the underserved—from young children and developmentally disabled adults, to the frail elderly and those suffering with dementia.

Sister is one of the most remarkable individuals I have been blessed to call friend. I might have never met and come to know her if not for my being Maggie's dad. Amazingly, Sister Edna knew at age three of having a vocation to serve, and she entered the convent at age 14. The intergenerational model she birthed and fostered as a focus of her calling has received many awards, including international recognition for its effective, innovative delivery of care services.

Cathy and I had the good fortune to cross paths with Sister Edna some years ago. Like many others in our community, we were unaware of this gem tucked away on Milwaukee's south side

until we toured St. Ann Center at the invitation of another remarkable woman and Center supporter, the late Mary Rose. Learning
that we were parenting a special needs child, Mary had wisely
suggested we visit St. Ann Center and become acquainted with the
indefatigable Sister Edna.

Upon arriving in the bustling, enclosed courtyard, Cathy and I
were greeted by Sister Edna and her radiant smile. Both the Center
and Sister Edna became another important door opening for our
family and a pathway that has enriched Maggie's life and our own.
Sister Edna is quite fashionable in dress and appearance and not
at all what I had imagined she would be. We soon learned among
her many talents is creating beautiful jewelry to raise funds for the
Center. But what touched me most profoundly was the dynamic
taking place within St. Ann. One special memory is that of a two-
year-old being cradled and rocked lovingly by an older woman.
Sister informed us this precious child started life as a baby ad-
dicted to crack cocaine.

In another area of the sprawling Center, one of dozens of selfless volunteers was gently spoon feeding a young man paralyzed
from the neck down. We learned it could take the better part of an
hour to feed him lunch. What struck me most was how his eyes
were fixed on the woman feeding him, their exchange of love a
beautiful sight. Lunch time at St. Ann amounts to what has been
aptly described as "a daily banquet of love." Many of the clients or
daily guests like those I saw are unable to eat without help.

Amazingly, St. Ann has 600 volunteers, the true "beating
hearts" of this caregiving facility. Once someone is exposed to the
joy that permeates St. Ann, it is not uncommon to want to be part
of this place as a volunteer.

In response to a definite need, St. Ann Center opened a 24/7
Respite Care Center in 2007. It is somewhat akin to an eight-room
bed and breakfast for people with special needs. This overnight
care facility allows harried parents and caregivers to get away for
a few days to a few weeks, knowing their loved one is being well

taken care of in a safe environment by St. Ann staff. Sister Edna counsels caregivers that acknowledging our feelings of frustration is a very real, very understandable experience. She advocates that we badly need a regular break from the constancy of caregiving.

Our Maggie has stayed at the St. Ann 24/7 Respite Care Center on multiple occasions over the past several years. For Maggie, these interludes are an adventure, something special, a treat. She packs her own suitcase, has her own room, and is independent from us. I once asked Maggie what she likes about St. Ann. Her quick reply: "Breakfast, lunch, and dinner."

For Cathy and me, these occasional sojourns foster a sense of independence in our girl of not being tethered to her mom. As aging parents, we have to prepare Maggie as well as us for the day when she may not live with us. Our hope and prayer for our first-born is that when the time comes, she will be happy and content in a safe, secure, and loving environment like St. Ann Center.

Similarly, my friends and clients Chip and Peggie Trampe depended on St. Ann Respite Care for 10 days last year to care for their adult son while the rest of the Trampe family travelled to South Korea for the wedding ceremony of his older sister. By all accounts, Jake enjoyed this experience, and the arrangement went well for everyone involved. Jacob "Jake" had suffered a brain aneurism at age 20 while in college. He was extremely fortunate to survive at all, but he was left paralyzed and brain damaged, and he now uses a wheelchair. Jake was a teen musician and continues to enjoy music. He has a good sense of humor and by all accounts is happy. To "Jacobize" their suburban home, his mom and dad invested a considerable sum to make their house work for their disabled son, including an accessible shower. Because of his health issues, Jacob does not fly, but each spring he accompanies his folks to Florida for a warm weather vacation in the family's SUV.

St. Ann Center is equal parts joy and love put into the caregiving equation. An example is the specially adapted bathing area.

I learned from Sister Edna that for many of their clients a warm water bath and shampoo might be the only one they receive all week. Clients also receive music and art therapy, albeit with St. Ann's special touch. Sister Edna, who holds a degree in occupational therapy and a master's degree in gerontology, told me about Benevolent Touch, a life enrichment program. They practice and teach Benevolent Touch using gentle massage and self-affirming song to enhance lives through tactile "hands on" contact for those with dementia, special needs, or sensory loss.

Maggie's new psychiatrist, Dr. Joseph O'Grady, is suggesting our girl could benefit from some occupational therapy, believing she has some sensory integration disorder issues.

What sets St. Ann Center apart is its intergenerational model. Sister told me they are constantly asking themselves how they can enhance the life experience for both young and old clients under their care. The daily guests in their memory care unit, Shepherd's House, look forward to regular visits and arranged tea parties with the youngsters. Pictures of adorable young children holding hands with and hugging gray-haired men in wheelchairs testify to the effectiveness of this special intergenerational interaction. The best time to visit St. Ann might be on a Friday morning to witness the joy of all the generations coming together as they assemble in the atrium for a spirited music concert.

Recently St. Ann Center constructed a new $22 million state-of-the-art center at 24th Street and North Avenue on Milwaukee's impoverished north side to bring compassionate quality care to an underserved area. Sister Edna shared with me that the genesis of the concept for a second center came to her in a dream. When she awoke from her slumber she was determined to replicate what is successful at St. Ann for the north side of the city.

Her dream was so big, bold, and daring it can legitimately be labeled audacious. Against long odds, Sister engaged generous supporters, city, community, and religious leaders and major foundations to make her dream a reality. Although this quest is monumental, Sister is a life force. Her unshakeable faith and fearlessness has miraculously moved this project of hope continually forward. She exudes an inescapable sense of urgency to bring the intergenerational brand of quality and dignified care to a neglected community that so desperately needs it. This magnificent new facility promises to be an oasis of hope, a beacon of light, and a bridge to help heal the racial and cultural divide in our fractured community.

The second campus on the north side also includes a medical and dental clinic. Sister has observed that people with severe disabilities and other special needs are often underserved because of income barriers or the nature of their disability.

Even with such a worthwhile project, the hard truth is raising money as a non-profit entity is extremely challenging. Reluctant to open this new facility in phases, Sister Edna and her board were forced to by the reality of awaiting millions in additional contributions before the full facility could be completed. Sister genuinely believes there is a higher power driving this project forward, and through her prayers she is convinced that God will somehow provide.

Her abundant faith brings to mind one of my all-time favorite movies, the 1945 classic, *The Bells of St. Mary's,* starring Bing Crosby as Father O'Malley and Ingrid Bergman as Sister Benedict. The Sister has a recurring dream of securing a new and badly needed school building. The mortgage holder is a wealthy aging businessman, Horace P. Bogardus, who also owns the neighboring new building, which the good sister is eyeing to replace the about-to-be condemned big city school. By the end of this touching film, Bogardus is miraculously persuaded to donate his new building.

My hope is that Providence continues to smile on Sister Edna, enabling her to find the resources to expand her new building and fulfill her dream of serving more of the community's underserved.

CHAPTER 28

GIVE IT AWAY

Through the years, our family has occasionally traveled to Arlington racetrack in the northwest suburbs of Chicago. Because my sister Nancy lives in nearby Arlington Heights, over the Labor Day weekend we like to organize a McCarthy family outing at the racetrack.

I am not much of a gambler but do enjoy seeing the beautiful thoroughbreds. Some years ago I took Maggie, Martha, and Jack down to the paddock area to get close to the horses as they were paraded around to warm up before racing. Maggie took a particular interest in "horsy number seven." It could well be she thought the animal winked at her. Her siblings decided we should bet on Maggie's choice. When number seven's red-haired jockey saddled up, I thought we might be onto something with the luck of the Irish. My noticing a shamrock embroidered on his racing silks clinched the deal.

While the kids headed up to the track to view the race, I went to place the bet. I was thinking of laying down a $5 wager until I learned to my dismay that "horsy number seven," Moneychanger, was a 35:1 long shot. Not wishing to completely throw away money, I opted to place the minimum $2 bet. I caught up with the gang at the rail as they excitedly waited to see Maggie's chosen horse run. I tried to tamp down any expectation of our having a winner. A cute young girl standing next to us asked what horse we were "voting" on to win.

The race started, and we viewed its progress from the big screen on the infield. It soon became evident that poor Moneychanger had, as race fans say, the best view of the field. Old number seven was running dead last. I felt smart that I would lose only $2. Yet, slowly but surely, our horse was moving up. Then, as the pack thundered into the final turn, Moneychanger took off as if shot from a cannon and amazingly went from last to first. The finish was exciting! Each of us jumped up and down celebrating our winner, and I felt especially happy for Maggie.

I took our jolly group with me to the ticket window to retrieve our improbable winnings. There I met up with my sister Mary Ann, who poked fun at my account for not knowing how to claim a winner. She then proceeded to ridicule me, saying she would never be so cheap as to make a mere $2 bet. The woman working at the counter came to my defense, saying how rare it is to have 35:1 odds pay off. For my cheap $2 bet she handed me three crisp $20 bills plus a $10 bill.

Flush with $70 in cash, I turned to Maggie and asked her what I should do with her winnings. Her quick reply was, "Give it away."

So I turned to our host Aunt Nancy and attempted, unsuccessfully, to slip her $20. She pushed it back in my pocket. I had better results with Martha and my niece Jamie. Jack who was then about 10, got handed the $10 bill. He looked at me open-mouthed, knowing he was being shortchanged compared to the $20 Martha and Jamie each received. If I'd had my wits about me, I would have instructed Jack to never look a gift horse in the mouth.

After several more races, striking out in all of them, Martha and Jack suggested we take Maggie back to the paddock area to have our lucky girl pick another winner. They apparently thought they had discovered a system. Unfortunately, lightning didn't strike twice. But we did have fun.

I had the opportunity of hearing the great investment master John Templeton speak to a group of financial planners and investment advisors at a conference in 1986. What has stayed with me over all these years and created a lasting influence on my approach to investing was his sincere belief that the absolute best investment, and ultimately the most rewarding, is to be generous to those less fortunate. A deeply spiritual man, Templeton believed in tithing 10 percent of one's income to charities.

Tony Robbins, in *MONEY Master The Game*, refers admirably to Templeton as "one of the greatest human beings who ever lived." A prominent philanthropist, John Templeton established the Templeton Prize with the aim that it be worth more than the Nobel Prize.

The first Templeton award went to the sainted Mother Teresa. This diminutive nun was renowned for helping the poorest of the poor. Mother Teresa felt strongly, "We can do no great thing; only small things with great love." Tony Robbins reminds us in his book that love is the ultimate wealth.

Templeton was knighted in 1987 by Great Britain's Queen Elizabeth for his humanitarian efforts. Sir John died in 2008 at the age of 92, but the spirit of this giant of a man lives on through his philanthropic legacy.

In following his wisdom as well as heeding Maggie's call to "give it away," I present two simple yet powerful tax-smart ways to be generous to those charities that touch your heart. You could well choose any of the more than a dozen referenced in this very book that serve and care for special needs individuals. Incidentally, I have pledged to donate 20 percent of the profits of this book to help support these worthy charitable causes.

Tax laws encourage charity. In the first of two tax-smart techniques, a monetary gift to a qualified charity (qualified means that it meets IRS requirements) is deductible from income taxes for those who itemize deductions. For example, my check made out to Special Olympics to sponsor my buddy Dougie in the Polar Plunge is deductible from what otherwise would be taxable income. For a taxpayer in the 25 percent tax bracket, every $1 gifted to a qualified charity such as Special Olympics reduces one's federal income tax bill by 25 cents.

A simple yet smart move is to donate or gift an *appreciated* asset—most commonly stock or mutual fund shares—to your chosen qualified charity. Your tax accountant or financial planner can readily identify those investments that from a tax, investment, and estate standpoint would be good candidates to gift.

Say for example you own XYZ stock in a taxable, non-retirement account that you purchased for $1 (its cost/tax basis) and that has grown in value since purchase to now be worth $3. If you sold XYZ, you would in this example be subject to a capital gain tax on the $2. If instead you directly gift XYZ to a qualified charity, you could deduct the full $3 on your tax return.

Cathy and I were happy to make a gift of mutual fund shares directly to St. Ann Center for Intergenerational Care to help fulfill Sister Edna's dream of building a new center on Milwaukee's north side. We owned mutual fund shares in a joint taxable account that had appreciated nicely over the years we owned it and was worth four times what we originally paid. This was an ideal candidate to gift.

The second simple yet powerful tax-smart gifting technique involves making a charity the beneficiary of your IRA. Based on current tax law, the vast majority of individuals will not face a federal estate tax upon death. This is because an estate valued up to $5.43 million is now exempt (free) of federal estate taxation with the 2015 inflation adjustment. Married couples will not be subject to a federal estate tax until their estate exceeds close to $11 million. In years past, the individual exemption cutoff was only $1 million. The estate tax is no longer the primary estate planning focus it had been. Now only the very wealthiest estates will face the so-called federal death tax, although more may experience it on the state level. Moreover, all individuals who inherit IRAs or retirement accounts as beneficiaries will still have to pay *income* taxes on distributions received. An important exception is when the beneficiary of an IRA is a charity.

Changing the beneficiary of an IRA is a very simple matter. A one-page form from your IRA custodian is all that is needed. Once made, you can also change your mind as well as any percentage allocations. Although you definitely do not need the services of an attorney to change a beneficiary election, I recommend that any significant estate planning matter be coordinated with your team of attorney, financial advisor, and the charity. For one, you want to make sure the charity is identified correctly.

For example, say you own an IRA valued at $100,000. Upon your death, this IRA goes to the named beneficiary (one who benefits from your bequest). This designation supersedes whatever your will states. In most cases, the beneficiary is your spouse or other family members, but it can be anyone you choose. Beneficiaries would then be required to pay regular income taxes at full ordinary (non tax-favored) rates on any and all retirement distributions received. Individuals cannot escape this taxation. However, if a charity is named as the beneficiary, the charitable organization receives these valuable funds without anyone paying any tax.

As I previously noted, most of us will not be subject to a federal death or estate tax. But the millions of taxpayers owning tax-deferred (postponed) IRA and retirement accounts might be surprised to learn their beneficiaries will have to pay federal income taxes on *all* distributions they receive from their inheritance.

If you have it in your heart to make a planned gift to occur at death, you should look hard at making your favored charities beneficiaries of your IRA.

Comedian Bob Hope, in all seriousness, was quoted as saying, "If you haven't got any charity in your heart, you have the worst kind of heart trouble."

My friend and a former St. Coletta board member Joe Duffey,

Monica's brother, tutored me about the daunting financial challenges to be overcome by this particular special needs charitable organization. Almost all its clients are benefit recipients, meaning they are on Medicaid. This is true of our Maggie. There exists a gap, or shortfall, between what the government covers and the true total cost of care. This shortfall must be raised by fundraising and other charitable means, or the charity might literally have to shut its door.

Sister Edna Lonergan informed me that St. Ann Center gets reimbursed just $55 per day per individual for quality day care services that cost them $75 to provide. Without the Center's scores of dedicated volunteers, this gap would be even wider. Sister proudly says they turn away no one due to inability to pay. Similar to St. Coletta, St. Ann Center must find a way to cover shortfalls through the generosity of their donors as well as from various fundraisers, such as raffles or other events.

Maggie happily attends Camp Pow Wow for one glorious week each summer. This camp is put on by ARCh, Association for the Rights of Citizens with handicaps. At a membership meeting I attended recently, Jennifer Horth, Executive Director for the past 30 years, laid out the precarious financial condition of this special needs charity that does so much good. As a telling example, the organization's office technology is truly from the last century and desperately needs to be updated.

We recently learned that Milwaukee County's six-week summer day camp Maggie attended for the past decade is cutting back due to financial constraints. As is too often the case, adult campers such as our girl "age out" of certain camps at 18, 22, or in this latest case, 30. We feel the adult special needs campers are too frequently getting squeezed out.

Unexpected expenses put even more of a strain on finances. My friend Diane Miller, who operates the B&B in Newburg, was surprised by a $10,000 bill for a new furnace. As non-government agencies, charities cannot simply raise taxes to cover costs. And as non-profit entities, they cannot easily raise their fees for services. Unlike colleges, they have no alumni network to tap for support. The individuals they care for are most likely to have little or no assets.

Charities such as Misericordia, St. Ann Center, and St. Coletta have three major financial areas they must address and frankly struggle to meet. The first and most pressing involves financing operations. This includes meeting a budget and making payroll, covering benefits and keeping the lights and heat on. By failing to accomplish this, these caregiving institutions would be forced to scale back and turn away clients and even do the unthinkable— close the facility.

The second financial matter involves capital campaigns. These efforts provide the necessary funds for expansions, major remodeling, or new buildings to replace outdated facilities that can serve more clients or offer new programming. Capital campaigns rely heavily on major gifts and foundation support.

The third leg of the financial stool involves the need to create an endowment fund capable of allowing the organization to carry on financially in the face of uncertainty. Sister Rosemary at Misericordia is on record voicing her great fear for her clients' futures: the financial uncertainty surrounding the distressed finances of the State of Illinois. In terms of financial health, the Land of Lincoln is rated fiftieth among states.

Sister Edna asked me to prayerfully consider accepting the challenge to lead the endowment for St. Ann Center. She suggested calling this the "Blessed Assurance Pledge," which happens to be the title of an inspirational Christian hymn familiar to her. This challenge is designed to sustain and assure that the good works and programming that take place at St. Ann's two centers can carry on. Sustainability is the capacity to endure, to hold up. The act of assurance is a statement or other form of indication that inspires confidence, a guarantee or pledge, and freedom from doubt.

Earlier in this chapter I explained about making tax-smart

gifts of appreciated securities (stocks and mutual funds) and the attractiveness of naming a charity as the beneficiary or contingent beneficiary of retirement accounts, such as IRAs. Another simple concept is similar to putting your savings on a disciplined regular plan such as PYF—paying yourself first. You could employ such a plan as this as a variation of charitable giving. It puts your giving on automatic pilot and can be budgeted by you and the charity together.

Say, for example you wish to gift $10,000 to a favorite charity that touches your heart, but this sum is currently beyond your financial reach. Recall John Templeton's principle that giving is the best and most rewarding investment you can make. To accomplish this level of giving, you could challenge yourself with a giving plan that involves spreading your gift over 10 years, thereby donating a total of 120 payments (10 years) of $83.33 ($1,000 a year) to be automatically deducted from your bank account each month.

Here's what my wife, Cathy, and I are doing to help sustain the worthwhile mission of St. Ann Center. Our simple but effective giving plan is to make regular donations over 15 years—180 monthly payments—to the *Blessed Assurance Plan* endowment. Others might prefer a 3-, 5-, or 10-year plan. On top of this, we named St. Ann Center as beneficiary of a portion of my IRA. This planning has built-in flexibility and can readily be altered to accommodate changes in family circumstances, tax laws, or financial markets.

The important thing is that our family is supporting a charity with a mission we believe in. An Arabic Proverb sums it up: "If you have much, give of your wealth, if you have little, give of your heart."

CHAPTER 29

SOME OF MY FAVORITE PEOPLE

Sometimes in my musings I construct an ideal group-home setting for our Maggie and others. One of the first residents of this idealized setting to come to mind is Kim Pawelski. Kim, a special needs individual and a teammate of Maggie in race walking in Special Olympics track, currently resides with her loving parents, Al and Pam, in their Milwaukee area home.

As you may have realized by now, Maggie being Maggie likes to alter people's preferred names. So whenever we refer to Kim, Maggie expands it to Kimberly. Mike becomes Michael, and Theo might be Theodore. A nice volunteer in her art class is Roz, whom Maggie insists on calling the more formal Rosalind. Lately, she has taken to referring to her mom, Cathy, as Cath, or as "your wife."

Kim/Kimberly is a sweet woman, now in her mid-thirties, whom I've had the pleasure of getting to know over the past 15 years. When I told Kim she is one of my favorite people, she blushed, which endeared her to me all the more. Kim has been a productive employee for all those 15 years and a valued volunteer for eight years at a local senior living and care facility.

Kim is an especially caring person. I have seen her put an arm around a friend whose boyfriend was showing interest in another girl at a Special Olympics dance. She is always a role model and a "mother hen" at track practice when our Maggie needs some redirection. At the State summer games, athletes and coaches stay in college dorm rooms, with the women's bathroom facilities separate from the men's on opposite ends of the hallway. Although Maggie is independent in her bathroom duties, she occasionally needs some general assistance, such as finding an open stall, locking and unlocking the door, accessing toilet paper, using the soap dispenser, making sure the water is not too hot, and finding the hand dryers or towels. Kim knows this help is needed and regularly offers to keep an eye on Maggie. As a father I am appreciative of Kim's assistance.

Kim possesses a high degree of emotional intelligence and honesty, is dedicated to her work, and is a determined athlete and all-around fun person. Like her friends the Maloneys, Kim enjoys bowling and taking trips with Able Trek Tours. Based in Reedsburg, Wisconsin, this firm offers exciting travel opportunities, from one-day excursions to multi-day vacations for people with special needs. Such supported trips promote independence, expand horizons, and break down travel barriers for the likes of Kim. This organization uses compassionate volunteers to make it all work.

Every year at the Milwaukee Yacht Club a Halloween party is hosted for Special Olympians and their families. These special athletes get a big charge out of putting on costumes and stepping into character. Our Maggie makes a charming Dorothy from the *Wizard of Oz*. She wears a simple blue and white checked dress and red shoes and carries her toy dog Toto in a wicker basket.

One year a religious sister in full habit approached me. Being a product of Catholic schools in the 1950s and sixties, I instinctively stood taller and respectfully replied, "Good afternoon, Sister."

"Peace be with you," came the reply from this pious sister.

To my complete surprise, I found myself addressing our own Kim Pawelski. In my humble opinion, Kim's holiday persona could not have been more apt. She always displays compassion and caring in the best tradition of nuns. She is surely worthy of being addressed as Sister Kimberly.

I once casually asked Maggie if she knew of any nuns and was pleasantly surprised when she answered yes, from the movie *The Sound of Music*. This epic family musical was an all-time favorite of my aunt Cassie. Starring Julie Andrews in the role of Maria, Cassie found the hills are alive theme from the title song to be very uplifting. For my part, I am partial to another song from the musical, "Climb Every Mountain," which implores us to take every path in reaching for our dreams.

Kim works at the Lutheran Home as a dishwasher and also serves there as a volunteer, helping to care for the elderly residents—which might involve moving residents in their wheelchairs to and from a Bingo game. She especially enjoys volunteer office duties, helping out by delivering mail and making photocopies. In fact, Kim proudly told me that at the home's annual awards dinner she received special recognition for 1,000 hours of volunteer effort. This is just one more reason why I think so highly of Kim—aka Kimberly, and "Sister."

Another of my favorite people—someone I would like living in a community housing setting along with our Maggie—is Theo Tarkowski. Theo and Maggie have known each other for most of their lives, ever since they were four-year-olds attending a special education preschool. They are also long-time teammates in Special Olympics. Theo, who grew into a strapping young man, chuckles remembering Maggie as a young girl being bigger and faster than he was.

Theo is a consummate gentleman and a wonderful person in every respect. At a couple of Special Olympics dances, with merely a hint from me, Theo asked Maggie to be his dance partner, taking her by both hands. They often have a good time dancing together. If not for Theo's attention, Maggie is content to stand alone near the deejay and rock back and forth to the music. Theo warmed my heart by telling me he has always loved my girl. Any father would be pleased by his daughter having a friend such as Theo.

Theo's mom Deb was five months pregnant with her firstborn

when she was in a bad car accident in her hometown of Ironwood, Michigan. Shamefully, she was struck by a 16-year-old repeat drunk driver. Soon after Theo was born, mom noted some abnormalities, especially that her baby's left arm was clutched. Later it was determined that the car accident had caused prenatal brain damage resulting in cerebral palsy.

There is no doubt this young man gets the most out of his ability. In Special Olympics track and basketball, Theo is a spirited competitor, giving it his all. He runs hard, his herky-jerky style and crooked left arm making it appear as if he will tumble and fall at any moment. One memorable year at State, Theo lost a shoe while competing in a relay. Undaunted, he kept running to the finish line. Theo laughs heartily recalling a race official later coming up to him and handing him his lost shoe. Theo's positive attitude is one of his best attributes.

Deb proudly points out that her special son never takes anything in life for granted. He is appreciative whenever he gets to go to State and never disappointed by his race results. At the most recent games Theo didn't immediately qualify but was able to compete as a substitute. He placed sixth in his event, calling it a tough division. No athlete exhibits better sportsmanship or has a better time in all the joy that surrounds State than Theo Tarkowski.

While in high school, he gamely tried out each year for the school basketball team. Although he did not make it, he nevertheless felt a part of the team all through high school as its manager.

When he graduated from Wauwatosa West High School, Theo's triumphant school story was profiled in the local community newspaper. At the ceremony, this popular student was given a standing ovation from his fellow classmates.

Theo was determined to go the community college route after high school. He had a sincere interest in becoming an alcohol and drug abuse counselor. Theo laughs, recounting that this pursuit, despite his best efforts, turned out "not as good as hoped."

He then found employment at the Milwaukee County Zoo, only

a mile from his house. There, among multiple food service duties, he ran a kiosk, solo. Theo was gainfully employed for over six years at the zoo. Unfortunately, he eventually ran into a supervisor who couldn't see his abilities. As a result, Theo reluctantly left this long-time employment position, and I, for one, am no longer as inclined as I used to be to visit the zoo.

Theo is popular with the girls. To hear him tell it he "has a lot of girlfriends." His favorite is Sarah. This nice couple enjoys dates, dining out, and attending movies and plays almost every weekend. Sarah, along with her brother, Dan, are also members of the Tosa Special Olympics track team.

Theo is fortunate—blessed, really—to have a loving brother in his life. Whereas Sarah and Dan have no other siblings, Theo's brother, Phil, only 13 months younger, is in many ways all that his older brother would be were it not for the considerable limits placed on Theo by his disability. Phil is a good athlete, has a college degree, and is happily married. It speaks volumes about Phil that he volunteers his time as the basketball coach for three teams of Special Olympians. He has designs on putting his sociology degree to work in a position that helps those going through life carrying an extra burden, as his big brother does.

With a passion for the game of basketball, Theo auditioned to become one of the superfans for the NBA's Milwaukee Bucks. His enthusiasm and spirit were recognized. He relishes being a part of the official cheering section for all the home games, attending free of charge. I asked Theo who his favorite player is and was not at all surprised when he offered the "Greek Freak," the athletically gifted almost seven-footer from Greece, 22-year-old Giannis Antetokounnmpo. Knowing his style of play, I teased the almost six-footer Theo if he could dunk like his favorite Buck. Theo laughed heartily, saying if he could dunk, he would have made his high school team.

Theo is approaching 30, and like most Special Olympians his future path is cloudy. On the matter of someday living independently of his parents, Deb and Scott, he admits it crosses his mind "now and then." Theo does have an interest in writing his own book and becoming a motivational speaker. With his positive outlook on life we could all benefit from his message.

Joy Piotrowski is another special person and a true joy in every sense of the word. Although this quiet, soft-spoken 42-year-old now leads a happy, productive, family-centered life, turbulence marked her earliest years. Joy arrived in the United States as an extremely sick infant from embattled South Vietnam on April 3, 1975, after the fall of Saigon. The very next day her adoptive parents, Paul and Pat, rushed their precious new child to Children's Hospital of Wisconsin. There Joy was diagnosed with cerebral palsy, a paralysis (hemiplegia) of her right side. This condition would also result in a cognitive disability. The story of her struggle made the front page of the former *Milwaukee Sentinel.*

What impresses me most about Joy, beyond her sweet and gentle demeanor, is her gainful employment of 30 hours a week at Kid Tech Day Care in Milwaukee. Having held this job since she was 24, she is now the most senior employee at this preschool facility. Joy relishes the camaraderie and socialization from her co-workers and the kids in her care.

Joy always brings to my mind the beautiful and inspiring Christmas carol, "Joy to the World." She is one more shining example of someone who has overcome her challenges and lives strong.

Another of my favorite residents for Maggie's ideal neighbor is Amy Kiesner. The more I get to know Amy, the more she and her exceptional life impress me. At 43, she lives a life of power and purpose with Down syndrome. A determined Special Olympics athlete, she is a 23-year veteran McDonald's employee whose job is to keep the restaurant's lobby clean. She is an eternally happy, loving daughter, sister, and friend.

A well-rounded individual, Amy started piano lessons at age 13, and now at 42 continues with twice-a-month lessons. Amy is far from a virtuoso, but she is dedicated, practicing every day.

The highlight of her athletic career was competing in the 2006 Special Olympics National Games held on the campus of Iowa State University. At the Wisconsin State summer games Amy is a perennial participant in race walking. With her short legs and pumping arms, she gets the absolute most out of her ability. She trains diligently year round, putting in three miles at a good pace five times a week on a treadmill in her home. She never slacks off in practice sessions because giving less than her best at all times is not in her makeup.

What most impressed me watching Amy compete in the 2015 long distance 800m and 1500m race walks was how smart, tenacious, disciplined, and strategic she was in each of these grueling, highly competitive events. In both races she found herself in a heated duel among two other equally determined women. In each event the first place leader had the top spot locked up early. Amy fought for second place and the silver medal. First she had to close the gap down the stretch, negotiate passing the competitor in front of her while probing on her left, then take the right side. There, she managed a tight turn around the cone and accelerated the last hundred yards to the finish line—all while holding off the opposing charge. Each race had an exciting finish and was a pleasure to watch. Our athlete could not have executed either race better than she did. Amy definitely earned those two silver medals.

During a lull in the activities, Amy Kiesner, Tim Maloney, and I reminisced about a karaoke contest held at State some years back during a rain delay. Not too many people were in the gym that afternoon, but those of us present remember Tim and Amy holding hands and performing a touching duet of the epic song, *"I Got You Babe."* Even in our retelling years later, I was aware of certain sparks flying between these two good friends.

Amy's devoted mom and dad, Mary Ellen and Dan Kiesner, have generously served the last 11 years as the agency managers for Wauwatosa Special Olympics, which is volunteer driven. The demand on and responsibilities of the agency manager amounts to a heavy load. This general manager role involves coordinating 100 athletes in 7 sports—bowling, basketball, bocce, golf, soccer, swim, and track—with 90 coaches and volunteers in up to 18 district, hometown, regional, and state game competitions. For this married couple, all of that amounts to one full-time job between them. They do it for their love of Amy, but it greatly benefits the rest of us, some 200 parents and guardians. As parents of Maggie, Cathy and I are extremely grateful.

For the past year, many of us involved with Special Olympics in Wisconsin became concerned over a new direction this esteemed organization is taking. Many suspect the cause is a new focus on Unified Partners, an initiative that combines, on the same teams, both intellectually disabled athletes and the nondisabled, referred to as partners. Our concern is that this unified movement, while well intentioned for promoting inclusion, appears to be taking away from the resources available to the adult, non-student special needs athletes. From our perspective, reduced quotas put in place in the last year led to our Maggie missing out on going to the 2015 State games, to her great disappointment. Special Olympics had worked so effectively serving well the individuals for whom it was founded. How disconcerting it is to see cutbacks that decrease opportunities compared with those existing in the recent past. I sincerely hope this organization can return to its roots.

CHAPTER 30

NICE YOUNG PEOPLE COMING OF AGE

Each summer for the past fifteen years, Maggie has eagerly participated in an informal soccer skills program held Monday nights at a nearby school. Its coach is David Dray, a soccer enthusiast and devoted father of Adriana (Ana), his beautiful 25-year-old special needs daughter. His wife, Diane, ably organizes this popular soccer program and important social outlet.

Maggie, who has been on board since the very beginning, has grown very fond of Coach Dave, good man that he is, and he of her. She likes to put on her soccer jersey and socks and strap on her shin guards. She collects her soccer ball, grabs her water bottle, and off we go. She particularly anticipates the snack treat at the end of each weekly session. Although the season-ending party has grown in popularity and is a big hit for the entire family, Soccer Monday has evolved into quite a social interaction of its own. We parents take our lawn chairs and watch from the sidelines as our children merrily kick the ball around, eventually splitting into our own conversation groups to discuss the weather, our families, and the fortunes or misfortunes of the Brewers, Milwaukee's baseball team. Inevitably, talk turns to our special loved ones, who at that moment are working up a sweat on the adjoining playing field.

Many of this crop of soccer players are five to ten years younger than our Maggie, a veteran who still owns—and insists on wearing—her original soccer jersey, vintage circa 2000. I have come to know better a new generation of special individuals in this happy social setting and to engage with their wonderful and committed parents.

This is how I came to know Jacob (Jake) Voss, with whom I also interacted at the State summer games where he was a team-mate of Maggie on the track team. He especially loves being part of the basketball team, but also competes in bowling as well as in track. His dedicated mother, Tricia, says she now wishes her youngest son had joined Special Olympics at a younger age than 18. Athletes become eligible at the age of eight.

What really intrigues me about Jacob is to observe him dutifully serving as an usher during church services at our St. Jude parish. A pious young man of 23, he has expressed a sincere interest in entering the priesthood. This idea went so far as having a discussion about it with the pastor. From this exchange, Jacob came to grips with the reality that becoming a priest requires years of rigorous academic study beyond his reach. That being said, there must nevertheless be a place in the Church for Jacob to practice and grow his faith, and be an active part of the church community.

Maggie's spiritual dimension, especially as she has grown older, misses the mark and is not truly meaningful. Therefore we were enthused to have discovered SPRED, which stands for special religious development. SPRED is expressly designed to meet the spiritual needs of individuals living with developmental disabilities.

Sam Dess, age 20, is a core member of the Monday night soccer group and represents the wave of nice young people now coming of age. Through the years I have observed how this cute little guy always said hello to Maggie at the back of church, or wherever else we ran into him. Now grown into a man, Sam has a deep voice, facial hair and muscles. Sam thrives in the SPRED community and his picture even appears on its promotional material. Cathy, her maternal antenna always tuned to finding opportunities for our girl, became aware of SPRED through Sam's mom, Mary, and social media postings. This rapidly expanding religious program was started in Chicago some 40 years ago by Father James McCarthy—no relation as far as I know. Its training and its materials are specially designed to appeal to children as well as teens and adults. Its innovative program encompasses a welcoming space, bonds of friendship, proclamation, and sacramental life. As parents, we are impressed by the warmth surrounding the SPRED community and feel blessed this door is opening for our young woman. For her part, Maggie is enthusiastic and likes to refer to it as spread cheese.

Amy Keisner's hearing impairment led to her learning sign language at an early age. This faith-filled woman now employs this talent as a ministry, signing music at church services. Particularly moving is her signing of the solemn Christian hymn "Here I Am Lord." Another highlight in her remarkable life was signing in front of an audience of 5,000 attending a Lutheran Women convention in San Antonio.

Getting back to Jacob's story, he is high functioning and quite capable despite his limitations. Jake was enrolled in Early Childhood Development at the age of three, having been identified as developmentally delayed. When he was five he experienced a near drowning incident that could well have set him further back. It definitely didn't help.

At age 22 Jacob "aged out" of the high school's special needs educational program. In Wisconsin, students such as Jacob, Ana, and Maggie have their high school extended until they reach age 22. This extension is designed to help students with learning disabilities transition to the next phase of their lives and build independence. Ideally, it includes preparation for some type of employment and related vocational training. As too often is the case for the disabled, this major life transition from school into gainful adult employment and added independence stumbles right at the gate.

A column in *The Wall Street Journal* captured the frustration, sense of loss, and anxiety that frequently accompanies the estimated 100,000 families of intellectually disabled loved ones who, after "graduating" from high school are "thrown into the unknown." Titled "The Graduates: What Happens After Young Disabled Adults Leave School," the story starts by chronicling the not uncommon dilemma of then 21-year-old Kirk from Illinois. According to his mom, Sue, "He is part of a generation that by law got an incredible start educationally, from specialized preschool to innovative mainstreaming programming." But, she laments, "He has been educated to the best of his ability so that he can sit on the couch in the basement for the next 70 years."

What parents of special education grads such as the thousands of Jacobs and Kirks discover is reality: job opportunities and meaningful day programs or services are limited for young adults with cognitive disabilities. This stands in stark contrast to the supportive environment they experienced in high school.

For the past three summers Jacob Voss has done landscaping work associated with a social agency, but the work is seasonal and part-time. Both Jake and his parents want him to land something more long term with a better and more interesting fit that uses his capabilities. In this quest, the Voss family has experienced considerable frustration with the Department of Vocational Rehabilitation, and with a certain bureaucrat in particular.

As an example, Jake was chided for not wearing a white dress shirt and tie to an interview—for landscape maintenance! To top this, he was also scolded for arriving to work half an hour *early*. Turns out his limited bus options meant he had to be early in order to arrive on time. These and other galling episodes convinced his very reasonable parents they needed to go in another direction for their son. All who take the time to know Jacob agree that he possesses a strong work ethic and is honest, dependable, and diligent. To me that sounds like an ideal employee. The plan now is to not give up but rather continue searching for the right job for their highly capable son. He is ready.

As a young man coming of age, Jacob has expressed an interest in stepping up his game socially and ideally finding a girlfriend. He has even taken to growing a moustache to signify his maturity. Although shy, he does show the courage to mingle by attending some of the social outlets available, such as dances or dinner and a movie. It would be icing on the cake if a nice young woman were to come into his life.

Mary Walz-Chojnacki, W.C. for short, is yet another strong mother of a special needs child. Sophia is high functioning and independent, with a whole lot going for her. I am impressed by Sophia's taking yoga classes alongside Cathy and W.C. She also regularly works out with a personal trainer at our health club. It seems to me that Sophia, though not quite there yet, is so close to realizing her full potential. As Mary tells us, her 27-year-old daughter has made strides in her maturity. Sophia would love to find a boyfriend, and to catch a break on the employment front. Somehow, some way, she needs to get over a couple of challenging hurdles. Mary shared with me her frustration that job placements for Sophia have been the result of their family's own personal network, not an agency's.

Cydney "Cyd" Ehlenbach is another charming young woman from a close and academically accomplished family who aged out of the public school system last year. I get a kick out of Cydney's preference for wearing shocking pink stockings with her soccer shorts. I am old enough to be her grandfather, yet she alternates between calling me Johnny and the more formal Mr. McCarthy.

Her loving mom, Jayne, feels distressed that since graduation her special daughter has suddenly fallen into a void. While in school Cyd followed a regular routine, enjoyed socializing, and had the support of a job and life skills coach. Her situation now seems more of a step backward than forward. Mom expressed the unfilled expectation that between her and her husband Chris—both intelligent and college educated—they should be able to find a way to secure suitable employment for their lovable special needs daughter. It is difficult for them to accept how much trouble they are experiencing with this transition.

Some years back, three families who were faced with the same dead ends after their special needs young adults got out of school took matters into their own hands. Pooling their resources, these proactive parents bought a struggling greenhouse business so their aged-out loved ones had a place to work and interact. Today, We Grow Dreams located in West Chicago, Illinois, employs and trains some 50 intellectually disabled people at its five-acre wholesale and retail greenhouse and garden center. This nonprofit aims to create a supportive environment with positive affirmations and specialized training. Their tagline, Planting Seeds of Opportunity, says it all.

In this age of countless social media communities two special needs moms, Jayne Ehlenbach and Mary Dess, each liked "A Very Special Needs Resource" on Facebook. From the same site, I found the following bedrock truths that resonate with so many of us who are blessed with special needs offspring. The first quote especially hits home:

"Special needs parents know they only have three choices: Give up, give in or give it all they've got."

The backdrop to many life stories is summed up by a second resolute statement:

"My child with special needs is my everything. I will give anything and stop at nothing."

Sarah Roegner is another young adult member of the Wauwatosa Special Olympians. Her dad, Mark, proudly tells me Sarah is a happy and joyful person. Her exuberance is always on full display at our community's Fourth of July parade. While marching with her Special Olympics teammates, she will break off to give spirited high fives to the little kids sitting on the curb along the parade route. A talented swimmer, Sarah also has a job as a bagger at our local grocery store. As I suspect others do, I make it a point to go through her checkout line, even if that means a longer wait. She knows me as Maggie's dad. The last time I saw Sarah at the store I casually asked her how she was doing.

"My birthday is coming up," she gushed.

"That's great. When is it?"

"November!"

I had to chuckle because the current date was August 15. She had another three months to go.

Sarah is not the only Special Olympian who gets excited about a birthday. These individuals are uniformly eager to mark their special days and celebrate life and living. It has been said, "A birthday is a voyage on the sea we call life."

This merry band of a half dozen Olympians—Jake, Ana, Sam, Cyd, Sophia, and Sarah—are blessed with wonderful moms and dads. Each of these 20-something coming-of-age happy warriors is looking to take the next step in life's journey. I am rooting for them.

CHAPTER 31

ANGELS AMONG US

"Ever felt an angel's breath in the gentle breeze? A teardrop
in the fallen rain? Hear a whisper amongst the rustle of
leaves? Or been kissed by a lone snowflake? Nature is an
angel's favorite hiding place."

Terri Guillemets

A friendship photo of our then 27-year-old child/woman
Maggie and 87-year-young Margaret Ball says a whole
lot. They are sitting together as natural as can be on a bed
at the Milwaukee Catholic Home. Although vastly different in age,
temperament, capabilities, and life experiences, it is evident that
Maggie shares a special bond with her new old friend Margaret.

Margaret sent a poignant thank you note to Maggie along
with the photo. While our cognitively disabled daughter is not
capable of reading the note herself, she seems to grasp its essential
message:

Dear Maggie,

What a wonderful young lady you are.

Thank you so much for being so kind to me.

How I love to have you visit me. It was especially nice to
have you come and visit me when I was recuperating from
surgery in the Milwaukee Catholic Home Rehab Center. That
really brightened my day. It was so kind of you to come by.

Thank you for visiting me yesterday and for the gift you gave me of the beautiful ceramic angel. How did you know how much I love angels? I know that we have our own special angels watching over us. I will always think of you when I look at this beautiful angel you gave me.

I think you are one of God's special angels. You are so kind, generous and full of God's love.

Thank you again, Maggie. I am looking forward to seeing you again soon.

Love,
Margaret

As I've repeatedly said, I have come to believe that angels come into Maggie's life on a regular basis. Margaret clearly believes in angels, as does Oprah. George Bernard Shaw pointed out that "In heaven an angel is nobody in particular."

Maggie's angels play a large role in her life, seemingly on an as-needed basis. Because of her age, we no longer refer to Maggie's caregivers as babysitters, but more appropriately as her companions. Leah, Rachel, Christina, Danie, and Karina are all flesh-and-blood angels who serve as individual companions to enrich Maggie's life and to offer Cathy—and me to a lesser extent—a welcome break and needed respite. All of these fine young women enjoy full and busy lives, whereas our Maggie seems frozen in place.

Danie O'Neill graduated from college this spring, and Christina Best, "the best girl" as referred to by Maggie, is engaged to be married. Karina will graduate next semester. She is eyeing graduate school in art therapy and maybe working at a psychiatric facility, perhaps with alcohol and drug patients. Leah, who was Maggie's summer camp counselor, has changed careers and is now enrolled in nursing school.

Rachel was married this summer. Cathy and Maggie attended a wedding shower for her, and we as a family were honored to be among guests invited to the wedding. We met Rachel when she was a high school student. Her mom, Linda Klann, conducted cooking classes that Maggie attended as a part of programming put on by Easter Seals. Maggie developed a special bond with Linda—and Cathy, a friendship. Once, Maggie overheard Cathy mentioning Linda's name. Our girl piped in, inquiring whether she was talking about "My Linda."

Rachel is now a special needs educator in the local high school. While in school herself, Rachel frequently helped us out, so Cathy and I could get out of the house. One time when we were discussing possible arrangements, Maggie let her preference be known: "I vote for Rachel."

I understand from the mother of a special needs 25-year-old it is much more difficult to find respite care for her son at his age. Virtually no young males are available. So this mom has been forced to provide almost all of her son's care herself.

Sister Edna is adamant that all caregivers need regular respite to be at their best. Otherwise, she says from personal experience, one is likely to "be pulling their hair out." We are extremely fortunate to have these young women come into Maggie's life, finding them as camp counselors, from school programs, and as student interns in art classes.

Eric Honeycutt wisely observed: "The wings of angels are often found on the backs of the least likely people."

It should come as no surprise that Cathy is the one who discovered, recruited, and continually administers these highly valued companions who take turns caring for our special girl. Maggie relishes spending quality one-on-one time with each of these patient caregivers, and she truly adores each of her companions. When any of them leaves for the day she tells them sweetly "I love you," and each responds the same. This exchange is always touching to witness.

A photo of our Maggie and the late angel Anna was taken in 2009 at Christmastime at Anna's house. I remember at the time asking Maggie if her severely disabled, wheelchair-dependent friend Anna was able to speak. Instead of answering in the negative, Maggie replied that Anna smiles. "And," she added, "she smiles at me."

Sadly, Anna died at age 26 from complications of a bowel obstruction. Maggie, accompanied by Cathy and me, attended the memorial service for her young friend, who departed this world much too soon.

A certain angel in Maggie's life these past 15 years has been Anna's devoted mother, Jean, who was an aide in our daughter's high school Special Education Program. I distinctly remember taking Maggie to the home of Anna and Jean for an overnight stay and noticing welcoming yard signs announcing that angels resided there. Jean routinely referred to her precious adopted Anna as an angel, as did our Maggie. It is highly likely Anna never would have lived as long as she did without the abundant love and quality care provided by her mother.

Another vivid memory I have is of Maggie, Cathy, and me approaching a grieving Jean at the funeral parlor. The room was adorned with Anna's many stuffed animals and pictures celebrating her important but too short life. Winnie the Pooh was her favorite character, and this fitting Pooh quote set the scene: "If there ever comes a day when we can't be together, keep me in your heart, I'll stay there forever."

On the table next to Jean, who was dressed in all black for mourning, was a small white ceramic angel that had stood sentry on the nightstand in Anna's bedroom. As we hugged Jean and offered our sympathies as best we could, Jean picked up Anna's angel and handed it to to Maggie, telling her she wanted her to have this remembrance. I don't have to tell you how deeply this beautiful gesture affected us.

Anna's angel now stands guard next to Maggie's bed, very close to where our girl rests her head on her pillow. On occasion, I point it out and Maggie always informs me it belonged to Anna. She also adds that Anna now rests peacefully in heaven.

Reflect on this from an unknown source. "While we are

sleeping, angels have conversations with our souls."

As a natural part of the life continuum, Maggie has experienced death. This has occurred on three sad occasions in the past few years. Coach Dave Dziedzic, age 55, the father of Erin, a Down syndrome daughter in her 20s, died suddenly while he was at work. Maggie was sitting in her familiar spot curled up on the couch in our family room on a Friday evening when Cathy received the phone call informing us of Dave's death. As Cathy handed the phone to me, Maggie, her antennae up, somehow surmised that her Coach was gone. Whenever she is sad her bottom lip protrudes.

Dave was Maggie's Special Olympics basketball skills coach. The athletes work at weekly practices in season to improve their dribbling, passing, shooting skills, and overall conditioning, should they go on to compete in regular basketball games. Maggie struggles mightily with dribbling, but is known for sinking a fair number of shots. Her shooting style is unorthodox, to say the least. She can get the ball up to the rim only by shooting underhand. Adding to the degree of difficulty of her shot, she doesn't even look at the basket. This is quite a feat for her, and when she manages to make a basket I get a huge rush. Maggie's triumphs are always accompanied by high fives all around.

At the start of each basketball skills practice, Coach Dave in his booming voice had instructed the athletes under his charge to put the balls down and assemble in a circle around him at half court. He then led them in a boisterous clapping session that ended in total silence and rapt attention. Maggie, having been charged up, inevitably continued talking. Dave would have to quiet her down with a stern, "Maggie!" This never failed to get her attention. She always replied contritely, "Sorry coach," thereby eliciting a big smile from Dave. Coach Dave could not hide that Maggie was one of his favorites. Basketball skills will never be the same without the giant presence of Coach Dave.

Earlier in chapter 7, I wrote a piece sharing the inspirational story of Maggie's friend and teammate Diane Schuller, who had amazingly won a gold medal at the Special Olympics State games. What always set Diane apart from others was her beautiful smile and resolute determination. Therefore, all of us found it so hard to reconcile her loveliness with the ugliness of a previous cancer that returned with a vengeance to claim her life.

I was at work in my office when Diane's grieving mother, Mary, called our house and told Cathy of this tragic ending of a young life. Cathy phoned me with the dread news. I will admit this loss hit me really hard. Diane was truly special. My first thought was how to tell Maggie. Cathy assured me that Maggie already knew. Once again she had overheard one side of a phone conversation from another room and somehow knew what was up. "Is she dead?" Maggie inquired in a somber tone, and a choked-up Cathy nodded yes.

Lest we forget Diane and her precious life, I searched for her obituary from 2011.

Diane Lynn "Dibbie" Schuller became an angel on 9/28/11 at age 23. Further survived by her loving K-9 companions Brittney and Godfrey, other relatives and friends. She was preceded in death by her beloved cat Mysty.

For someone who doesn't usually get her age right or the correct day of the week when asked, Maggie does comprehend the element of death. In discussing Diane, Maggie knows she is no longer alive and was placed in a coffin box. To her, Diane is now far up in the clouds in heaven (Maggie will look skyward) next to her deceased grandfathers. However, they were old and sick, but Diane was only sick. Maggie knows she will never see her friend again, and that makes her sad.

Cheryl Hetzel, an older Special Olympian, was one of the many angels that Maggie and I came to know. We often drove Cheryl to practices, events, and athletic competitions. Sadly, Cheryl lost her battle with brain cancer in 2015 at the age of 65. Now, whenever we drive past her house, Maggie reminds me that is where Cheryl lived, but now she is dead. Maggie told me her friend is now in heaven with Anna and the other angels.

Like Diane, Cheryl loved animals. She was an active Wisconsin Humane Society volunteer and helped care for cats and dogs at the shelter. A music fan like Maggie, she was especially fond of the Beatles. Cheryl was also well known for the collection of souvenir pins that adorned her ever-present Special Olympic baseball cap.

Cheryl lived with her younger sister, Janan, also a Special Olympian. Janan confided to me that Cheryl struggled with depression. This is not an uncommon phenomenon. Many older Special Olympians are burdened with anxiety and depression, but Cheryl fought against it with her many activities and interests. Cheryl had a variety of friends. For instance, despite their age difference, Cheryl and Diane Schuller became close friends. I have a vivid mental picture of Cheryl sitting somberly in the front row as a mourner at Diane's memorial service. At Cheryl's own service, it was apparent from the display of photos and the many teammates, coaches, and parents in attendance that the Special Olympics family was the major force in her life.

Standing tall at just four feet nine inches, Cheryl was only a fair athlete, but she gave it her all. Lacking confidence, she always sought assurances from us coaches, asking repeatedly, "I did good, didn't I?" Yes, Cheryl. You inspired others by living a fulfilling and active life, and you were a friend to many. You will be missed. You did good.

CHAPTER 32

A SPECIAL KIND OF LOVE STORY

"Angels are never too distant to hear you."
Author Unknown

Aone-of-a-kind individual is John "Chin" Klein, so nick-named owing to his square-jawed look and rock-like rugby player demeanor. A veteran special education teacher, he works with emotionally and behaviorally challenged high school students. His only sibling, his older sister, Marie, is intellectually disabled.

Although I have come across scores of people whose brother or sister lives with cognitive disabilities, and I know and respect many special education teachers, what sets John apart is something exceedingly rare. Both of his loving parents, Rudy and Geraldine (Gerry) Klein, are cognitively disabled. They are unable to read, write, or drive. As John told me over lunch one day, "I don't know anyone like me. I've never heard of anyone like me."

Few would ever expect his mentally challenged parents to marry, much less live independently and have and nurture two children, Marie and John. Life wasn't easy for the four members of the unlikely Klein family, which nevertheless survived in a tough Milwaukee neighborhood.

Yet, young Johnny, as he is still called today by his family, never felt deprived. In fact he feels genuinely blessed to have grown up in such a loving home with amazing parents. Dad Rudy worked at a minimum wage job as a nursing home orderly to provide as best he could for his young family. Gerry worked as a stay-at-home mom to care for Marie and Johnny, born less than a year apart.

Rudy met the love of his life while both were taking adult remedial reading classes at a local community college. It was love at first sight for Rudy, 15 years Gerry's senior. "I met her and I loved her, that's what," he matter-of-factly explains.

They were married in 1973, and baby Marie arrived rather unexpectedly in 1974. According to Geraldine, "I fooled them all. Nobody told me I could get pregnant." The following year they welcomed another miracle, their son John.

It wasn't until Johnny was about 7 or 8 years old that this extraordinarily bright and confident youngster came to realize his family life wasn't the norm. "It's hard to put into words. I think growing up you don't recognize your family is different because it's family, and that is all you know."

He grew up fast because he took on major responsibilities for his special needs family, such as reading the mail to his mom and dad. Remarkably, he was managing the household finances before he became a teenager. "Even though I had extra responsibilities, I did not see it as an extra burden," this dutiful son told me.

While contemplating the amazing story of the Klein family, I happened to view again the cult classic film *Forrest Gump,* which our family enjoyed on one of many camp weekends sponsored by the Wisconsin Lions. I was struck by certain similarities.

Forrest Gump, played by Tom Hanks, is the fictional lead character, a simple, naive, intellectually challenged only child of a devoted single mother, Mama, played by Sally Fields. The setting is Alabama in the turbulent 1960s and seventies, and a dynamite soundtrack sets the mood. Forrest's true love and best friend is Jenny, the beautiful but deeply troubled victim of abuse he has known since childhood.

Twice in the plot, local bullies chase after Forrest. On both occasions Forrest is with Jenny, who excitedly encourages her outmatched and in-danger friend to escape their clutches, screaming "Run, Forrest, run!" In the first of the two episodes, three young boys on bicycles come after Forrest, taunting him as "dummy." His heavy metal leg braces fall off—literally but also symbolically—and these get discarded as he gains speed and eludes his tormentors.

When he grows into a young man, the bullies again come after him in a pickup truck, yelling "Hey, stupid!" This time his elusive speed earns him the notice of the famed Alabama football coach. As Forrest tells it, "I could run like the wind blows."

To this day, those who attended family camp that rainy weekend distinctly remember viewing *Forrest Gump.* In the darkness of the makeshift theater, our girl Maggie was so moved she shouted out at the top of her lungs, "Run, Forrest, run!"

As Forrest and Jenny mature into young adults they drift apart. When they do meet again, Forrest expresses his love for her. Unable to accept his sincere proclamation of affection, Jenny hurts him, by saying, "You don't know what love is."

Later, a determined Forrest asks Jenny to marry him. Predictably, she refuses his heartfelt proposal, saying, "You don't want to marry me."

In a poignant scene, the slow-witted Forrest replies, "I'm not a smart man, but I know what love is."

Despite his intellectual shortcomings, Forrest Gump indeed knows how to love. We see his love tenderly shown to his mama and troubled lifelong friend Jenny. We see his love for his fallen Vietnam War buddy Bubba, and the embittered double-amputee Lieutenant Dan. At the end of the movie, we also view him as a loving solo parent to his own son, Forrest Jr. The last line in this tender scene has Forrest telling little Forrest, as he puts the boy on the school bus, "I want to tell you that I love you."

Our girl Maggie clearly knows how to love and to be loved,

as does the Klein quartet of Rudy, Gerry, John, and Marie, as does the vast community of special needs individuals I have had the privilege of getting to know. Love is the glue that held the Klein family together. It allowed each of them to survive intact and also to succeed as a unit. As John, with deep emotion, has shared with me, "I was loved."

Unconditional love and loving is what those with cognitive disabilities do best. They excel at loving. Every conversation John has with a family member ends with the phrase, "I love you."

The Klein family is a special kind of love story. It is moving to hear John, gifted and talented yet humble, describe his amazing mom and dad: "They don't know how to write a check. They don't know how to read. But my parents know how to love somebody. And, as long as you feel loved, anything is possible."

CHAPTER 33

LEARN TO LOVE THEM ALL
THE MORE

"No I never saw an angel, but it is irrelevant whether I saw one or not. I feel their presence around me."

Paul Coelho

Another film I enjoyed and would recommend is the 2003 movie *Radio,* starring two of my favorite actors, Cuba Gooding and Ed Harris. Gooding plays the lead character, James Robert Kennedy, born in Anderson, South Carolina, in 1946. Living with an intellectual disability, the young man we meet at 23 is known throughout town as "Radio" because he is always seen with a big box transistor radio wherever he goes.

Based on a 1996 piece in *Sports Illustrated,* the storyline of "Somebody to Lean On" has Harold Jones, the local high school football coach, played by Ed Harris, befriending and taking a personal interest in Radio after he discovers him being bullied by some of his players. Coach Jones slowly builds Radio's trust, visits his home, and meets his widowed mother. As the relationships develop, Radio assists Coach Jones with the football team. Coach even gets the young man enrolled in high school. Remarkably, with effort and attention, Radio learns to read on a basic level.

However, all the warmth and attention focused on Radio does not please everyone in this small southern town—most notably

Johnny, the gifted star athlete, and his overbearing father.

Coach Jones confides to his only child, a cheerleader daughter, that he cares so much about Radio because of an incident from his own childhood. Early one morning, as a young teenager delivering newspapers in a remote wooded area, he happened across a mentally disabled young boy locked up and kept hidden by his family under the porch of an isolated house. This discovery has stayed with him all these years, and he feels remorse over doing nothing to help that criminally neglected boy. He was determined to help Radio no matter the pushback from a vocal but influential minority in town. Ultimately, Coach Jones takes a moral stand and resigns as football coach.

This sentimental but true story concludes with Radio teaching the townspeople, students, and the school a positive lesson on inclusion and the triumph of ability over disability. This story is one I have seen repeated in real life by untold special needs heroes.

In 2015 at age 65, James Robert Kennedy, aka Radio, continues at T.L. Hanna High School helping to coach and inspire the football and basketball teams. He is well known for his trademark inquiry of students, "We gonna win tonight?" This favorite son and overall goodwill ambassador for the school and the town additionally helps patrol the cafeteria, effectively keeping students in line. And this original 65-year-old Radio is a regular participant in Special Olympic track meets, running the 100-meter dash, and is also a top competitor with a strong arm in the softball throw.

I consider my friend Bob Kult a mentor of sorts—someone who has experienced a lot of life and from whom I can learn and discuss life lessons. I have gotten to know this good family man, husband of Laurel for 50 years, father of five, and grandfather "Bapa" of 11. This semi-retired CPA and people-person has worked with our firm for the past 15 years preparing tax returns for clients during tax season. Over this span, I witnessed Bob survive a serious cancer and mourn the passing of his own beloved parents, younger brother, and a cherished aunt. What is by far the toughest chapter in his otherwise blessed life was the death of his first grandchild. Five-year-old Spencer, despite a heart transplant, lost out to a congenital heart condition. Bob keeps Spencer's memory alive, knowing how truly precious a young life is.

Bob has known our Maggie for half her life and always makes a point of reaching out to her. Like many others who have regular interactions with our girl, he gets a kick out of her special brand of humor. He has also gotten to know the remarkable Maloney family and feels genuine empathy for people with special needs and disabilities, as well as for their parents.

I have always enjoyed my talks with Bob. Aware of and supportive of my work on this book, he discussed the movie *Radio* with me. Bob recounted a story seared into his memory from his youth that shows how much we as a society have evolved for the better on certain social issues.

Bob Kult grew up in West Allis, Wisconsin, a working-class manufacturing community just west of Milwaukee. As a fresh-faced boy of 11, in the years immediately following World War II, he was best friends with Greg, who lived two doors away. They spent much of their boyhoods together, playing ball and roaming the neighborhood. His buddy Greg was a frequent visitor to the busy Kult family home, where Bob was the second of seven children.

One memorable day, Bob was briefly in Greg's house, having been told by his friend to wait in the kitchen while he retrieved something from his room. While Bob waited alone, a young girl appeared in the hallway crying and making a commotion. Bob was surprised. Greg had never mentioned a sister. Bob hadn't ever heard her name spoken. She was never seen outside, attended school, or went to church. Without any tangible identity and seeming hidden away in his friend's house only 25 yards from his own, Bob looked at this young mystery girl as if she didn't exist.

Greg's mother quickly appeared, ushered the girl away, and was visibly upset with her son, perhaps for allowing his friend into their home to discover the family secret. As a fifth grader, Bob had no first-hand knowledge of Down syndrome, but he was somehow able to recognize this disabled child by her distinguishing features. This fleeting encounter was one he never forgot.

Not until 1958 did scientists learn that Down syndrome was a genetic abnormality caused by an extra chromosome. Mothers whose children were identified in those days as mongoloid felt great shame over having "caused" this in some way during their pregnancy. My Cathy shared with me her own fears as a first-time mother that she was somehow responsible for Maggie's condition. Was it by something she did or didn't do, or was it by exposure to something during pregnancy? Such feelings often led to the secrecy evidenced by Bob's neighbor. Many mentally disabled children were hidden away in locked attics, in basements, or—as Coach Jones had discovered—under a porch. As Bob and I talked about this significant episode occurring in his life 60 years earlier, it seemed to him as fresh as yesterday. He told me that in those days he also wouldn't have had close contact with a person of color, such as Radio. And when a young unmarried woman became pregnant she would have been sent away and the birth hushed up. Neither would someone like Maggie's art teacher, Kurt, a wonderful human being with a big heart, have been able to be open about his sexual identity and partnership with Ben, another fine human being.

A turning point for disabled children occurred in the 1960s when Vice President Hubert Humphrey, TV cameras rolling in the White House, proudly introduced the nation to his granddaughter with Down syndrome. Vicky Solomonson had been born to Humphrey's daughter Nancy, on election night 1960, a Senate race in which Humphrey had been victorious—which is how this beloved grandchild came to be named Victoria.

When Vicky was 10 years old, grandmother Muriel Humphrey wrote a piece that appeared in the *Chicago Tribune* provocatively headlined, "Our Vicky is Retarded."

The lead-in to this guest editorial shows how much has changed since it was written some 45 years ago. For one, we no longer use the "R" word, because "retarded"—then the slang "retard"—became coopted as derogatory, derisive, slanderous. It also spoke of one being a *victim* of what was then popularly labeled mongolism, based on the single feature of slanted eyes, similar to that seen among Asian populations. Actor and musician Chris Burke, in a book published 20 years later, champions that he lives a happy life with "Up" syndrome, adding that Down syndrome is not a disease and he doesn't suffer from it.

Writing about her granddaughter, Muriel Humphrey says, "Our family has always looked upon Vicky as a cherished member, but one with a special handicap." She relates how crushing it was for her to take this beautiful child out in public and witness the stares.

Those reactions are what prompted Muriel to editorialize and come to the defense of sweet Vicky. "I felt then, as I do now, that every time a new person met Vicky and got to know her, a tiny but important step would be taken toward breaking down the age-old barriers of fear, superstition and prejudice against mongoloid children. Eventually, I look for the day when enlightenment and understanding will become widespread enough for other retarded persons and their families to obtain their rightful share of life's joys and fulfillment."

Vicky Solomonson died in 2010 at age 49 from early onset Alzheimer's disease. She was symbolic of those courageous special needs families who clearly advanced the rights of the disabled. Vicky's sister, Jill Gillis, lovingly noted, "Her life has been full. We truly felt she was our sunshine."

While reading an interview in a weekend edition of *The Wall Street Journal,* I discovered a most remarkable human being and untiring advocate for people with intellectual disabilities. Born in 1928, Jean Vanier is a philosopher, Catholic theologian and humanitarian.

Raised in Canada, Vanier's career started in the British Navy. He ultimately abandoned the military to answer the call of the gospel and follow Jesus. While earning a doctorate in ethics from the Catholic Institute of Paris in 1962, Vanier developed a friendship with a Dominican priest, Father Thomas Philippe. Their close association changed Vanier's life.

At the time, Father Thomas was serving as chaplain at an institution for the severely mentally retarded outside Paris. While visiting this institution Vanier recalled, "I discovered this world." He witnessed violence and abuse among the 80 men living in facilities intended to house 40. Visiting another site, he was aghast to see a teenager chained in a garage. As Vanier remarked in this interview, "People locked up in institutions. Parents feeling ashamed, pained."

Vanier optimistically finds hope about the place of people with special needs in today's world. "There's a desire to respect people with disabilities, which reflects progress after centuries of persecution." He puts this progress in context, saying, "the idea was that disability was a punishment from God. And now we are saying that people with disabilities are a way to God." He refers to the disabled as "people of the heart." This progress is encouraging. I recall in my own childhood those with the physical features of Down syndrome were often referred to, shamefully, as mongoloid idiots.

Having been made aware of the plight of thousands of people institutionalized with developmental disabilities, Vanier felt called by faith to make it his mission to serve this isolated and neglected population. In 1964, Vanier purchased a small house in Trosly-Breviol, France, and invited two mentally disabled adult men, whom society had shunned and institutionalized, to live as friends with him in community.

From this simple beginning of one man's courage and vision, L'Arche, or the Ark, was founded. In the ensuing 52 years the seeds planted in this social movement have grown to 140 member communities in 36 countries. Some 5,000 disabled men and women find a true home in these communities and are encouraged to develop their unique gifts to the fullest. Currently, 18 residential communities in the United States are aligned with the International Federation of L'Arche. The two disabled men Vanier took into his home, Raphael Simi and Philippe Seux, are now identified, along with Jean Vanier, as co-founders of L'Arche. This is in keeping with its philosophy of treating the disadvantaged as equals and peers. Speaking of his co-founders, Vanier noted that Raphael spoke only a few words, whereas Philippe was known to talk too much.

In his interview, philosopher Vanier said, "The great thing about people with intellectual disabilities is that they're not people who discuss philosophy . . . what they want is fun and laughter, to do things together and fool around, and laughter is at the heart of community."

For his lifetime of compassionate work surrounding L'Arche, Vanier was at age 87 awarded the 2015 Templeton Prize. This award was in recognition of his advocacy for people with disabilities and his contribution to a broader exploration of helping the weak and vulnerable. Receiving this prestigious 1.7 million dollar award, Vanier said, "This prize honors primarily the most vulnerable among us, often marginalized in our societies." It is to them he attributes his advocacy. It is these people who revealed to him that any person who has been previously rejected, when welcomed, becomes a source of dialogue, of healing, of unity, and of peace for our societies and our religions.

The previously mentioned *Wall Street Journal* interview is titled "The Gift of Living with the Not Gifted." Vanier and his organization remind us that we have much to learn from the intellectually disabled. They are important, they are extraordinary teachers, and they have a message to give all of humanity about what it means to be accepted and valued. Vanier believes "what people with disabilities want is to relate. They care about the relationship. So they have a healing power, a healing power of love."

In a letter he penned on a life shared with those who are most fragile, Vanier admits it is rewarding, but often not easy. "These links that bind me to each person have opened my heart, giving me strength in love that makes patience and the other demands easier and lighter. But, that does not preclude occasional struggles, those moments of tiredness or discouragement, which are more or less bearable. It is the same for us all. For me, life with those who are often seen as the lowest of the low is leading me to rise up with a joy that comes from God."

Owing perhaps to our Irish ancestry, Maggie can readily identify Irish folk music. As a family, we McCarthy's make it a point to attend Milwaukee's annual Irish Fest held each August on the lakefront, billed as the world's largest Irish music festival. It was in the early years of this festival that I first became acquainted with Dublin-born balladeer Paddy Reilly.

When Cathy and I celebrated our 15th wedding anniversary in Ireland, I picked up the CD *The Fields of Athenry* by Paddy Reilly, because I so liked his rendition of the title song. Through the years, over many hours of listening to this CD, I became acquainted with and curious about a more obscure cut, "Scorn Not His Simplicity."

This song spoke to me as a father of a special needs child. Someone else anonymously posted a comment online in reference to how this emotional song also spoke to her, observed, "Music is amazing in its ability to hold our attention and make us pause and consider."

Investigating its roots, I discovered this song was written by Northern Ireland musician and songwriter Phil Coulter. It all made sense to me to learn that Coulter's first son was born with Down syndrome. He penned this very personal song several months after the birth of his son in an attempt to convey his strong emotions, including these words:

Simple Child
He looks almost like the others
Yet they know he's not the same

Phil Coulter's special son died in the 1970s at the age of four, but his memory lives on. His song has been performed by the cream of Irish musicians, including Sinead O'Connor, The Irish Tenors, The Dubliners, and Paddy Reilly.

The refrain is what most touches me. It reflects a poignant thought on which I choose to focus:

Scorn not his simplicity
But rather try to love him all the more

I have come to interpret the repetition of this refrain as a call to action for us as parents to be sure we do indeed throw off the guilt, despair, and sense of helplessness we may feel and to concentrate instead on loving our special child *all the more.*

One of the artists Maggie is most frequently exposed to from my listening to satellite radio while in the car is singer songwriter James Taylor. If I say James, Maggie quickly pairs it with Taylor. A personal favorite among his litany of hits over the decades is "Carolina In My Mind."

I was driving with Maggie when this song came on the car radio. My girl made me feel jazzed by asking that I turn it up. At that very moment came the lyrics:

There ain't no doubt in no one's mind that love's the finest
thing around...

These few words sum up for me the essence of our humanity. There is no doubt. Love is the finest thing around. If we "learn to love" the special people in our life "all the more," we can empower them to realize their highest aspirations. In the process, we become our finest selves. Surrounded by her many angels, our sweet Maggie would admonish us one and all, "Don't forget."

To order copies direct of Maggie's Angels simply go to our website:

www.maggiesdad.com

20% of book profits go to charities serving the special needs community mentioned in Maggie's Angels.

Special discounts are available for bulk purchase.
Please inquire on the website.

The website www.maggiesdad.com is a resource and includes a photo gallery and additional information related to topics covered in the book.

An E-book version of Maggie's Angels is scheduled to be available by the end of 2016.

———

Maggie's Dad, John T. McCarthy, is available as a speaker to professional, industry, business, civic, charitable, educational or church organizations on topics surrounding the book's subject matter.

The author of four books, John is a financial educator and veteran certified financial planner.

He can be reached at: John@maggiesdad.com or 414-530-7963